Asian American Panethnicity

Bridging Institutions and Identities

In the series
Asian American History and Culture
edited by Sucheng Chan

TEMPLE
UNIVERSITY
PRESS
Philadelphia

Asian American Panethnicity

Bridging Institutions and Identities

Yen Le Espiritu

Temple University Press, Philadelphia 19122
Copyright © 1992 by Temple University
All rights reserved. Published 1992
Printed in the United States of America

Library of Congress Cataloging-in-Publication Data
Espiritu, Yen Le.
   Asian American panethnicity: bridging institu-
tions and identities /
   Yen Le Espiritu.
   p.   cm.—(Asian American history and culture
series)
   Includes bibliographical references and index.
   ISBN 0-87722-955-4
   1. Asian Americans—Ethnic identity. 2. Asian
Americans—Politics and government. I. Title.
II. Series.   91-37374
E184.06E87   1992   CIP
305.895'073—dc20   Rev

To **Thel F. Taylor**
The forever teacher

Contents

Tables and Figures

Tables

Figures

Preface

As a Vietnamese American who is married to a Filipino American, I have a personal interest in pan–Asian American ethnicity. This personal interest has led to theoretical questions: How, under what circumstances, and to what extent can groups of diverse national origins come together as a new, enlarged panethnic group? This book is my attempt to answer these questions.

After four years of researching, thinking and rethinking, writing and rewriting, I still find pan–Asian American ethnicity a complex and changing topic, often defying sociological interpretations and generalizations. This is because Asian Americans are a complex and changing population: far from homogeneous, we are a multicultural, multilingual people who hold different worldviews and divergent modes of interpretation. Thus, although this book tells the story of the construction of pan-Asian ethnicity, it is not about obscuring our internal differences, but rather about taking seriously the heterogeneities among our ranks. Only in doing so can we build a meaningful solidarity as a pan-Asian group—one that allows us to combat systems of chauvinism and inequality both within and beyond our community.

A few words about terms. I use the term *Asian American* to refer to American-born Asians and to post-1965 arrivals, most of whom come to this country with the intention of settling permanently. Prior to this period, I call Asians in this country immigrants. Because pan-Asian American (pan-Asian for the sake of brevity) ethnicity has taken root primarily among Asian Americans, I use the term *Asian American* rather than *Asian Pacific American*, except in Chapters 4 and 5, where this term is used by government agencies for their administrative convenience. Because there is no consensus on the preferred terms to describe the major ethnoracial groups in this country, I use *Indian* and *Native American, white* and *Euro-American, black* and *African American,* and *Hispanic* and *Latino American* interchangeably.

As much as we would like to think so, no scholarly product is ever the work of just one individual. This is certainly true in my own case. Without the collaboration of supportive institutions, informants, teachers, friends, and family, I never would have been able to write this book. I owe all of them a great deal.

At the University of California, Los Angeles, where I did my graduate work, I am grateful for the support of the Institute of American Cultures, the Asian American Studies Center, and the Hortense Fishbaugh Memorial Scholarship Fund. I also received three years of financial support (1987–90) from the American Sociological Association Minority Fellowship Program. A 1990–91 postdoctoral fellowship from the University of California President's Fellowship Program provided me the much-needed time to turn an unwieldy manuscript into this book.

I am indebted to the people I interviewed (whose names are listed at the end of this book) for their time, ideas, and assistance. Their keen observations forced me to rethink much of what I had assumed about Asian Americans and about the process of group formation.

In particular, I want to acknowledge the late Beverly Yip, founder of the Union of Pan Asian Communities in San Diego, for her contribution to this project and, more important, for her tireless efforts on behalf of the immigrant communities in San Diego. I also thank Joanna Su, former executive director of the Detroit-based Asian American Center for Justice, for providing me with the archival data needed to compile Tables 6.2, 6.3, 6.4, and 6.5.

A host of people have lent me ideas and stimulation at various stages of this project. Although vastly grateful for their help, I bear responsibility for any errors of fact or opinion. I wish to acknowledge, in particular, four persons who shaped the content of this work: Ivan Light, Lucie Cheng, David Lopez, and Paul Ong. This book is a tribute to their skills as intellectual mentors and supportive colleagues. I thank them for their counsel and friendship. While not directly involved with this project, Michael Schudson had an important influence on my development as a sociologist. Rubén Rumbaut sparked my interest in the sociology of migration and adaptation. I have also benefited from discussions with Edna Bonacich, José Calderón, E. Antoinette Charfauros, Steve Cornell, Yuji Ichioka, Russell Leong, George Lipsitz, John Liu, Lisa Lowe, and the New Asian Immigration group at UCLA.

I also thank Russell Leong for coining the subtitle of this book, and Jean Yonemura and Elaine Kim for helping me to find a suitable image for the jacket.

Sucheng Chan was the catalyst for the publication of this book. She read every word of earlier drafts with enthusiasm, keen insight, and amazing speed. Michael Omi provided incisive and detailed suggestions that greatly improved this work, both theoretically and substantively. Their invaluable assistance underscores the importance of having works on Asian Americans reviewed by specialists in the field of Asian American studies.

Of a more personal nature, I offer my gratitude to Sonja de Lugo, Leigh Ann Fan, Susan Lewis, and Ruby Wirfs for the remarkable quality of their friendship. My deepest thanks go to my husband and best friend, Abe, who did things for me beyond the call of duty—all with his usual good cheer. Most important, he gave me a gift of wonder: a beautiful baby girl, Evyn Christine (Ngọc-Vân), who arrived on 16 January 1991. Into my busy world Evyn brings sunshine, joy, and chaos; I am truly enriched. Having a daughter has brought me ever closer to my own mother, a remarkable lady who truly puts my needs before hers—in all situations. I hope to be as loyal, giving, and forgiving in raising my own daughter.

Finally, this book is dedicated to Thel Taylor, who became my father upon marrying my mother. Defying all negative stereotypes of stepparents, he has been a wonderful friend, supporter, and advisor. Most of all, he has been an effective *teacher* (in the widest sense of the word) who truly believes that *all* children's questions deserve answers. For all the difference that he has made in my life, this book is for him: the forever teacher.

Asian American Panethnicity

Bridging Institutions and Identities

Chapter 1

Ethnicity
and Panethnicity

In November 1969, eighty-nine American Indians seized Alcatraz Island in San Francisco Bay, invoking an 1868 Sioux treaty that promised the return of unused federal property to the Indians. Identifying themselves as "Indians of All Tribes," the island occupiers represented a large number of Indian tribes, including the Sioux, Navajo, Cherokees, Mohawks, Puyallups, Yakimas, and Omahas. They occupied the island for nineteen months, intending to turn it into a cultural, educational, and spiritual center for all American Indians (Nagel 1989: 1–2).

In June 1971, twenty-three Puerto Rican and Mexican American community organizations in Chicago formed the Spanish Coalition for Jobs (La Coalición Latinoamericana de Empleos) to fight for better employment opportunities for Spanish-speaking workers. Charging job discrimination, the coalition mobilized as a "Latino group" against two Chicago employers (Illinois Bell and Jewel Tea). These protests led to job openings and job-training programs for Latinos at the two companies (Padilla 1986: 164–167).

In the mid-1980s, Asian Americans of various socioeconomic backgrounds and ethnic origins came together to campaign against possible discrimination in college admissions. Prompted by reports of declining acceptance rates of Asian Americans at the University of California and Ivy League colleges, community leaders charged that informal quotas were being imposed on Asian American university admissions (Chan 1991: 179–180). Asian American protest led to federal and university investigations of possible anti-Asian bias at the University of California, Berkeley and other colleges (Millard 1987; Woo 1988; Wang 1989).

These events call attention to the changing scope of ethnic identities, as linguistically, culturally, and geographically diverse groups come together in the interest of panethnic, or all-ethnic, solidarity. These developments cannot be explained adequately by studies of ethnicity[1] that focus on the quantitative transformations of ethnic consciousness. Though it is important to examine the degrees to which immigrant and minority groups retain their community-of-origin ties (Bonacich and Modell 1980; Reitz 1980) or assimilate into mainstream American life (Park 1950; Gordon 1964; Sowell 1981), we need also to look at the qualitative transformations of what constitutes ethnicity, that is, changes in who belongs to the ethnic groups (see Light 1981: 70–71).

Pan (the Greek word for "all") has been used primarily to characterize macronationalisms, movements seeking to extend nationalism to a supranational form (Snyder 1984: 4). Examples of such movements include the quest for religious unity (Pan-Islam), hemispheric cooperation (Pan-Americanism), and racial solidarity (Pan-Africanism). Whatever their basis of affinity, pan-movements involve shifts in levels of group identification from smaller boundaries to larger-level affiliations. Focusing on the idea of extension, *panethnic group* is used here to refer to a politico-cultural collectivity made up of peoples of several, hitherto distinct, tribal or national origins.

In the United States, examples of newly forged panethnic groups include the Native American, the Latino American, and the Asian American. These groups enclose diverse peoples who are nevertheless seen as homogeneous by outsiders: the Native American label unites people of linguistically and culturally distinct tribes; the Latino American category combines colonized Mexicans, Puerto Ricans, Cuban refugees, and documented and undocumented immigrants; and the Asian American unit comprises groups of different national origins that continue to be divided along class, linguistic, and generational lines. Despite their distinctive histories and separate identities, these ethnic groups have united to protect and promote their collective interests. They need not do so always. But as these examples indicate, for certain purposes, panethnic organization takes precedence over tribal or national affiliation.

Focusing on Asian Americans, this study asks how, under what circumstances, and to what extent groups of diverse national origins can come together as a new, enlarged panethnic group. The theoretical question concerns the construction of larger-scale affiliations, where groups previously unrelated in culture and descent submerge their differences and assume a common identity. Whereas most studies of ethnicity have focused on the maintenance of ethnic boundaries (Barth 1969; Bonacich and Modell 1980) and intergroup conflict (Bonacich 1972; Banton 1983), the study of panethnicity deals with the creation of new ethnic boundaries and intergroup cooperation (see Padilla 1985). As such, it calls attention to the unforeseen persistence of ethnicity and the mutability of ethnic boundaries in the modern world. Most important, as an emergent phenomenon, panethnicity focuses attention on ethnic change and thus allows one to assess the relative importance of external, structural conditions, as opposed to internal, cultural factors in the construction and maintenance of ethnicity (Lopez and Espiritu 1990: 198).

Theories of Ethnicity: An Overview and Assessment

Ethnic consciousness continues to thrive in contemporary societies, despite Marxist and functionalist predictions that modernization and industrialization will bring about a decrease in the importance of ethnic ties (Park 1950; Lipset and Rokkan 1967). As Edna Bonacich and John Modell (1980: 1) put it, "Almost every society in the world has some degree of ethnic diversity and for most, ethnicity appears to be a pivotal point of division and conflict." In the United States, the civil rights movement of the 1950s and 1960s and the subsequent radical minority movements (Black, Brown, Red, and Yellow Power) reawakened sociologists and others to the continuing importance of cultural and racial divisions in defining lines of social order. A variety of theories have sought to explain the tenacity of ethnic boundaries. Two divergent approaches dominate this literature: the primordialist focus on "communities of culture" and the instrumentalist emphasis on "communities of interests."[2]

Primordialism: Communities of Culture

Primordialists focus on culture and tradition to explain the emergence and retention of ethnicity. Ethnic cohesion is deemed sentimental; that is, people form ethnic groups because they are or regard themselves as bound together by a "web of sentiment, belief, worldview, and practice" (Cornell 1988b: 178). Scholars taking this approach claim that this "intuitive bond" originated in the primordial past—at the beginning (Connor 1978: 377; also Isaacs 1975: 45; van den Berghe 1981: 80). This "beginning" gives ethnicity a special tenacity and emotional force. In other words, the meaningfulness of ethnic identity derives from its birth connection; it came first. Capturing the emotive aspects of ethnicity, primordialism offers a plausible reason for the durability of such attachments.

Nonetheless, primordialism has several shortcomings. First, primordial ties do not always lead to ethnic solidarity. For example, the strained relationship between Canadian-born Chinese and Vietnamese-born Chinese in Canada suggests that groups sharing the same ancestry do not necessarily fraternize (Woon 1985). Second, primordial explanations of ethnicity cannot readily account for variations in the intensity of ethnic awareness. As Ivan Light (1981: 55) observed, these variations "indicate that living people are making a lot or a little of their 'primordial' ties according to present convenience."

Finally, in the primordialist literature, issues of economic and political inequalities are often treated as epiphenomenal (McKay 1982: 399). Focusing on the psychological origin of ethnicity, simple primordialism overlooks the economic and political interests that are so tightly bound up with ethnic sentiment and practice (Glazer and Moynihan 1963; Greenberg 1980). Because conscious ethnic identity emerges and intensifies under situations of intergroup competition, what need to be addressed are the structural conditions that produce ethnic groups—not only the cultural variables themselves.

Instrumentalism: Communities of Interest

Unlike primordialists, who assume that participation within the confines of one's ethnic group is valuable in and of itself (Lal 1990), instrumentalists treat ethnicity as a strategic tool or resource. Scholars taking this approach argue that populations remain ethnic when their ethnicity yields greater returns than other statuses available to them. The functional advantages of ethnicity range from "the moral and material support provided by ethnic networks to political gains made through ethnic bloc voting" (Portes and Bach 1985: 24). In other words, ethnic groups are not only sentimental associations of persons sharing affective ties but also interest groups.

The most extreme variant of the instrumentalist approach takes whatever attributes are associated with particular ethnic groups to be primarily situational, generated and sustained by members' interests. Thus membership in one group is only for the sake of obtaining comparative advantage vis-à-vis membership in another. As Orlando Patterson (1975: 348) stated, "The strength, scope, viability, and bases of ethnic identity are determined by, and are used to serve, the economic and general class interests of individuals." A more moderate version combines an analysis of the external activators of ethnic behavior with their specific cultural form and content. For example, Abner Cohen (1969: 3) argued that because ethnic groups are culturally homogeneous, they can more effectively organize as interest groups. In either case, rational interests are assumed to play an important role in the retention or dissolution of ethnic ties (Glazer and Moynihan 1963; Bonacich and Modell 1980).

Rethinking Primordialism and Instrumentalism

Whatever their differences, primordialists and instrumentalists both assume that ethnic groups are largely voluntary collectivities defined by national origin, whose members share a distinctive, integrated culture. The phenomenon of panethnicity challenges these assumptions, calling attention instead to the coercively imposed nature of ethnicity, its multiple layers, and the continual creation and re-creation of culture.

Voluntary and Imposed Ethnicity

Focusing on sentimentality and rational interests, primordialists and instrumentalists posit that ethnicity endures because individuals derive psychological or material support from their ethnic affiliations. But the obverse is also true: once sentimental and economic ties disappear, ethnics will vanish into the acculturated main-stream. These propositions imply that ethnicity is largely a matter of choice—in the sense that individuals and groups can choose to keep or discard their ethnicity according to their changing psychological and material needs.

However, to conceptualize ethnicity as a matter of choice is to ignore "categorization," the process whereby one group ascriptively classifies another. Categorization is intimately bound up with power relations. As such, it characterizes situations in which a more power-ful group seeks to dominate another, and, in so doing, imposes upon these people a categorical identity that is defined by reference to their inherent differences from or inferiority to the dominant group (Jenkins 1986: 177–178). Thus, while ethnicity may be an exercise of personal choice for Euro-Americans, it is not so for nonwhite groups in the United States. For these "visible" groups, ethnicity is not always voluntary, but can be coercively imposed. As Mary Waters (1990: 156) concluded, "The ways in which identity is flexible and symbolic and voluntary for white middle-class Americans are the very ways in which it is not so for non-white and Hispanic Ameri-cans." Her conclusion echoes the internal colonialism perspective, which maintains that white ethnics differ from nonwhites in the re-duced severity of oppression they experience (Blauner 1972: 60–66).

Panethnicity—the generalization of solidarity among ethnic sub-groups—is largely a product of categorization. An imposed cate-gory ignores subgroup boundaries, lumping together diverse peoples in a single, expanded "ethnic" framework. Individuals so catego-rized may have nothing in common except that which the cate-gorizer uses to distinguish them. The Africans who were forcibly brought to the United States came not as "blacks" or "Africans" but as members of distinct and various ethnic populations. As a result of slavery, "the 'Negro race' emerged from the heterogeneity of Afri-can ethnicity" (Blauner 1972: 13; also Cornell 1990: 376–379). Di-verse Native American tribes also have had to assume the pan-Indian label in order to conform to the perceptions of the American state (Keyes 1981: 25; Nagel 1982: 39). Similarly, diverse Latino popula-tions have been treated by the larger society as a unitary group with common characteristics and common problems (Moore and Pachon 1985: 2). And the term Asian American arose out of the racist dis-course that constructs Asians as a homogeneous group (Lowe 1991:

30). Excessive categorization is fundamental to racism because it permits "whites to order a universe of unfamiliar peoples without confronting their diversity and individuality" (Blauner 1972: 113).

When manifested in racial violence, racial lumping necessarily leads to protective panethnicity. Most often, an ethnic group is sanctioned for its actual or alleged misconduct, as when middleman minorities are attacked for their own entrepreneurial success (Bonacich 1973). But minority groups can also suffer reprisal because of their externally imposed membership in a larger grouping. Because the public does not usually distinguish among subgroups within a panethnic category, hostility directed at any of these groups is directed at others as well. In 1982, for example, as detailed in Chapter 6, a Chinese American was beaten to death by two white men who allegedly mistook him for Japanese. Under the force of necessity, ethnic subgroups put aside historical rivalries and enroll in a panethnic movement. According to Tamotsu Shibutani and Kian Kwan (1965: 210), groups often join forces when they recognize that the larger society does not acknowledge their differences.

This is not to say that panethnicity is solely an imposed identity. Although it originated in the minds of outsiders, today the panethnic concept is a political resource for insiders, a basis on which to mobilize diverse peoples and to force others to be more responsive to their grievances and agendas. Referring to the enlarged political capacities of a pan-Indian identity, Stephen Cornell (1988a: 146) stated that "the language of dominant-group categorization and control has become the language of subordinate-group self-concept and resistance." Thus, group formation is not only circumstantially determined, but takes place as an interaction between assignment and assertion (Ito-Adler 1980). In other words, panethnic boundaries are shaped and reshaped in the continuing interaction between both external and internal forces.

Multiple Levels of Ethnicity

In general, primordialists and instrumentalists have used national origin to designate ethnic groups (Parsons 1975: 56). This approach ignores the range of ethnicity—from small, relatively isolated kin groups to large categories of people bound together by symbolic attachments (Yinger 1985: 161). Addressing this oversight, recent studies of ethnicity have been more attentive to internal ethnicity, or ethnic differences within a national origin group (Bhachu 1985; Desbarats 1986). At the other end of the spectrum is panethnicity, in which groups of different national origins merge into new larger-scale groupings (Nagel 1982; Padilla 1985; Cornell 1988a).

Although prevalent, the movement from small-scale to large-scale organization is by no means unilinear (Horowitz 1985: 64–65). Among Native Americans, ethnic organization occurs along three boundaries: subtribal, tribal, and supratribal (Nagel 1982; Cornell 1988a). Similarly, in a study of Latino politics in Chicago, Felix Padilla (1985) reported a shifting of identity between Cuban or Mexican American on the one hand, and Latino American on the other, based on the political context. In the Asian American case, researchers have noted both the rise of pan-Asian organization and the increase in conflict among constituent populations (Trottier 1981). The ebb and flow of panethnic tendencies indicates that ethnic organization is multitiered, situational, and partly ascribed.

Ethnic Group and Cultural Group

Primordialists and instrumentalists agree that a distinctive, integrated culture is the principal antecedent and defining characteristic of ethnic groups (Horowitz 1985: 66). This assertion ignores the emergent quality of culture: culture not only is inherited but can also be created and re-created to unite group members (Roosens 1989: 12). As Lisa Lowe (1991: 27) points out, "Culture may be a much 'messier' process than unmediated vertical transmission from one generation to another, including practices that are partly inherited, partly modified, as well as partly invented."

According to Susan Olzak (1985: 67), the majority of ethnic groups in contemporary societies are fundamentally new, making claims to cultural traditions that are symbolic or mythical, or that no longer exist. With the changing positions of groups within society, old forms of ethnic cultures may die out, but new forms may also be generated (Yancey, Ericksen, and Juliani 1976: 391). Calling attention to the emergent quality of culture, Abner Cohen (1981: 323) reported that when different cultural groups affiliate themselves in opposition to other groups, their differences quickly disappear. As group members borrow customs from one another, intermarry, and develop a common lifestyle, a common culture emerges. Donald Horowitz (1985: 69) similarly concluded that "culture is more important for providing *post facto* content of group identity than it is for providing some ineluctable prerequisite for an identity to come into being."

The above discussion suggests that, in some cases, culture is used to define a boundary; in others, it is ultimately the product of a boundary. Hence, objective cultural differences need to be distinguished from the socially constructed boundaries that ultimately define ethnic groups (Hechter 1975: 312–326). Cultural differences are merely *potential* identity markers for the members of those groups. When this potential is taken up and mobilized, a cultural group—a group of people who share an identifiable set of meanings, symbols, values, and norms—is transformed into an ethnic group, one with a conscious group identity (Barth 1969: 15; Patterson 1975: 309–310).[3]

Because panethnic groups are new groups, any real or perceived cultural commonality cannot lay claim to a primordial origin. Instead, panethnic unity is forged primarily through the symbolic reinterpretation of a group's common history, particularly when this history involves racial subjugation. Even when those in subordinate positions do not initially regard themselves as being alike, "a sense of identity gradually emerges from a recognition of their common fate" (Shibutani and Kwan 1965: 208). Drawing on the experiences of blacks, Robert Blauner (1972: 140–141) argued that cultural orientations not only are primordial but can also be constructed from a shared political history: "The centrality of racial subjugation in the black experience has been the single most important source of the developing ethnic peoplehood" and "the core of the distinctive ethnic culture." Similarly, Lowe (1991: 28) maintains that "the boundaries and definitions of Asian American culture are continually shifting and being contested from pressures both inside and outside the Asian origin community." Thus the study of panethnicity suggests that culture is dynamic and analytic rather than static and descriptive.

Ethnic Change: The Construction of Panethnicity

In moving away from cultural explanations of ethnicity, the study of panethnicity directs research and theoretical debate to those structural conditions that lead to the construction of ethnic boundaries in the first place. For the most part, structural theorists have focused on the effects of economic conditions on ethnic solidarity such as the existence of a cultural division of labor or a split labor market (Bonacich 1972; Hechter 1978; Nielsen 1985). While important, economic explanations of ethnic solidarity are incomplete because they largely ignore the similarly paramount role played by political organization and processes. Noting the important role of the polity in modern societies, Daniel Bell (1975: 161) suggested that "competition between plural groups takes place largely in the political arena."

Ethnic groups are formed and changed in encounters among groups. To interact meaningfully with those in the larger society, individuals have to identify themselves in terms intelligible to outsiders. Thus, at times, they have to set aside their national or tribal identities and accept the ascribed panethnic label. Since the central government is the most powerful ascriptive force in any state, "there is a strong political character to much modern ethnic mobilization" (Nagel 1986: 96). According to Joane Nagel (1986: 98–106), ethnic resurgences are strongest when political systems structure political access along ethnic lines and adopt policies that emphasize ethnic differences. When the state uses the ethnic label as a unit in economic allocations and political representations, ethnic groups find it both convenient and necessary to act collectively. In other words, the organization of political participation on the basis of ethnicity provides a rationale for, and indeed demands, the mobilization of political participation along ethnic lines. As Jeffrey Ross (1982: 451) suggested, ethnic groups are most likely to exist where multiple access points into the political systems are available. Thus instead of declining, ethnicity is politicized and legitimized in modern states.

One possible explanation for the development of panethnicity in modern states is the competitive advantage of large-scale identities. The formation of larger ethnic units "gives people more weight in playing ethnic politics at the higher level" (van den Berghe 1981: 256; also Hannan 1979: 271). While valid, this ecological perspective is incomplete. Panethnic coalition is not only an efficacious organizational strategy but also a response to the institutionally relevant ethnic categories in the political system. When the state uses a unitary panethnic label—rather than numerous national or tribal designations—to allocate political and economic resources, it encourages individuals to broaden their identity to conform to the more inclusive ethnic designation. Over time, these individuals may see themselves as more than just an artificial state category, but rather "as a group which shares important common experiences: oppression, deprivation, and also benefits" (Enloe 1981: 134). Thus, shifts in ethnic boundaries are often a direct response to changes in the political distribution system.

To conceptualize panethnicity as a political construct is not to deny its economic function. On the contrary, panethnic organization is strongest when given economic reinforcement by the politically dominant group. The state's recognition of "legitimate" groups directly affects employment, housing, social program design, and the disbursement of local, state, and federal funds (Omi and Winant 1986: 3–4). According to Paul Burstein (1985: 126), "Politics revolves around economic issues more than anything else."

Another economic dimension is the constraint of social class on panethnic solidarity. In general, similar class position enhances the construction of panethnic consciousness whereas intense class stratification works against it (Lopez and Espiritu 1990: 204). Ironically, class divisions are often most evident within the very organizations that purport to advance panethnic unity: the leaders and core members of these organizations continue to be predominantly middle-class professionals (Padilla 1985: 156–157). This class bias undercuts the legitimacy of the organizations and the use of panethnicity as their organizing principle. As argued in Chapters 3 and 4, however, the dominance of the professional class in panethnic organizations is rooted in the very way the state has responded to minority demands. Because the political and funding systems require and reward professionalism, the ability to deal effectively with elected officials and public agencies has become a desirable qualification for leadership—a development that favors more politically sophisticated, articulate, and well-educated persons (Espiritu and Ong 1991). Thus, once again, economics is linked to the politics of panethnicity.

The emphasis on the political nature of panethnicity does not ignore culture either. While panethnic groups may be circumstantially constructed, they are not simply circumstantially sustained (Cornell 1988b). Once established, the panethnic group—as a result of increasing interaction and communication among its members—can produce and transform panethnic culture and consciousness. As persons of diverse backgrounds come together to discuss their problems and experiences, they begin to develop common views of themselves and of one another and common interpretations of their experiences and those of the larger society (Cornell 1988b: 19). In other words, they begin to create a "political history," which then serves as the core of the emerging panethnic culture—and a guide to action against the dominant groups (Blauner 1972: 141). Culture building is essential in consolidating ethnic boundaries because it promotes group consciousness, reminding members constantly "of the disproportionate importance of what they shared, in comparison to what they did not" (Cornell 1990: 377). In so doing, it levels intergroup differences and inspires sentiments conducive to collective action. Excellent examples may be found in the recent history of the United States.

Panethnicity in the United States

In the 1960s, the discordance between the American promise of fairness and the experience of discrimination led to organized struggles against racism, sexism, poverty, war, and exploitation. These social and political struggles led minority groups to realize that their interests could be better advanced by forming coalitions. In particular, the Black Power movement sensitized minority groups to racial issues and set into motion the Yellow Power, Red Power, and Brown Power movements. International struggles also contributed to panethnic mobilization. The visibility and success of anticolonial nationalist movements in Asia, Africa, and Latin America stirred racial and cultural pride and provided a context for panethnic activism (Blauner 1972).

As a result of the 1960s movements, ethnicity was institutionalized. Civil rights and the subsequent minority movements forced the state to redefine and expand the rights of minorities. Before these social movements erupted, the approved role of government was to ensure that people were not formally categorized on the basis of race. However, after the early 1970s, antidiscrimination legislation moved away from emphasizing the equality of individual opportunities to focusing on the equitable distribution of group rights. This move led to the implementation of government-mandated affirmative action programs designed to ensure minority representation in employment, in public programs, and in education (Wilson 1987: 112–114). Because affirmative action programs are oriented to group membership, they provide a compelling material interest for minority groups to resurrect dormant ethnic ties or to create new ones in order to pursue interests that may or may not relate to culture (Lal 1990).

Unwilling or unable to listen to myriad voices, government bureaucracies (and the larger society) often lump diverse racial and ethnic minority groups into the four umbrella categories—blacks, Asian Americans, Hispanics, and Native Americans—and treat them as single units in the allocation of economic and political resources (Lowry 1982: 42–43). In response, members of the subgroups within each category begin to act collectively to protect and to advance their interests. Tracing the development of Latino ethnic consciousness in Chicago during the 1970s, Padilla (1986: 163) reported that affirmative action policy "enabled nonunited groups [Mexican Americans and Puerto Ricans] to transcend the boundaries of their individual ethnic groups and assert demands as a Latino population or group." Along the same line, Nagel (1982: 39) concluded that the various levels of American Indian mobilization "are responses to a particular incentive structure largely determined by US Indian policies."

Thus, panethnic groups in the United States are products of political and social processes, rather than of cultural bonds (Lopez and Espiritu 1990). For these groups, culture has followed panethnic boundaries rather than defined them. Even for Latino Americans who share a common language, the designation of the Spanish language as the defining ingredient of Latino consciousness—its "primordialization"—is largely a response to the structural commonalities shared by the subgroups. Padilla (1985: 151) reported that Latino identity is related more to the *symbolism* of Spanish as a separate language than to its actual use by all members of the group. This is not to say that the state is an entirely independent force. Depending on its political strength and resources, a panethnic group can pressure political institutions to advance the material interests of its members. In a political system in which numbers count, this political strength is derived from a unified front rather than from the separate efforts of individual subgroups. Thus, panethnicity is not only imposed from above but also constructed from below as a means of claiming resources inside and outside the community.

To be sure, panethnic groups are still full of internal divisions. Within the broad panethnic boundary, constituent communities compete for members and loyalty and fight for the modicum of political power and material resources generated by government-sponsored programs (Nagel 1982: 44; Cornell 1988a: 161–163). Historical intergroup enmities, cultural differences, and class divisions exacerbate these conflicts, at times polarizing the panethnic coalition. For the Latino and the Asian American communities, intergroup conflicts have been further aggravated by continuing immigration. This influx creates new constituencies that may feel inadequately represented by established panethnic groups; it also rejuvenates ethnic cultures, reinforces national allegiances, and reminds ethnic members of how little they have in common with members of other ethnic groups (Lopez and Espiritu 1990: 205). Hence the study of panethnicity is a study of the process of fusion as well as of fission.

Goals, Definitions, and Scope

Pan-Asian American ethnicity is the development of bridging organizations and solidarities among several ethnic and immigrant groups of Asian ancestry. Although subject to the same general prejudice and similar discriminatory laws, Asians in the United States have rarely conceived of themselves as a single people and many still do not. "Asiatic," "Oriental," and "Mongolian" were merely convenient labels used by outsiders to refer to all Asians. The development of panethnicity among Asian Americans has a short history. While examples of white oppression of Asian Americans stretch back over a century, a meaningful pan-Asian movement was not constructed until the late 1960s (Daniels 1988: 113). This book tells the story of this construction—of the resultant unity and division, and corresponding benefits and costs. The emphasis here is on the *political* nature of panethnicity, that is, on the distribution and exercise of, and the struggle for, power and resources inside and outside the community. Panethnicity is political not only because it serves as a basis for interest group mobilization but also because it is linked with the expansion of the role of the polity (Enloe 1980: 5).

Panethnicity has not been well studied. Moreover, the few existing works on panethnicity have dealt primarily with Native American and Latino American panethnicities (Nagel 1982; Padilla 1985; Cornell 1988a). Except for several essays from the proponents of the 1960s Asian American movement (Uyematsu 1971; P. Wong 1972), the process of pan-Asianization has not been well documented. While social scientists have devoted substantial attention to individual Asian groups (Montero 1979; Bonacich and Modell 1980; Kim 1981), few have focused on Asian Americans as a collectivity. Yet a host of pan-Asian organizations testify to the salience of pan-Asian consciousness, as do the numerous cooperative efforts by Asian American groups and organizations on behalf of both subgroup and pan-Asian interests.

There are two dimensions of groupness: the conceptual and the organizational. The conceptual refers to individual behavior and attitude—the ways group members view themselves; the organizational refers to political structures—the ways groups are organized as collective actors. The boundaries of these two dimensions usually but do not necessarily coincide (Cornell 1988a: 72). Some key indicators of pan-Asian consciousness include self-identification, pan-Asian residential, friendship, and marriage patterns, and membership in pan-Asian organizations. Given the multiple levels of Asian American ethnicity, a study of individual ethnicity can also document "ethnic switching"—the relabeling of individuals' ethnic affiliation to meet situational needs. That is, a person is a Japanese American or an Asian American depending on the ethnic identities available to him or her in a particular situation. Sometimes the individual has a choice, and sometimes not (see Nagel 1986: 95–96). While recognizing the importance of the conceptual dimension of panethnicity, this work is primarily a study of the organizational dimension: the institutionalization of Asian American consciousness, and not the state of panethnic consciousness itself. Thus, most of the evidence is drawn from the level of formal organizations. The research methods are basically those of the historically grounded community study, combining organization archives, public records, interviews with the leaders of organizations, participant observation, and library research.

15

Naturally, the rank and file's level of Asian American consciousness influences its institutionalization. On the other hand, grassroots consciousness does not necessarily precede the process of organizational consolidation. As this study documents, panethnic organizations need not merely reflect existing panethnic consciousness but can also generate and augment it. In building themselves, pan-Asian organizations also build pan-Asian consciousness. Thus, the organizational level is intrinsically worthy of examination because it tells us about the directions of the populations supposedly represented.

Moreover, pan-Asian institutions cannot survive without support; their very existence presupposes some amount of consensus. One research strategy would to be to quantify this consensus. Another would be to identify the individuals who may have vested interests in promoting pan-Asian ethnicity, and in so doing name the dominant groups and sectors in the pan-Asian coalitions.[4] The research question then becomes not who identifies with pan-Asian ethnicity, but who benefits the most from it—and at whose expense? Such an approach allows us to look beyond numbers to the power struggles and the resultant intergroup conflicts and competition.

The influx of the post-1965 Asian immigrants and refugees—who are distinct in ethnic and class composition from the more "established" Asian Americans—has exacerbated intergroup conflicts. The determination of what and whose interests will be defended often factionalizes the pan-Asian collectivity, as newcomers and old-timers pursue their separate goals (Lopez and Espiritu 1990: 206). On the other hand, the pan-Asian concept is now so well institutionalized that new Asian immigrants and refugees often encounter extensive pressure to consider themselves Asian Americans, regardless of whether or not they see themselves in such terms. For example, Southeast Asian refugees have had to adopt the Asian American designation because this category resonates in the larger society (Skinner and Hendricks 1979; Hein 1989). Accordingly, this study examines the benefits as well as the limitations of pan-Asian coalitions.

Scholars and laypersons alike have argued that Asian Americans are not a panethnic group because they do not share a common culture (Ignacio 1976; Trottier 1981). While Native Americans can trace their common descent to their unique relationship to the land, and Latino Americans to their common language, Asian Americans have no readily identifiable symbols of ethnicity. This view involves the implicit assumption that ethnic boundaries are unproblematic. However, as Frederick Barth (1969) suggested, when ethnic boundaries are strong and persistent, cultural solidarity will result. But ethnic groups that are merging need not exhibit such solidarity. Discussing the ongoing efforts to build an Asian American culture, John Liu (1988: 123–124) stated, "The admonition that we can no longer assume that Asian Americans share a common identity and culture is not a setback in our efforts, but rather a reminder that the goals we set for ourselves need to be constantly struggled for."

The construction of pan-Asian ethnicity involves the creation of a common Asian American heritage out of diverse histories. Part of the heritage being created hinges on what Asian Americans share: a history of exploitation, oppression, and discrimination. However, individuals' being treated alike does not automatically produce new groups. "Only when people become aware of being treated alike on the basis of some arbitrary criterion do they begin to establish identity on that basis" (Shibutani and Kwan 1965: 210). For Asian Americans, this "arbitrary criterion" is their socially defined racial distinctiveness, or their imposed identity as "Asians." As such, an important task for pan-Asian leaders is to define racist activities against one Asian American subgroup as hostilities against all Asian Americans. In her call for pan-Asian organization, Amy Uyematsu (1971: 10–11) referred to the internment of Japanese Americans as a "racist treatment of 'yellows,'" and the mistreatment of Chinese immigrants in 1885 as mistreatment of *Asians* in America (emphasis mine). More recently, Asian American leaders characterized the 1982 fatal beating of Chinese American Vincent Chin as a racial attack against all Asian Americans (Zia 1984a). Thus, following Barth (1969), the task at hand is to document the process of culture building and its function in the construction and maintenance of panethnic boundaries— not to define and inventory cultural symbols.

The Steps Ahead

This study examines the continuing interaction between internal and external factors that forms and transforms pan-Asian ethnicity. Chapter 2 documents the confrontational politics that led to the emergence of pan-Asian ethnicity in the late 1960s and the early 1970s. Although the pan-Asian concept was first coined by young Asian American activists on college campuses, it was subsequently institutionalized by the larger society. Chapters 3 to 5 examine several settings—electoral politics, social service funding, and census classification—within which the pan-Asian concept was institutionalized. Government efforts to reduce the number of Asian American groups by lumping them together for the purpose of working with them in electoral politics, distributing funds, and counting them in the census represent the external forces shaping the emergence of a pan-Asian consciousness. As a result of the institutionalization of the pan-Asian concept, the confrontational politics of the activists eventually gave way to the conventional and electoral politics of the professionals, lobbyists, and politicians. Finally, Chapter 6 analyzes Asian American response to the most threatening form of external imposition: anti-Asian violence.

Groups are forged and changed in encounters among groups. Thus the study of pan-Asian ethnicity is primarily a study of social relations, of fusion and fission between Asian and non-Asian Americans as well as among Asian American subgroups. Because the sociopolitical environment and the Asian American world are organized in different terms, Asian Americans often have to manipulate their own organizational structure to adapt to the changing social and political reality. Such manipulation can violate zealously guarded boundaries and long-established power structures, leading to intergroup factionalism and infighting. But intergroup divisions are not news. What is important is that these divisions have rarely led to formalized factions. Because of the need to present a united front to the public, internal conflicts are often handled privately—within the confines of the Asian American community. In sum, this study is about the power—as well as the limitations—of external, structural factors to bridge dissimilar lives.

Chapter 2

Coming Together:
The Asian American
Movement

Arriving in the United States, nineteenth-century immigrants from Asian countries did not think of themselves as "Asians." Coming from specific districts in provinces in different nations, Asian immigrant groups did not even consider themselves Chinese, Japanese, Korean, and so forth, but rather people from Toisan, Hoiping, or some other district in Guandong Province in China or from Hiroshima, Yamaguchi, or some other prefecture in Japan. Members of each group considered themselves culturally and politically distinct. Historical enmities between their mother countries further separated the groups even after their arrival in the United States. Writing about early Asian immigrant communities, Eliot Mears (1928:4) reported that "it is exceptional when one learns of any entente between these Orientals." However, non-Asians had little understanding or appreciation of these distinctions. For the most part, outsiders accorded to Asian peoples certain common characteristics and traits that were essentially supranational (Browne 1985: 8–9). Indeed, the exclusion acts and quotas limiting Asian immigration to the United States relied upon racialist constructions of Asians as homogeneous (Lowe 1991: 28).

Mindful that whites generally lump all Asians together, early Asian immigrant communities sought to "keep their images discrete and were not above denigrating, or at least approving the denigration of, other Asian groups" (Daniels 1988: 113). It was not until the late 1960s, with the advent of the Asian American movement, that a pan-Asian consciousness and constituency were first formed. To build political unity, college students of Asian ancestry heralded their common fate—the similarity of experiences and treatment that Asian groups endured in the United States (Omi and Winant 1986: 105). In other words, the pan-Asian concept, originally imposed by non-Asians, became a symbol of pride and a rallying point for mass mobilization by later generations. This chapter examines the social, political, and demographic factors that allowed pan-Asianism to take root in the 1960s and not earlier.

Ethnic "Disidentification"

Before the 1960s, Asians in this country frequently practiced ethnic disidentification, the act of distancing one's group from another group so as not to be mistaken and suffer the blame for the presumed misdeeds of that group (Hayano 1981: 162). Faced with external threats, group members can either intensify their solidarity or they can distance themselves from the stigmatized segment. Instead of uniting to fight anti-Asian forces, early Asian immigrant communities often disassociated themselves from the targeted group so as not to be mistaken for members of it and suffer any possible negative consequences (Hayano 1981: 161; Daniels 1988: 113). Two examples of ethnic disidentification among Asians in this country occurred during the various anti-Asian exclusion movements and during World War II. These incidents are instructive not only as evidence of ethnic disidentification but also as documentation of the pervasiveness of racial lumping. Precisely because of racial lumping, persons of Asian ancestry found it necessary to disassociate themselves from other Asian groups.

Exclusion Movements

Beginning with the first student laborers in the late nineteenth century, Japanese immigrants always differentiated themselves from Chinese immigrants. Almost uniformly, Japanese immigrants perceived their Chinese counterparts in an "unsympathetic, negative light, and often repeated harsh American criticisms of the Chinese" (Ichioka 1988: 191). In their opinion, the Chinese came from an inferior nation; they also were lower-class laborers, who had not adapted themselves to American society. In 1892, a Japanese student laborer described San Francisco's Chinatown as "a world of beasts in which . . . exists every imaginable depravity, crime, and vice" (cited in Ichioka 1988: 191).

Indeed, the Japanese immigrants were a more select group than their Chinese counterparts. The Japanese government viewed overseas Japanese as representatives of their homeland. Therefore, it screened prospective emigrants to ensure that they were healthy and literate and would uphold Japan's national honor (Takaki 1989: 46).

More important, Japanese immigrants distanced themselves from the Chinese because they feared that Americans would lump them together. Aware of Chinese exclusion, Japanese immigrant leaders had always dreaded the thought of Japanese exclusion. To counteract any negative association, Japanese immigrant leaders did everything possible to distinguish themselves from the Chinese immigrants (Ichioka 1988: 250). For example, to separate themselves from the unassimilable Chinese laborers, some Japanese immigrant leaders insisted that their Japanese workers wear American work clothes and even eat American food (Ichioka 1988: 185). In 1901, the Japanese in California distributed leaflets requesting that they be differentiated from the Chinese (tenBroek, Barnhart, and Matson 1970: 23).

However, under the general rubric Asiatic, the Japanese inherited the painful experiences of the Chinese.[1] All the vices attributed to the Chinese were transferred to these newest Asian immigrants (Browne 1985). Having successfully excluded Chinese laborers, organized labor once again led the campaign to drive out the Japanese immigrants. In 1904, the American Federation of Labor adopted its first anti-Japanese resolution. Charging that the Japanese immigrants were as undesirable as the Chinese, the unions' resolution called for the expansion of the 1902 Chinese Exclusion Act to include Japanese and other Asian laborers. By mid-1905, the labor unions of California had joined forces to establish the Asiatic Exclusion League (Hill 1973: 52–54; Ichioka 1988: 191–192).

Since the Japanese immigrants considered themselves superior to the Chinese, they felt indignant and insulted whenever they were lumped together with them. In 1892, a Japanese immigrant wrote in the *Oakland Enquirer* that he wished "to inveigh with all my power" against American newspapers that compared the Japanese to "the truly ignorant class of Chinese laborers and condemned them as bearers of some mischievous Oriental evils" (cited in Ichioka 1988: 192). Instead of joining with the Chinese to fight the anti-Asian exclusion movement, some Japanese leaders went so far as to condone publicly the exclusion of the Chinese while insisting that the Japanese were the equals of Americans (Daniels 1988: 113). Above all else, Japanese immigrant leaders wanted Japanese immigration to be treated on the same footing as European immigration (Ichioka 1988: 250).

In the end, Japanese attempts at disidentification failed. With the passage of the 1924 Immigration Act, Japanese immigration was effectively halted. This act contained two provisions designed to stop Japanese immigration. The first barred the immigration of Japanese wives even if their husbands were United States citizens. The second prohibited the immigration of aliens ineligible for citizenship. Because the Supreme Court had ruled in 1922 that persons of Japanese ancestry could not become naturalized citizens, this provision effectively closed the door on Japanese and most other Asian immigration (U.S. Commission on Civil Rights 1986: 8–9). The Japanese immigrants felt doubly affronted by the 1924 act because it ranked them, not as the equals of Europeans, but on the same level as the lowly Chinese, the very people whom they themselves considered inferior (Ichioka 1988: 250). Thus, despite all their attempts to disassociate themselves from the Chinese, with the passage of the act, the Japanese joined the Chinese as a people deemed unworthy of becoming Americans. Little did they foresee that, in less than two decades, other Asian groups in America would disassociate themselves from the Japanese.

World War II and Japanese Internment

Immediately after the bombing of Pearl Harbor, the incarceration of Japanese Americans began. On the night of December 7, the Federal Bureau of Investigation (FBI) began taking into custody persons of Japanese ancestry who had connections to the Japanese government. Working on the principle of guilt by association, the security agencies simply rounded up most of the Issei (first-generation) leaders of the Japanese community. Initially, the federal government differentiated between alien and citizen Japanese Americans, but this distinction gradually disappeared. In the end, the government evacuated more than 100,000 persons of Japanese ancestry into concentration camps, approximately two-thirds of whom were American-born citizens. It was during this period that the Japanese community discovered that the legal distinction between citizen and alien was not nearly so important as the distinction between white and yellow (Daniels 1988: ch. 6).

Like the Japanese, the Chinese understood the importance of the distinction between white and yellow. Fearful that they would be targets of anti-Japanese activities, many persons of Chinese ancestry, especially in the West, took to wearing buttons that proclaimed positively "I'm Chinese." Similarly, many Chinese shopkeepers displayed signs announcing, "This is a Chinese shop." Some Chinese immigrants even joined the white persecution with buttons that added "I hate Japs worse than you do" (Daniels 1988: 205; Takaki 1989: 370–371). The small Korean and Filipino communities took similar actions. Because of Japan's occupation of Korea at the time, being mistaken as Japanese particularly angered Koreans in the United States. Cognizant of Asian lumping, the United Korean Committee prepared identification cards proclaiming "I am Korean." During the early months of the war, women wore Korean dresses regularly to distinguish themselves from the Japanese (Melendy 1977: 158; Takaki 1989: 365–366). Similarly, persons of Filipino ancestry wore buttons proclaiming "I am a Filipino" (Takaki 1989: 363).

Given the wars between their mother countries and Japan, it is not surprising that the Chinese, Koreans, and Filipinos distanced themselves from the Japanese. But their reactions are instructive not only as examples of ethnic disidentification but also as testimonies to the pervasiveness of racial lumping. Popular confusion of the various Asian groups was so prevalent that it was necessary for Chinese, Filipinos, and Koreans to don ethnic clothing and identification buttons to differentiate themselves from the Japanese. Without these *visible* signs of ethnicity, these three Asian groups would probably have been mistaken for Japanese by anti-Japanese forces. As Ronald Takaki (1989: 370) reported, Asian groups "remembered how they had previously been called 'Japs' and how many whites had lumped all Asians together." But there are also examples of how Asian groups united when inter-Asian cooperation advanced their common interests.

Inter-Asian Labor Movements

The most notable example of inter-Asian solidarity was the 1920 collaboration of Japanese and Filipino plantation laborers in Hawaii. In the beginning, plantation workers had organized in terms of national origins. Thus, the Japanese belonged to the Japanese union and the Filipinos to the Filipino union. In the early 1900s, an ethnically based strike seemed sensible to Japanese plantation laborers because they represented about 70 percent of the entire work force. Filipinos constituted less than 1 percent. However, by 1920, Japanese workers represented only 44 percent of the labor force, while Filipino workers represented 30 percent. Japanese and Filipino union leaders understood that they would have to combine to be politically and economically effective (Johanessen 1950: 75–83; Takaki 1989: 152).

Because together they constituted more than 70 percent of the work force in Oahu, the 1920 Japanese–Filipino strike brought plantation operations to a sudden stop. Although the workers were eventually defeated, the 1920 strike was the "first major interethnic working-class struggle in Hawaii" (Takaki 1989: 154).[2] Subsequently, the Japanese Federation of Labor elected to become an interethnic union. To promote a multiethnic class solidarity, the new union called itself the Hawaii Laborers Association (Takaki 1989: 154–155).

Although the 1920 strike was a de facto example of pan-Asian cooperation, this cooperation needs to be distinguished from the post-1960 pan-Asian solidarity. The purported unifying factor in 1920 was a common class status, not a shared cultural or racial background (Takaki 1989: 154). This class solidarity is different from the large-scale organization of ethnicity that emerged in the late 1960s. For most Asian Americans, the more recent development represents an enlargement of their identity system, a circle beyond their previous national markers of identity. True, like working-class unions, pan-ethnic groups are interest groups with material demands (Glazer and Moynihan 1963; Bonacich and Modell 1980). However, unlike labor unions, panethnic groups couch their demands in ethnic or racial terms—not purely in class terms. In other words, their ethnicity is used as a basis for the assertion of collective claims, many but not all of which are class based.

Social and Demographic Changes: Setting the Context

Although Asians in the United States have long been engaged in political action, their efforts never drew public attention until the 1960s (Chan 1991: 171). Prompted by broader political struggles and internal demographic changes, college students of Asian ancestry spearheaded the Asian American movement. Critical to its development was the mobilization of American blacks. Besides offering tactical lessons, the civil rights and the Black Power movements had a profound impact on the consciousness of Asian Americans, sensitizing them to racial issues (Uyematsu 1971). The anticolonial nationalist movements in Asia also stirred racial and cultural pride and provided a context for the emergence of the Yellow Power movement (P. Wong 1972). Influenced by these broader political struggles, Americans of Asian ancestry united to denounce racist institutional structures, demand new or unattended rights, and assert their cultural and racial distinctiveness. Normal urban issues such as housing, education, and social welfare began to take on ethnic coloration.

While important, these broader societal developments alone do not explain why the Asian American movement became panethnic. To understand this development, we first need to understand the underlying social and demographic factors that allowed pan-Asianism to take root in the 1960s but not earlier. Before World War II, pan-Asian unity was not feasible because the predominantly foreign-born Asian population did not share a common language. During the postwar years, increasing intergroup communication and contact facilitated the emergence of a pan-Asian consciousness. The breakdown of economic and residential barriers during the postwar period provided the first opportunity for an unprecedented number of Asian Americans to come into intimate, sustained contact with the larger society— and with one another.

TABLE 2.1

Chinese and Japanese American Foreign-Born Population in the United States, 1860–1940

	Chinese		Japanese	
Year	Number	Percentage Foreign-Born	Number	Percentage Foreign-Born
1900	80,853	90	24,057	99
1910	56,596	79	67,655	94
1920	43,107	70	81,383	73
1930	44,086	59	70,477	51
1940	37,242	48	47,305	37

Source: U.S. Bureau of the Census (1943: tables 4 and 6).

From an Immigrant to a Native Population

Before 1940, the Asian population in the United States was primarily an immigrant population (see Table 2.1). Immigrant Asians faced practical barriers to pan-Asian unity. Foremost was their lack of a common language. Old national rivalries were another obstacle, as many early Asian immigrants carried the political memories and outlook of their homelands. For example, Japan's occupation of Korea resulted in pervasive anti-Japanese sentiments among Koreans in the United States. According to Brett Melendy (1977: 155), "Fear and hatred of the Japanese appeared to be the only unifying force among the various Korean groups through the years." Moreover, these historical enmities and linguistic and cultural differences reinforced one another as divisive agents.

During the postwar period, due to immigration restrictions and the growing dominance of the second and third generations, American-born Asians outnumbered immigrants. The demographic changes of the 1940s were pronounced. During this decade, nearly twenty thousand Chinese American babies were born. For the first time, the largest five-year cohort of Chinese Americans was under five years of age (Kitano and Daniels 1988: 37). By 1960, approximately two-thirds of the Asian population in California had been born in the United States (Ong 1989: 5–8). As the Asian population became a native-born community, linguistic and cultural differences began to blur. Although they had attended Asian-language schools, most American-born Asians possessed only a limited knowledge of their ethnic language (Chan 1991: 115). By 1960, with English as the common language, persons from different Asian backgrounds were able to communicate with one another (Ling 1984: 73), and in so doing create a common identity associated with the United States.

Moreover, unlike their immigrant parents, native-born and American-educated Asians could muster only scant loyalties to old world ties. Historical antagonisms between their mother countries thus receded in importance (P. Wong 1972: 34). For example, growing up in America, second-generation Koreans "had difficulty feeling the painful loss of the homeland and understanding the indignity of Japanese domination" (Takaki 1989: 292). Thus, while the older generation of Koreans hated all Japanese, "their children were much less hostile or had no concern at all" (Melendy 1977: 156). As a native-born Japanese American community advocate explained, "By 1968, we had a second generation. We could speak English; so there was no language problem. And we had little feelings of historical animosity" (Kokubun interview).

As national differences receded in subjective importance, generational differences widened. For the most part, American-born Asians considered themselves to have more in common with other American-born Asians than they did with foreign-born compatriots.[3] According to a third-generation Japanese American who is married to a Chinese American, "As far as our experiences in America, I have more things in common than differences with a Chinese American. Being born and raised here gives us something in common. We have more in common with each other than with a Japanese from Japan, or a Chinese from China" (Ichioka interview). Much to their parents' dismay, young Asian Americans began to choose their friends and spouses from other Asian groups. Eui-Young Yu (1983: 47) related that second- and third-generation Koreans "identify and intermingle as much with other Asian minorities as with fellow Koreans, especially with the Japanese and Chinese." Similarly, Stephen Fugita and David O'Brien (1991: 146) reported that the Sansei (third-generation) were much more likely than the Nisei (second-generation) to see themselves as Asian Americans. This muting of cultural and historical divisions distressed their parents, who, more often than not, had supported these divisions for most of their lives. As a young Chinese American asserted:

> My parents mean well and I try to respect them, but they do not understand what it's all about. We have buried the old hatreds between Chinese and Japanese, and my friends and I must go beyond our parents' "hang-ups." My mother is upset because I'm engaged to a Japanese girl but she knows she can do nothing about it. (Cited in Weiss 1974: 235)

The Watershed of World War II

Before World War II, Asian immigrant communities were quite distinct entities, isolated from one another and from the larger society. Because of language difficulties, prejudice, and lack of business opportunities elsewhere, there was little chance for Asians in the United States to live outside their ethnic enclaves (Yuan 1966: 331). Shut out of the mainstream of American society, the various immigrant groups struggled separately in their respective Chinatowns, Little Tokyos, or Manilatowns. Stanford Lyman (1970: 57–63) reported that the early Chinese and Japanese communities in the western states had little to do with one another—either socially or politically. Although statistical data do not exist, ethnographic accounts confirm the ethnic homogeneity of each early Asian immigrant community. For example, according to a study of New York's Chinatown in the 1890s, "The entire triangular space bounded by Mott, Pell, and Doyers Streets and Chatham Square is given to the exclusive occupancy of these Orientals" (cited in Yuan 1966: 323). Within these enclaves, diversity among Asian nationalities was more salient than commonality.

Economic and residential barriers began to crumble after World War II. The war against Nazism called attention to racism at home and discredited the notions of white superiority. The fifteen years after the war was a period of largely positive change as civil rights statutes outlawed racial discrimination in employment as well as housing (Daniels 1988: ch. 7). Popular attitudes were also changing. Polls taken during World War II showed a distinct hostility toward Japan: 74 percent of the respondents favored either killing off all Japanese, destroying Japan as a political entity, or supervising it. On the

West Coast, 97 percent of the people polled approved of the relocation of Japanese Americans. In contrast, by 1949, 64 percent of those polled were either friendly or neutral toward Japan (Feraru 1950).

During the postwar years, Asian American residential patterns changed significantly. Because of the lack of statistical data,[4] a longitudinal study of the changing residential patterns of Asian Americans cannot be made. However, descriptive accounts of Asian American communities indicate that these enclaves declined in the postwar years. Edwin Hoyt (1974: 94) reported that in the 1940s, second-generation Chinese Americans moved out of the Chinatowns. Although they still came back to shop or to see friends, they lived elsewhere. In 1940, Rose Hum Lee found twenty-eight cities with an area called Chinatown in the United States. By 1955, Peter Sih found only sixteen (Sung 1967: 143–144). New York's Chinatown exemplifies the declining significance of Asian ethnic enclaves. In 1940, 50 percent of the Chinese in New York City lived in its Chinatown; by 1960, less than one-third lived there (Yuan 1966: 331). Similarly, many returning Japanese Americans abandoned their prewar settlement in old central cities and joined the migration to suburbia (Daniels 1988: 294). In the early 1970s, Little Tokyo in Los Angeles remained a bustling Japanese American center, "but at night the shop owners [went] home to the houses in the suburbs" (Hoyt 1974: 84).

Although single-ethnic communities were still the norm, residential segregation between Asian nationalities declined in the postwar years. Formerly homogeneous, the ethnic enclaves started to house other Asian groups—as well as non-Asian groups. In 1957, driving past 7th and H streets in Washington, D.C., Betty Lee Sung (1967: 142–143) reported, "I passed the length of Chinatown before I suddenly realized that the place was almost deserted. The faces that I did see on the street were not Chinese but Filipinos." In 1970, due to the influx of Japanese and Filipinos, there was a proposal to rename Oakland Chinatown "Asiantown" (Sano 1970). Multigroup urban centers also emerged. Paul Wong (1972: 34) reported that since the early 1960s, Asian Americans of diverse national origins have moved into the suburbs outside the major Asian communities such as Berkeley or San Mateo, California. Although a small proportion of the local population, these Asian Americans tended to congregate in pockets; consequently, in some residential blocks a majority of the residents were Asian Americans.

TABLE 2.2

Mean Segregation Indices for Chinese and Japanese Americans in 822 U.S. Suburbs, 1960, 1970, and 1980

Ethnic Groups	1960	1970	1980	Change, 1960–80
Chinese–White	38.83	31.45	28.22	−10.61
Chinese–Black	54.02	50.42	49.43	−4.59
Japanese–White	34.00	22.16	26.77	−7.23
Japanese–Black	48.62	48.46	45.97	−2.65
Chinese–Japanese	39.11	27.70	24.97	−14.14

Source: Lam (1986: tables 1, 2, and 3).

Moreover, recent research on suburban segregation indicates that the level of segregation between certain Asian American groups is often less than that between them and non-Asians. Using Standard Metropolitan Statistical Area (SMSA) data[5] for 1960, 1970, and 1980, Frankie Lam (1986) computed indices of dissimilarity (ID)[6] among Chinese, Japanese, black, and white Americans in 822 suburbs. As indicated in Table 2.2, from 1960 to 1980 the level of segregation between Chinese and Japanese Americans was much less than that between these two groups and blacks and, in one case, less than that between these groups and whites. But the actual level of segregation is only one issue. The decline of segregation over time is another. From 1960 to 1980, Chinese segregation from the Japanese shows a more pronounced decline (−14.14) than that of Chinese or Japanese from whites (−10.61 and −7.23 respectively) and from blacks (−4.59 and −2.65 respectively).[7] Though not comprehensive, these studies together suggest that Asian residential segregation declined in the postwar years.

As various Asian groups in the United States interacted, they became aware of common problems and goals that transcended parochial interests and historical antagonisms. One recurrent problem was employment discrimination. According to a 1965 report published by the California Fair Employment Practices Commission, for every $51 earned by a white male Californian, Japanese males earned \$43 and Chinese males \$38—even though Chinese and Japanese American men had become slightly better educated than the white majority (Daniels 1988: 315). Moreover, although the postwar period marked the first time that well-trained Chinese and Japanese Americans could find suitable employment with relative ease, they continued to be passed over for promotion to administrative and supervisory positions (Kitano and Daniels 1988: 47). Asians in the United States began to see themselves as a group that shared important common experiences: exploitation, oppression, and discrimination (Uyematsu 1971).

Because inter-Asian contact and communication were greatest on college campuses, pan-Asianism was strongest there (P. Wong 1972: 33–34). Exposure to one another and to the mainstream society led some young Asian Americans to feel that they were fundamentally different from whites. Disillusioned with the white society and alienated from their traditional communities, many Asian American student activists turned to the alternative strategy of pan-Asian unification (Weiss 1974: 69–70).

The Construction of Pan-Asian Ethnicity

Although broader social struggles and internal demographic changes provided the impetus for the Asian American movement, it was the group's politics—confrontational and explicitly pan-Asian—that shaped the movement's content. Influenced by the internal colonial model, which stresses the commonalities among "colonized groups," college students of Asian ancestry declared solidarity with fellow Asian Americans—and with other Third World[8] minorities (Blauner 1972: ch. 2). Rejecting the label "Oriental," they proclaimed themselves "Asian American." Through pan-Asian organizations, publications, and Asian American studies programs, Asian American activists built pan-Asian solidarity by pointing out their common fate in American society. The pan-Asian concept enabled diverse Asian American groups to understand their "unequal circumstances and histories as being related" (Lowe 1991: 30).

From "Yellow" to "Asian American"

Following the example of the Black Power movement, Asian American activists spearheaded their own Yellow Power movement to seek "freedom from racial oppression through the power of a consolidated yellow people" (Uyematsu 1971: 12). In the summer of 1968, more than one hundred students of diverse Asian backgrounds attended an "Are You Yellow?" conference at UCLA to discuss issues of Yellow Power, identity, and the war in Vietnam (Ling 1989: 53). In 1970, a new pan-Asian organization in northern California called itself the "Yellow Seed" because "Yellow [is] the common bond between Asian-Americans and Seed symboliz[es] growth as an individual and as an alliance" (Masada 1970). This "yellow" reference was dropped when Filipino Americans rejected the term, claiming that they were brown, not yellow (Rabaya 1971: 110; Ignacio 1976: 84). At the first Asian American national conference in 1972, Filipino Americans "made it clear to the conferees that we were 'Brown Asians'" by forming a Brown Asian Caucus (Ignacio 1976: 139–141). It is important to note, however, that Filipino American activists did not reject the term "yellow" because they objected to the pan-Asian framework. Quite the contrary, they rejected it because it allegedly excluded them from that grouping (Rabaya 1971: 110).

Other community organizers used the term "Oriental" to define their organizations and service centers. In Southern California, the Council of Oriental Organizations (COO) became the political base for the diverse Asian American communities. In 1968, COO lobbied for federal funding to establish the Oriental Service Center in Los Angeles County, serving Chinese, Japanese, Filipinos, and Koreans. But Asian American activists also rejected *Oriental* because the term conjures up images of "the sexy Susie Wong, the wily Charlie Chan, and the evil Fu Manchu" (Weiss 1974: 234). It is also a term that smacks of European colonialism and imperialism: *Oriental* means "East"; Asia is "east" only in relationship to Europe, which was taken as the point of reference (Browne 1985). To define their own image and to claim an *American* identity, college students of Asian ancestry coined the term *Asian American* to "stand for all of us Americans of Asian descent" (Ichioka interview). While *Oriental* suggests passivity and acquiescence, *Asian Americans* connotes political activism because an Asian American "gives a damn about his life, his work, his beliefs, and is willing to do almost anything to help Orientals become Asian Americans" (cited in Weiss 1974: 234).

The account above suggests that the creation of a new name is a significant symbolic move in constructing an ethnic identity. In their attempt to forge a pan-Asian identity, Asian American activists first had to coin a composite term that would unify and encompass the constituent groups. Filipino Americans' rejection of the term "yellow" and the activists' objection to the cliché-ridden Oriental forced the group to change its name to Asian American. The history of the Sansei Concern, a UCLA student group, provides a telling example. In the summer of 1968, as we have seen, Sansei Concern organized the "Are You Yellow?" conference. At the end of the conference, in an effort to incorporate other Asian subgroups, Sansei Concern changed its name to Oriental Concern. In 1969, reflecting its growing political sophistication, the group changed its name once more to Asian American Political Alliance, a name adopted by a group of activists at the University of California at Berkeley the year before (Ling 1989: 53). It is noteworthy that while Yellow, Oriental, and Asian American connote different ideologies, all three terms signify panethnicity.

Pan-Asian Organizations

Influenced by the political tempo of the 1960s, young Asian Americans began to join such organizations as the Free Speech Movement at the University of California at Berkeley, Students for a Democratic Society, and the Progressive Labor Party. However, these young activists "had no organization or coalition to draw attention to themselves as a distinct group" (P. Wong 1972: 33). Instead, they participated as individuals—often at the invitation of their white or black friends (Chin 1971b: 285; Nakano 1984: 3–4). While Asian American activists subscribed to the integrationist ideology of the 1960s and 1970s social movements, they also felt impotent and alienated. There was no structure to uphold their own identity. As an example, when the Peace and Freedom Party was formed on the basis of black and white coalitions, Asian American activists felt excluded because they were neither black nor white (P. Wong 1972: 34; Yoshimura 1989: 107).

In the late 1960s, linking their political views with the growth of racial pride among their ranks, Asian Americans already active in various political movements came together to form their own organizations (Nakano 1984: 3–4). Most of the early pan-Asian organizations were college based. In 1968, activists at the University of California, Berkeley founded one of the first pan-Asian political organizations: the Asian American Political Alliance (AAPA). According to a co-founder of the organization, its establishment marked the first time that the term "Asian American" was used nationally to mobilize people of Asian descent (Ichioka interview). AAPA was formed to increase the political visibility and effectiveness of Asian American activists:

> There were so many Asians out there in the political demonstrations but we had no effectiveness. Everyone was lost in the larger rally. We figured that if we rallied behind our own banner, behind an Asian American banner, we would have an effect on the larger public. We could extend the influence beyond ourselves, to other Asian Americans. (Ichioka interview)

AAPA differed from the traditional Asian cultural groups on most college campuses in two primary ways: its political activism and its pan-Asian emphasis. Reflecting the various political movements from which its members had come, AAPA took progressive stands against the war in Vietnam and in support of other Third World movements (Ichioka interview). Espousing a pan-Asian framework, AAPA brought together young Chinese, Japanese, and Filipino American activists (Nishio 1982: 37).[9] Shortly after AAPA was formed at the University of California at Berkeley, a sister organization was established at San Francisco State College (now University). Like its Berkeley counterpart, San Francisco State AAPA "was a vehicle for students to share political concerns in a pan-Asian organization" (Umemoto 1989: 17). AAPA's influence also spread to Southern California as Asian American students formed similar organizations on the UCLA and California State University, Long Beach campuses (Ling 1984; Yoshimura 1989).

Pan-Asian organizations also mushroomed in other parts of the country. In 1969, through the initiative of West Coast students, Asian American organizations began to form on East Coast campuses. For example, in New York, young Asian Americans organized Asian

Americans for Action, or Triple A. At Columbia University, Asian Americans involved in white radical politics came together to found their own Asian American Political Alliance. Students at Yale prepared and taught a course on "Asians in America" (Chin 1971b: 285). Similarly, in the Midwest, the civil rights, antiwar, and United Farm Workers movements drew Asian Americans together. Out of these political gatherings emerged a group of Asian American activists who subsequently formed Madison's Asian Union, Illinois' Asian American Alliance, and Minneapolis' Asian American Political Alliance (*Rice Paper* 1975).

Not only did pan-Asian organizations reinforce the cohesiveness of already existing networks, but they also expanded these networks. By the mid-1970s, *Asian American* had become a familiar term (Lott 1976: 30). Although first coined by college activists, the pan-Asian concept began to be used extensively by professional and community spokespersons to lobby for the health and welfare of Americans of Asian descent. In addition to the local and single-ethnic organizations of an earlier era, Asian American professionals and community activists formed national and pan-Asian organizations such as the Pacific/Asian Coalition and the Asian American Social Workers (Ignacio 1976: 162; Kuo 1979: 283–284). Also, Asian American caucuses could be found in national professional organizations such as the American Public Health Association, the American Sociological Association, the American Psychological Association, the American Psychiatric Association, and the American Librarians Association (Lott 1976: 31). Commenting on the "literally scores of pan-Asian organizations" in the mid-1970s, William Liu (1976: 6) asserted that "the idea of pan-Asian cooperation [was] viable and ripe for development."

Asian American Studies

On college and university campuses, the most important legacy of the Asian American movement was the institutionalization of Asian American studies.[10] Beginning in 1968, under the slogan of self-determination, Asian American and other U.S. Third World students fought for an education more relevant and accessible to their communities. Reflecting the larger national struggle over cultural hegemony, these students demanded the right to control their educational agenda, to design their own programs, and to evaluate their instructors (Umemoto 1989: 3–4). In 1968, after the most prolonged and violent campus struggles in this country's history, Asian American studies programs were established at San Francisco State College (now University) and at the University of California at Berkeley. These campus struggles emboldened students at other colleges to fight for ethnic studies courses, programs, and departments and forced college administrations to heed such demands (Murase 1976a: 205–209). In succeeding years, Asian American Studies programs were established on major campuses throughout the country.[11] Since 1968, the field has progressed from experimental courses to degree programs. For example, UC Berkeley and UCLA now offer B.A. and M.A. degree programs in Asian American Studies respectively (Nakanishi and Leong 1978: 6).

Although varied in their curriculum development and course offerings, Asian American Studies programs built, and continue to build, an Asian American heritage, putting courses and reading selections together and expounding similarities—as well as differences—in the experiences of Asian peoples in the United States. Indeed, the curriculum was designed to help students "know who they are as Asian Americans" (Contemporary Asian Studies Division 1973: 38). Clearly part of the heritage being created hinges on Asian Americans' shared history of racial discrimination. Many courses stress an Asian American identity and experience, yielding highly emotional discussions on subjects dealing with discrimination, alienation, and racism (Weiss 1974: 241). Such an emphasis is evident in the following statement of curriculum philosophy for Asian American Studies:

> Throughout much of America's history, Asians in this country have been the victims of contempt and exploitation. Often they were singled out as scapegoats in periods of severe economic depression, such as the nation-wide anti-Chinese agitations and riots in the 1870's and 1880's, and Asian Americans were regarded as enemies during times of international conflicts, particularly the Second World War and the Korean War. (Contemporary Asian Studies Division 1973: 35)

This statement links together the experiences of Chinese, Japanese, and Korean Americans; in so doing, it calls attention to their collective identity.

TABLE 2.3

Percentage of Studies on Specific Asian Groups for Bibliographies and Publications Released during the 1970s and 1980s

Ethnic Group	Total Number	Percentage of Total Studies for Century	Percentage Published 1970s–80s
Asian	208	15	37
Chinese	460	33	23
East Indian	53	4	17
Filipino	96	7	26
Japanese	514	37	18
Korean	32	2	75
Pacific Islander	8	0.6	75
Southeast Asian	6	0.4	83

Source: Asians in America (1983: vii).

Also, Asian American scholars began to reinterpret Asian history in the United States to bring out what is common to all Asian Americans. These histories highlight a record of violence against Asians, who were denied the rights of citizenship, forbidden to own land, interned in relocation camps, and forced to live in poverty-stricken enclaves (Jensen and Abeyta 1987: 406). For example, in discussing discriminatory laws and informal acts perpetrated against Chinese, Korean, Filipino, and Japanese immigrants, Lowell Chun-Hoon (1975: 47) concluded that "what is significant [about this exploitation] is that all of these varied Asian groups, each representing a separate country and unique culture, encountered a similar or identical pattern of racial oppression and economic exploitation." Also, Asian Americans were treated increasingly as a single unit of analysis in academic studies. A survey of studies on Asian groups in the United States indicates that works dealing with "Asians" increased dramatically during the 1970s and 1980s (see Table 2.3). Articles published in these decades represent 37 percent of such articles published in this country, "almost three times as many works" as might have been expected (*Asians in America* 1983: viii).

Along the same lines, in addition to explaining specific group experiences, Asian American writers have turned their attention to those experiences shared by the various Asian peoples. In the 1971 publication *Roots: An Asian American Reader*, the autobiographies and poems that appear in the "Identity" section "express the increasing commitment of Asian Americans to redefine and articulate their individual and collective identity. While they reflect a wide range of backgrounds and responses to American society, there can be found a common level of experience with which all Asians in America can identify" (Tachiki 1971: 4). This new direction enlarged the context of Asian American writing, and led to the use of the term "Asian American literature" (E. Kim 1982). As Jesse Hiraoka (1986: 95) stated, the overriding objective "became that of establishing an Asian American heritage in terms of the arrival and stay of the Asians in the United States, and the changes that occurred as they consolidated their presence in American society."

In sum, Asian American Studies provides an institutional means to reach more Asian American students and to create "an Asian American awareness expressing a unity of all Asians, Chinese, Japanese, Filipino, Korean, Samoan, and Hawaiian" (E. Wong 1971: 248). Its by-products—the Association for Asian American Studies, national conferences, research centers, and publications—further stimulate pan-Asian solidarity because they provide a forum for Asian Americans to discuss common problems and experiences.[12] In these settings, "the experiences of different Asian groups were compared and recognized as historically intertwined" (Ling 1989: 73).

Asian American News Media

The 1960s and 1970s also saw the rapid growth of a pan-Asian news medium directed toward the largest possible Asian audience, covering both ethnic and panethnic developments and concerns (see Table 2.4). Ethnic publications are important because they promote ethnic ideology and keep alive ethnic symbols and values, heroes, and historical achievements. It is the very business of the ethnic media to be concerned with the events and progress of the ethnic group (Breton 1964: 201). Until the late 1960s, most of the Asian newspapers and periodicals were concerned primarily with local and single-ethnic issues.

TABLE 2.4
Partial Listing of Asian American Periodicals, Late 1960s–Early 1970s

Publication	Place of Publication
AACTION	Philadelphia, Pa
AASA	California State University at Northridge
AASA	Cornell University, Ithaca, N.Y.
Aion	San Francisco
Amerasia Journal	Yale University, New Haven, Conn. (now UCLA)
Ameri-Asia News	Forest City, Fla.
Asian American for Equal Employment Newspaper	New York City
Asian Expression	California State University at Dominguez Hills
Asian Family Affair	Seattle, Wash.
Asian Spotlight	College of San Mateo, Calif.
Asian Student, The	Berkeley, Calif.
Asian Student	City College of New York
Asian Student Voice	San Francisco State
Bridge: An Asian American Perspective	New York City
Crosscurrents	Los Angeles
East Wind	Los Angeles
Eastern Wind	Washington, D.C.
Getting Together	New York City Chinatown
Gidra	Los Angeles
Jade: The Asian American Magazine	Los Angeles
Pacific Ties	Los Angeles
Rice Paper	Madison, Wis.
Rodan	San Francisco

Source: Compiled by author.

Pan-Asian periodicals came out of the Asian American movement, the efforts of Asian American student organizations on university campuses across the country. In fact, "these newspapers, pamphlets, and magazines were the lifeblood of the movement" (Quinsaat 1976: 267). While the traditional ethnic press continued to be important, its neglect and disdain of such political issues as civil rights, the Vietnam war, and ethnic studies prompted young dissidents to launch their own publications. Much of their journalism was committed to the empowerment of the Asian American people.

Although not always successful, some publications attempted to formulate a pan-Asian perspective rather than any singular ethnic outlook (Quinsaat 1976). In 1969, five UCLA students put up $100 each to launch the monthly publication *Gidra*, the first and most widely circulated pan-Asian publication. In all, during its five years of publication, about two hundred individuals participated in producing *Gidra* (Murase 1976b). On the East Coast, *Getting Together*, a New York Chinatown newspaper, expounded Asian American issues from a militant orientation; its stated purpose was to "further advance the just causes of Asian people in this country" (Chin 1971a: 30; *Getting Together* 1972: 1). These movement periodicals covered both ethnic and panethnic concerns. For example, the first issue of *Getting Together* included the following stories: "Chinatown and Its Problems," "Serving the People," "Yellow Power," and "Concentration Camps in the USA." Emphasizing its Chinese American as well as Asian American identity, the staff of *Getting Together* wrote, "We are not a bunch of 'do-gooders' out to save somebody else; we only know that our freedom and happiness are tied-in with the freedom and happiness of every Chinese and every Asian person" (cited in Chin 1971b: 286). Initiated in 1971 by the Yale Asian American Students Association, *Amerasia Journal* (now housed at UCLA) became the only national scholarly publication devoted exclusively to the study of the experience of Asians in America.

Besides functioning as a source of news for young Asian American activists, these media efforts also forged pan-Asian consciousness. Through articles, poetry, and photographs in a variety of publications, and by meeting together, these young Asian Americans across the country began to communicate with one another and to share their frustrations and their dreams. From these efforts, they began "to formulate their own values, establish their own identities and sense of pride, and create a new 'culture' which they can truly call Asian American" (Chin 1971a: 29). In the final issue of *Gidra*, Mike Murase (1976b: 319) described the solidarity that emerged from this collective experience:

> It has been an experience in sharing—in giving and receiving—in a sisterly and brotherly atmosphere. It has meant a chance to work for something we really believe in. It has meant a chance to express ourselves in a variety of ways. . . . It has meant working with people who care about people, and genuinely feeling the strength that can only come out of collective experience.[13]

By the mid-1970s, due to inadequate manpower and funding, many of the movement publications had folded. In their place came slicker and more business-minded publications. The transition from radical to "bourgeois" journalism reflects broader changes in pan-Asian political consciousness in the last two decades—from the confrontational to the more orthodox. For example, founded in the late 1980s, both *Rice* and *AsiAm* were nationally distributed magazines geared toward young and upper-income Asian American professionals.[14] Among the pan-Asian newspapers, *Asian Week*, published in San Francisco since 1979, has been the most stable. According to the weekly's managing editor, the management team decided to name the newspaper *Asian Week* instead of the proposed *Chinese Week* to "reflect the widespread acceptance of the pan-Asian concept" (Andersen interview). In recent years, some single-ethnic newspapers have also broadened their scope to cover additional Asian communities. For example, in the mid-1980s, *East/West* dropped its subtitle "A Chinese American Newspaper" and devoted more space to national Asian American issues. A content analysis of the longstanding Japanese American publication *Pacific Citizen* indicates that, from 1955 to 1985, the newspaper became more pan-Asian. As Table 2.5 indicates, the surge in Asian articles coincided with the Asian American movement of the late 1960s.

Although varied in their successes, these pan-Asian journals testify to the salience of a generalized Asian American readership. They are also important because they bring the news of the entire Asian American population to the various Asian American subgroups. In so doing, they enlarge the scope of Asian American awareness and dialogue beyond the boundaries of province and nationality.

TABLE 2.5
Number of Pacific Citizen **Articles Covering Asian Stories,**
April, August, and December 1955–85

Year	April	August	December	Total
1955	0	0	1	1
1960	0	0	0	0
1965	1	0	0	1
1970	12	5	8	25
1975	2	2	1	5
1980	4	4	4	12
1985	12	5	7	24

Source: Compiled by author from *Pacific Citizen*, 1955–85. An Asian story is defined as one that covers a non-Japanese Asian group or one that covers all Asian groups. Only the first issue of each month was examined.

An Asian American Perspective: In Quest of Identity

Although an offshoot of the mass struggles of the late 1960s, the Asian American movement was not only a political movement but one that emphasized "race," as that term is conventionally understood. Like their non-Asian peers of the time, young Asian American activists joined in the struggles against poverty, war, and exploitation. However, they often viewed these struggles from an Asian American perspective, emphasizing race and racism directed against Asian Americans. This racial perspective bound them to other Asian groups as well as to other minorities, while separating them from whites. The importance of race (or racial ideology) is most evident in Asian American participation in and interpretation of the antiwar, New Left, and women's movements.

Antiwar Movement

The antiwar movement united Asian Americans along racial lines. For many Asian American activists, the American invasion of Vietnam involved more than the issues of national sovereignty or imperialism; it also raised questions of racism directed against Asian people (Kwong 1987: 148). Watching the images of war on the evening television news, "an increasing number of Asian American college and high school students realized with a shock that the 'enemy' whom American soldiers were maiming and killing had faces like their own" (Chan 1991: 174). Seeing unarmed, unresisting civilians napalmed in Vietnam angered young Asian Americans and stirred them to protest the prevailing assumption that Asian lives were cheap. To emphasize the racist nature of the war, Asian American protesters discarded the popular slogans "Give peace a chance" and "Bring the GIs home," and touted their own "Stop killing our Asian brothers and sisters" and "We don't want your racist war" (P. Wong 1972: 35–36). According to Asian American antiwar activists, the slogan "Bring our boys home" clearly proclaimed that the primary concern was to avoid American, not Vietnamese, casualties (*Bridge* 1973: 3).

As Asian people fighting in an Asian country, Asian American G.I.s were particularly repulsed by the atrocities committed against the Vietnamese people:

> For some G.I.'s in Vietnam, there are no Vietnamese people. To them the land is not populated by people but by "Gooks," considered inferior, unhuman animals by the racist-educated G.I. Relieved in his mind of human responsibility by this grotesque stereotype, numerous barbarities have been committed against these Asian peoples, since "they're only 'Gooks.'" (Nakamura 1971: 24)

Because of their racial similarity to the "enemy," Asian American G.I.s also endured anti-Asian racism. Many Asian Americans complained that their superior officers and fellow G.I.s lumped them together with other Asian groups: regardless of their ethnic background, Asian American soldiers were indiscriminately called Gook, Jap, Chink, or Ho Chi Minh. An Asian American G.I. related that, upon entering basic training, he was called a "Gook" and was made to stand in front of his platoon as an example of "what the enemy looked like" (Yoshimura 1971). The "Gook" stereotype "portrays Koreans, Vietnamese, Cambodians, Laotians, and other Asians as subhuman beings who do not value individual human life and who all look like the treacherous Chinese Communist enemy" (Tachiki 1971: 2–3).

The stereotype angered and ethnicized Asian American G.I.s. As a former American G.I. of Japanese ancestry related, "I became ethnicized when I was in Vietnam. I saw how whites were treating the Vietnamese, calling them Gooks, running them over with their trucks. I figured I am a Gook also" (Watanabe interview).

At times, the race question alienated Asian Americans from the majority of the antiwar protesters. An Asian American activist recounted the tension in the antiwar camp:

> In the early stage, there was a debate on what would be the main slogan. One slogan was "Bring the GIs home." The white component felt that this would unite the greatest amount of concern. But the Asian community felt that this slogan ignored what the U.S. was doing over there in Asia. Asian Americans were the only group that pushed the question of racism toward Asians. They wanted to know why the U.S. was involved in Asia in World War II and in Vietnam now. (Omatsu interview)

In 1971, the Asian American contingent refused to join the main antiwar march in Washington, D.C. because the coordinating committee failed to adopt the contingent's antiracist statement for the march. On other occasions, the contingent's appeals "were met with hostility and rejection" (P. Wong 1972: 34–36). When Asian Americans did take part in the white-dominated marches, they passed out their own leaflets, which denounced racism and imperialism. A Japanese American antiwar protester described the Asian flavor of the Asian American contingent:

> I marched in the April 24 [antiwar] demonstration in San Francisco with the Asian contingent. That was everybody: Filipinos, Chinese, Koreans, and Japanese. We marched together, waving red books and carried the People's Chinese flag, a Pathet Lao flag, some North Korean flags, Vietnamese flags, and a Chinese flag—and it was good. (Sumi 1971: 259)

In sum, Asian American emphasis on race and racism differentiates their antiwar protest from that of whites. In characterizing the Vietnam war as a racist act against Asians, Asian American activists proclaimed racial solidarity not only with each other but also with the Vietnamese people, their "Asian brothers and sisters" (*Bridge* 1973: 3). In the process, pan-Asian political consciousness became transnationalized, encompassing the political struggles not only in

America but also in Asia. As an Asian American activist stated, "As long as there are U.S. troops in Asia, as long as the U.S. government and the military wage wars of aggression against Asian people, racism against Asians will serve the interest of this country. Racism against them is often racism against us" (Yoshimura 1971: 29).

New Left Movement

In the late 1960s and early 1970s, a significant number of Asian Americans also became active in New Left activities and organizations such as the Free Speech Movement (FSM), Students for a Democratic Society (SDS), the Weathermen, and the Progressive Labor Party. Asian American Marxist organizations grew out of these New Left activities (Nakano 1984: 2–3). Diverging from the Old Left emphasis on the working class as the leading revolutionary stratum, the New Left sought to organize people across class lines. The New Left also looked away from the Soviet Union and to the Vietnamese National Liberation Front and the People's Republic of China as new models of socialism. It was the New Left's version of socialism and the movements growing admiration for Asian countries that influenced the thinking of Asian American Marxists (Liu and Cheng 1986: 144–145).

As in the antiwar movement, the Asian American New Left separated itself from the dominant New Left movement over the issues of racism and national oppression. It was over these questions that Asian American working people acquainted themselves with Marxism—a Marxism that emphasized race as well as class (Liu and Cheng 1986: 148). Influenced by the call for national liberation by the Black Power movement and Asian socialist countries, Asian American Marxists added racial self-determination to their revolutionary agenda (Nakano 1984: 4–5). For many Asian American community activists, there was no contradiction between a Marxist–Leninist approach and the prominence given to race. Because race constitutes such a fundamental category in American society, Asian Americans (and other racial minority groups) often view class issues from a racial perspective (Lipsitz 1988: 235). For example, the ethnic consciousness of the Red Guard in San Francisco's Chinatown "usually supersedes and sometimes clashes with their alleged attachment to a class-oriented ideology" (Lyman 1973: 29).[15] The centrality of race is evident in the following call for Marxist–Leninist organizing in the Asian American communities:

> The situation in the Asian communities is so deplorable that a Marxist-Leninist Party must begin to take firm root among the people. It is necessary that this party does not alienate the people or create any factions among the budding Asian American movement as we do not even make up 1% of the total population of America. The purpose of this party is to educate the people on the fact that the Asian communities in America are included in the genocidal American foreign policy in Asia. (Hing 1970: 9–10)

In contrast, other white-dominated groups like the Revolutionary Union (now the Revolutionary Communist Party) considered the national oppression question to be of secondary importance to the "bread and butter" issues that affected all workers (*East Wind* 1979: 111).

Varied in their understanding and application of Marxism, Asian American Marxist organizations struggled over the relative importance of nation building and party building. Despite their desires for revolutionary change and socialism, the issue of national liberation continued to be the guiding principle for many Asian American community groups. This position is evident in the following statement issued by the I Wor Kuen (IWK),[16] the largest revolutionary organization in the Asian American community in the 1970s:

> Our organization, like many others in America, arose as a response to national oppression and racial discrimination, and as part of the growing anti-imperialist movement in the 1960s. We formed as an Asian organization because, in 1968–69, the national oppression and corresponding national struggles of Third World peoples was the sharpest in the nationwide progressive movements. Furthermore, the bankruptcy of the Communist Party, USA and Progressive Labor Party, among others, especially in relation to the national question, made joining their ranks out of the question. (I Wor Kuen 1974: 6–7)

The IWK also combined the goal of racial self-determination with the goal of socialism. For example, in 1969, the organization issued a twelve-point program and platform that included demands for self-determination for Asian Americans and Asians as well as the establishment of a socialist party (Liu and Cheng 1986: 147).

In 1972, in an attempt to apply Marxism to the national question, the Marxist-oriented organization East Wind adopted the "Asian nation" line. Echoing the separatist call in the black community, East Wind declared that as a racially oppressed minority, Asian Americans were entitled to form their own nation. Although East Wind dropped the Asian nation line in 1975, it continued to stress the importance of national liberation (Nakano 1984: 10–12). On the other hand, organizations such as the New York–based Asian Study Group advocated party building and criticized other Asian American revolutionary groups for their preoccupation with "band-aid" social service programs (Nakano 1984: 14–17). Many of these differences remained unresolved, eventually dissolving friendships as well as organizations (Ling 1984).

In short, as in the antiwar movement, Asian American Marxists added a racial perspective to the New Left movement. This racial perspective bound them to other Asian Americans as it separated them from other non-Asian components. Just as women in other social movements were identifying barriers that restricted their roles, Asian American women activists began to challenge sexism and introduce gender-related issues into the Asian American movement.

Women's Movement

Although Asian American women had been involved in each stage of the Asian American movement, they were often restricted to such subordinate tasks as taking minutes, typing, making coffee, and answering phones. The small number of Asian American women who achieved leadership positions in the movement found themselves called "bossy" and "unfeminine" (*Rodan* 1971; Ling 1989: 53). Asian American feminists who challenged Asian American sexism were often cast as betraying Asian American nationalism—as assimilationists (Lowe 1991: 31).

Sexist oppression prevailed even in the most revolutionary Asian American organizations. For example, the San Francisco–based Red Guards initially claimed that women's worth was only in staying at home and in producing children (Nakano 1984: 13). Along the same lines, the Marxist-oriented I Wor Kuen championed forsaking monogamy to liberate relations between men and women and to build collective solidarity. In actuality, this sexual liberation was "a cover for degeneracy and the most blatant forms of male supremacy and the oppression of women" (cited in Nakano 1984: 13). Rebelling against the sexual oppression of women in the Asian American movement, an angry Asian American poet wrote:

> so you come to me for a spiritual piece
> my eyes have the ol' epicanthic fold
> my skin is the ideologically correct color
> a legit lay for the revolutionary
> well, let me tell you, brother
> revolution must be total
> and you're in its way
> yeah, yeah, I'm all sympathy
> your soul and your sexuality has
> been fucked over by Amerika
> well, so has mine
> so has ours
> we chronic smilers
> asian women
> we of the downcast almond eyes
> are seeing each other
> sisters now, people now
> asian women. (T. Tanaka 1971)

Frustrated with male chauvinism, Asian American women began meeting separately from men to discuss feminist concerns. Their collective anger was nurtured by the progressive ideology of the women's movement of the late 1960s. Although they borrowed heavily from the general women's movement, Asian American women seldom joined these middle-class, white-dominated organizations. Like black, Chicana, and Native American women, Asian American women felt alienated and at times exploited by these women's organizations.

In its early development, the women's movement was in fact insensitive to the issues of minority and lower-class women (Ling 1989). In contrast, Asian American and other Third World feminists emphasized the "triple oppression" concept: their gender was inextricably linked to their race and class. As an Asian women's studies instructor reflected, "The writings of white middle-class women on 'women's lib' . . . failed to speak relevantly to Asian American women. Many Asian women faced discrimination not only as women, but also on the basis of race, cultural background or low socio-economic status" (Chen 1976: 235). In the provocative "Yellow Prostitution," an Asian American feminist chastised Asian women who tried to be white:

> It is not enough that we must "kow tow" to the Yellow male ego, but we must do this by aping the Madison Avenue and Hollywood version of *White* femininity. All the peroxide, foam rubber, and scotch tape will not transform you into what you are not. . . . Whether this is a conditioned desire to be white, or a desperate attempt to attain male approval, it is nothing more than Yellow Prostitution. (Gil 1968)

Because "their ethnic identity was a critical component of their feminism" (Ling 1989: 52), Asian American feminists refused to advocate a non-Asian alliance—despite the fact that white feminists could offer important resources and shared similar concerns. Distancing themselves from the general feminist movement, Asian American women organized their own movement. For Asian American women activists, the ideology of feminism had to be incorporated into the larger identity of being Asian American. According to Susie Ling (1989: 63), "The Asian Women's Movement's umbilical cord was still very much attached to the larger Asian American Movement." Asian American women chose two major paths of activism: they worked within the Asian American community or within Marxist–Leninist groups. In 1971, Asian American women in Los Angeles organized Asian Sisters to address the drug problems of young Asian American women. It was one of the first social service projects for Asian American women by Asian American women. In 1972, they established Little Friends Playground to provide childcare for the community (Ling 1989). The Marxist–Leninist groups that Asian American women were involved in remain Asian American–oriented today (Ling 1984: 209). Asian American women were also concerned with the social conditions of their Asian sisters in China and Vietnam. For example, in 1971, the Los Angeles Asian women's movement sent delegates to the Vancouver Indochinese Women's Conference to express their solidarity with these women (Ling 1989: 55).

The Limits of Pan-Asianism

Although pan-Asian consolidation certainly has occurred, it has been by no means universal. For those who wanted a broader political agenda, the pan-Asian scope was too narrow and its racial orientation too segregative (P. Wong 1972: 33; Lowe 1991: 39). For others who wanted to preserve ethnic particularism, the pan-Asian agenda threatened to remove second- and third-generation Asians "from their conceptual ties to their community" (R. Tanaka 1976: 47). These competing levels of organization mitigated the impact of pan-Asianism.

Moreover, pan-Asianism has been primarily the ideology of native-born, American-educated, and middle-class Asians. Embraced by students, artists, professionals, and political activists, pan-Asian consciousness thrived on college campuses and in urban settings. However, it barely touched the Asian ethnic enclaves. When the middle-class student activists carried the enlarged and politicized Asian American consciousness to the ethnic communities, they encountered apprehension, if not outright hostility (Chan 1991: 175). Conscious of their national origins and overburdened with their day-to-day struggles for survival, most community residents ignored or spurned the movement's political agenda (P. Wong 1972: 34). Chin (1971b: 287) reported that few Chinatown residents participated in any of the pan-Asian political events. Similarly, members of the Nisei-dominated Japanese American Citizens League "were determined to keep a closed mind and maintain their negative stereotype" of the members of the Asian American Political Alliance (J. Matsui 1968: 6). For their part, young Asian American activists accused their elders of having been so whitewashed that they had deleted their experiences of prejudice and discrimination from their history (Weiss 1974: 238). Because these young activists were not rooted in the community, their base of support was narrow and their impact upon the larger society often limited (P. Wong 1972: 37; Nishio 1982: 37).

Even among those who were involved in the Asian American movement, divisions arose from conflicting sets of interests as subgroups decided what and whose interests would be addressed. Oftentimes, conflicts over material interests took on ethnic coloration, with participants from smaller subgroups charging that "Asian American" primarily meant Chinese and Japanese American, the

TABLE 2.6
Asian American Studies Instructors in the United States
by Ethnic Group, 1973

Ethnic Group	Total	Doctorate	Master's	Bachelor's or less	Don't Know
Chinese	27	1	10	12	4
Filipino	9	1	1	4	3
Japanese	33	6	14	6	7
Korean	3	1	1	1	0
White	5	4	0	0	1
Don't Know	5	0	1	0	4

Source: Chun-Hoon, Hirata, and Moriyama (1973: 85). Chun-Hoon, Hirata, and Moriyama (1973) sent about twenty-five questionnaires to select institutions across the country. The table is based on the eight responses received.

two largest and most acculturated Asian American groups at the time (Ignacio 1976: 220; Ling 1984: 193–195). For example, most Asian American Studies programs did not include courses on other Asian groups, but only on Chinese and Japanese. Similarly, the Asian American women's movement often subsumed the needs of their Korean and Filipina members under those of Chinese and Japanese women (Ling 1984: 193–195). Chinese and Japanese Americans also were the instructors of Asian American ethnic studies (see Table 2.6), directors and staff members of many Asian American projects,[17] and advisory and panel members in many governmental agencies (Ignacio 1976: 223–224).

The ethnic and class inequality within the pan-Asian structure has continued to be a source of friction and mistrust, with participants from the less dominant groups feeling shortchanged and excluded. As discussed in subsequent chapters, the influx of the post-1965 immigrants and the tightening of public funding resources have further deepened the ethnic and class cleavages among Asian American subgroups.

Conclusion

The development of a pan-Asian consciousness and constituency reflected broader societal developments and demographic changes, as well as the group's political agenda. By the late 1960s, pan-Asianism was possible because of the more amicable relationships among the Asian countries, the declining residential segregation among diverse Asian groups in America, and the large number of native-born, American-educated political actors. Disillusioned with the larger society and estranged from their traditional communities, third- and fourth-generation Asian Americans turned to the alternative strategy of pan-Asian unification. Through pan-Asian organizations, media, and Asian American Studies programs, these political activists assumed the role of "cultural entrepreneurs" consciously creating a community of culture out of diverse Asian peoples.[18] This process of pan-Asian consolidation did not proceed smoothly nor did it encompass all Asian Americans. Ethnic chauvinism, competition for scarce resources, and class cleavages continued to divide the subgroups. However, once established, the pan-Asian structure not only reinforced the cohesiveness of already existing networks but also expanded these networks. As later chapters indicate, although first conceived by young Asian American activists, the pan-Asian concept was subsequently institutionalized by professionals and community groups, as well as government agencies. The confrontational politics of the activists eventually gave way to the conventional and electoral politics of the politicians, lobbyists, and professionals, as Asian Americans continued to rely on the pan-Asian framework to enlarge their political capacities.

Chapter 3

Electoral Politics

When the pan-Asian concept was first formulated in the late 1960s, it represented the confrontational politics of the community activists. In recent years, as racial politics has evolved from political protest to mainstream political participation (Omi and Winant 1986), pan-Asian ethnicity has come to signify the "bourgeois" politics of the professionals, lobbyists, and politicians. This chapter discusses Asian American involvement in electoral politics; the next two examine advocacy politics, focusing on pan-Asian lobbying efforts in social service funding and census classification.

Roughly speaking, electoral power is the product of a group's size and its coalition-building aptitude and achievement. Other things being equal, the larger the group, the more politically influential it is likely to be. When small, a group obtains access to political influence by combining forces with kindred groups. If Asian American subgroups can come together, then the united pan-Asian group will have more members and thus more political power than would any Asian American subgroup operating alone. But the need for more numbers is only one reason for pan-Asian political organization. The other is common destiny—as outsiders continue to treat Asian Americans as a largely undifferentiated racial category. For these reasons, politically minded Asian Americans find it expedient—and at times necessary—to aggregate Asian American subgroups when seeking to recast their history of disfranchisement and obtain political recognition.

Asian American Political Participation

Legislative discrimination has stunted the political mobility of Asian Americans in this country. The Naturalization Act of 1790 denied first-generation Asian immigrants the right to vote or to hold elected positions. Moreover, the 1882 Chinese Exclusion Law, a clause in the 1917 Immigration Act that delineated a "barred zone" (a triangular area encompassing most of the Asian continent) from which no one could immigrate into the United States, and the 1924 Immigration Act cut off immigration from Asia by permitting only individuals eligible for citizenship to immigrate. Lacking numbers and ineligible to vote, members of early Asian communities wielded little voting power. Because these discriminatory laws were not nullified until the passage of the 1952 McCarran–Walter Act and the 1965 Immigration and Nationality Act (Chan 1991: ch. 3), Asian American participation in the electoral arena is primarily a post–World War II phenomenon.

In a political system in which numbers count, a population increase can boost a group's electoral leverage. Because of the high level of immigration since 1965, Asian Americans have become the fastest growing segment of the U.S. population. During the 1970s, when the total U.S. population increased by only 11 percent, the Asian American population grew by 141 percent (Gardner, Robey, and Smith 1985: 7). According to the first 1990 census figures released in March 1991, the Asian American population more than doubled during the 1980s. In contrast, the Hispanic and black populations grew by 53 and 13 percent respectively, the white population declined by almost 3 percent. California led the nation in the growth of the Asian American population, increasing by 1.5 million people, or 127 percent (Clifford 1991).

While the Asian American growth rate has been dramatic, the percentage of Asians in the total population continues to be small in many states. Only in Hawaii do Asian Americans predominate, comprising close to 62 percent of the population in 1980 and also in

1990. California, the state with the next highest proportion of Asian Americans, was just 5.5 percent Asian in 1980 and 9.6 percent in 1990 (Gardner, Robey, and Smith 1985: 11; Clifford 1991). Asian American growth also is concentrated geographically. In 1990, more than two-thirds (67 percent) of all Asian Americans lived in just five states. California, with 40 percent of the nation's total, remained the state with the biggest share, up from 35 percent in 1980. Hawaii, which historically has had a large Asian American population, ranked second with 11 percent, down from 16 percent in 1980. New York, Illinois, and New Jersey rounded out the top five. Moreover, nearly half (47 percent) of the nation's Asian American population lived in one of six metropolitan areas: Honolulu, Los Angeles–Long Beach, San Francisco–Oakland, New York, Chicago, and San Jose (O'Hare and Felt 1991: 6). This geographical concentration means that Asian American political leverage is greatest in certain Asian-populated pockets in California and in Hawaii. Outside these areas, it is nearly impossible for Asian American candidates to be elected without the support of non-Asian voters.

Political Participation as Voters

Whatever their numbers, Asian Americans must vote to be politically effective. In general, minority groups are less likely to vote than white Americans. As indicated in Table 3.1, from 1964 to 1988, voter turnout had consistently been higher among whites than among either blacks or Hispanic Americans. Unfortunately, comparable data were not collected for the Asian American population. Aside from occasional newspaper articles and a few studies in California, little empirical data exist on the electoral participation of Asian Americans.

Although preliminary, available evidence also suggests that Asian Americans make little use of the vote. A 1984 analysis of the voter registration lists for three areas of high Asian American concentration in San Francisco revealed that Chinese and Japanese Americans registered to vote at far lower levels than did their neighbors in their districts and in the city as a whole (Din 1984). In Los Angeles, Asian Americans' overall registration rate of 29 percent in 1984 was substantially lower than that of the county's overall rate of approximately 60 percent (Nakanishi 1986). A 1990 California survey

TABLE 3.1

Percentage Reported Voting by Race and Hispanic Origin,
November 1964–November 1988

| | Voting Rates | | |
Year	White	Black	Hispanic Origin
PRESIDENTIAL ELECTIONS			
1964	70.7	58.5	NA
1968	69.1	57.6	NA
1972	64.5	52.1	37.5
1976	60.9	48.7	31.8
1980	60.9	50.5	29.9
1984	61.4	55.8	32.6
1988	59.1	51.5	28.8
CONGRESSIONAL ELECTIONS			
1974	46.3	33.8	22.9
1978	47.3	37.2	23.5
1982	49.9	43.0	25.3
1986	47.0	43.2	24.2

Source: U.S. Bureau of the Census (1989a: table A).

indicated that Asian Americans had the state's lowest registration rate of all groups: 39 percent compared to 65 percent for non-Hispanic whites, 58 percent for blacks, and 42 percent for Hispanic Americans (Field Institute 1990; also see Cain and Kiewiet 1986). Thus, in California and in the state's two most heavily populated Asian American areas (Los Angeles and San Francisco), Asian Americans' electoral participation—and thus their political influence as voters—is much lower than that of the general population.

Why individuals vote or fail to vote is a longstanding concern among social scientists. Students of political participation have argued that differences in voting behavior result primarily from differences in socioeconomic status. In general, the rate of voting increases with increased income, education, and status (Moore and Pachon 1985: 173; Cain and Kiewiet 1986: I-29). For example, in the

TABLE 3.2
Asian American Foreign-Born Population, 1980

	Percentage Foreign-Born of Group		
Ethnic	*United States*	*California*	*Los Angeles County*
Total Asian	73.0	66.8	63.1
Asian Indian	70.4	73.6	75.8
Chinese	63.3	62.3	70.3
Filipino	66.3	67.7	72.8
Japanese	28.4	28.8	28.5
Korean	81.8	83.8	85.9
Vietnamese	90.5	92.0	92.9

Source: U.S. Bureau of the Census (1988*a:* tables 3 and 5).

1988 presidential election, college graduates were more than twice as likely to report having voted (78 percent) than were persons who had attended only elementary school (37 percent). Higher income groups were also more likely to vote than lower income groups; 76 percent of voting-age persons living in families with yearly incomes of $50,000 or more voted, compared with only 35 percent of those in families with incomes of less than $5,000 (U.S. Bureau of the Census 1989*a:* 2). However, the relationship between socioeconomic characteristics and voting behavior is much weaker for Asian Americans. Although Asian Americans score high on the demographic indicators that predict high political participation, their actual participation rates are comparatively low (Nakanishi 1986: 13; Cain 1988: 28).[1]

To understand the relatively low electoral participation of Asian Americans, one needs to take into account their sizeable foreign-born population. In 1980 the proportion of foreign-born Asian Americans was 73 percent in the United States, 67 percent in California, and 63 percent in Los Angeles County (see Table 3.2). Preliminary research has indicated that the higher the percentage of foreign-born residents in an area, the lower the electoral participation rate (Din 1984: 83; Nakanishi 1986 :1). New immigrants face numerous obstacles that limit their electoral participation, including limited English ability,[2] unfamiliarity with the political system, and ignorance of the political

TABLE 3.3
Citizenship Status of the Asian Population in the United States, 1980

Ethnic Group	Persons 15 Years Old and Over	Percentage Citizen
Total U.S.	175,307,629	96.6
Total Asian	2,572,147	55.2
Asian Indian	282,417	39.6
Cambodian	10,450	6.2
Chinese	640,563	58.9
Filipino	569,903	57.5
Hmong	2,775	13.7
Indonesian	7,740	34.7
Japanese	597,787	81.2
Korean	241,962	39.4
Laotian	25,794	6.8
Thai	33,080	18.0
Vietnamese	159,676	12.2

Source: U.S. Bureau of the Census (1988*b:* table 7).

issues. Moreover, continuing concern for the politics of their mother countries often supersedes interest in the politics of the United States, leading to low electoral participation. For example, recent Asian immigrants and refugees continue to be active in opposition movements against both right-wing and communist regimes in the Philippines, Korea, India, and Vietnam (Bello and Reyes 1986–87; Waldman 1988).

Also, like Hispanic Americans, a high percentage—nearly 45 percent in 1980—of Asian Americans cannot vote because they are not yet citizens (see Table 3.3).[3] When controlling for citizenship, Bruce Cain and Roderick Kiewiet (1986: I–24) found that the proportion of Asian American respondents in California who voted in the 1984 election increased from 48 to 69 percent, prompting them to conclude that the relatively low rate of Asian American electoral participation "is due principally to their large numbers of noncitizens." But Asian immigrants are fast becoming citizens. Between 1976 and 1986, immigrants from Asia represented the largest group of newly naturalized citizens, constituting 43 percent of all immigrants naturalized during this period (Portes and Rumbaut 1990: 117). The naturalization rate of Asian Americans also increases with their length of residence. An analysis of the 1980 census indicates that while the naturalization rate was only 36 percent for Asians who had been in the country from five to ten years, it was 80 percent for those who had been here for more than fifteen years (Ong, Espiritu, and Azores 1991: 10).

As Asian immigrants become citizens, learn English, and familiarize themselves with the political system, they may become more involved in electoral politics. Not content to wait, community organizations and political parties have attempted to speed up the process. In major urban areas in California, Illinois, New York, and Texas, Asian American advocacy organizations have launched voter registration drives to increase Asian American electoral participation.[4] The Republican and Democratic parties have both hired Asian American recruiters to assist them in courting Asian American voters (*Asian Week* 1989b; Andersen 1990b).

Political Attitudes and Partisanship

Voting alone, however, does not ensure political power unless group members vote en bloc. Jewish, Irish, and black American communities have been effective politically because they have tended to vote as a bloc—almost solidly for liberal Democrats (Glazer and Moynihan 1963; Lieberson 1980). Similarly, Japanese Americans in Hawaii have enhanced their political prowess by voting largely for Democratic candidates (Haas 1987: 658–659). Outside Hawaii, however, single-ethnic and pan-Asian bloc voting has largely been ineffective because the Asian American electorate has been too small to make any difference at most governmental levels.

Beyond purely mathematical considerations, the weak partisanship of Asian Americans dilutes their potential impact as a voting bloc. As a group, Asian Americans have not aligned themselves with either the Republicans or the Democrats. Cain and Kiewiet (1986: I–18) reported that, in 1984, California's registered Asian Americans were evenly split between the Democrats and the Republicans, 42 and 41 percent, respectively. Moreover, a higher percentage of Asian Americans than other racial and ethnic groups declared themselves to be independents or mild partisans (Cain 1988: 30). According to Grant Din (1984) and Don Nakanishi (1986), among Chinese, Vietnamese, Korean, and Asian Indian registered voters, approximately one in five declined to specify a party affiliation.[5]

Unity at the polls is also elusive because Asian American subgroups often diverge on political issues. In addition to national origin and socioeconomic position, generation divides Asian Americans. In general, Asian subgroups that have been in the United States for similar amounts of time are more likely to share similar political concerns, whereas groups differing markedly along generational lines lack a basis for cooperation (Lopez and Espiritu 1990: 206). In their 1984 survey of minorities in California, Cain and Kiewiet (1986) found that first-generation Asian Americans were more likely than subsequent generations to favor bilingual education, bilingual ballots, amnesty for undocumented immigrants, increased arms expenditure, gun control, and school prayer.[6] Ironically, the very force that has boosted Asian American political clout—immigration—has also produced a population more divided along ethnic, class, and generational lines.

Foreign politics further separates Asian American groups. Whereas homeland politics has sometimes been a unifying issue for Irish and Jewish Americans, it has been a divisive factor within and between many Asian American groups. The Chinese, Filipino, Korean, Asian Indian, and Vietnamese American communities continue to be divided among themselves over the politics of their countries of origin (Bellow and Reyes 1986–87; Cain 1988; Lopez 1988). Some of these political differences have sparked violence. For example, in the Vietnamese American community, far-right extremists have claimed responsibility for arson fires, shootings, and other attacks on Vietnamese who support renewed diplomatic relations with Vietnam (Wilkinson 1989).[7] More important, homeland politics rarely generates pan-Asian solidarity. Coming from different homelands, Asian immigrant groups share no foreign policy interests. For instance, while domestic politics in India continues to be extremely important to Asian Indians in the United States (Lopez 1988), it is of limited interest to other Asian Americans. Assessing the political prospects of Asian Americans, California State Assemblyman Floyd Mori (1980: 25) stated, "One of the biggest problems that we face in the Asian community is its diversity. Everybody has his own agenda, and this makes any unified, cohesive effort difficult."

Campaign Contributions

The preceding discussion suggests that small numbers, limited participation, and inter-Asian political differences dilute Asian American political power. However, voting is only one means by which constituents communicate their political views to public officials. Donating to campaigns is another. To contribute to political campaigns, one does not have to be a registered voter, or even a citizen. As a group, Jewish Americans have been important contributors to political campaigns and hence enjoy enhanced political leverage (Lieberson 1980: 92–93). Money can also be used to support political candidates from one's own group. Because political campaigns are expensive, populations that are able to draw on wealthy contributors have an important political advantage. According to Stanley Lieberson (1980: 93), differentials in political achievements among the various European groups and blacks can be partially explained by differentials in wealth.

Although comprehensive data are not available, Asian Americans are believed to be the second most generous political donors after Jewish Americans (W. Wong 1988a). Comparing rates of political involvement between Japanese Americans in a California sample and the general population in a national sample, Fugita and O'Brien (1991: 151–152) found a higher proportion of campaign contributors among Japanese Americans than among the general population (39 versus 13 percent). Asian Americans have donated funds disproportionate to their numbers, though not necessarily disproportionate to their wealth. According to the director of the Field Institute for Public Policy, while 10 percent of the voters in a campaign in California may be Asian Americans, 20–30 percent of a candidate's campaign money may come from Asian Americans (Lew 1987).[8]

Political candidates have openly begun to court Asian American funders. For example, in 1985, Asian Americans made up less than 1 percent of the guests at fund-raising dinners in Texas; two years later, political candidates there were holding fund-raisers just for Asian Americans (Lew 1987). Indeed, three months before the June

1990 elections in California, *Asian Week* (1990), a widely circulated Asian American newspaper, proclaimed that San Francisco's Asian Americans were "besieged with candidates' pleas for money" and that "members of the Chinatown and greater Asian American communities don't need a calendar to see that there are some elections coming. They can just tell by the huge volume of mail inviting them to candidates' fundraisers."

Although concrete political attainments are few, Asian Americans, via their pocketbooks, have increased their capacity to influence the political process—to place their concerns on the political agenda, and to be consulted rather than ignored. Instead of bypassing Asian American communities and neglecting Asian American issues, major political candidates now campaign in Asian American neighborhoods, headlining Asian American concerns. In 1987, the National Democratic Council of Asian and Pacific Americans[9] convention lured three Democratic presidential hopefuls (Jesse Jackson, Michael Dukakis, and Paul Simon), who "made splashy appearances, hoping to convince Asian Americans that their money, their votes, and their opinions are valued" (Iwata 1987). Ten years ago, it would have been unlikely for presidential candidates to have felt compelled to attend such a gathering (W. Wong 1988*a*). Similarly, in 1990, all three candidates for governor of California (Pete Wilson, John Van de Kamp, and Dianne Feinstein) brought their campaigns to Asian American communities, pledging to fight quotas on Asian enrollment in higher education, to support small business programs, and to appoint Asian Americans to policy-making positions in government (Andersen 1990*a*; Lyons 1990*b*; Siao 1990).

Political donations notwithstanding, Asian Americans continue to rely on the pan-Asian framework to obtain political influence. The Pacific Leadership Council provides an example. An arm of the Democratic Senatorial Campaign Committee, the Council raised close to $1.2 million in 1988 to support Democratic candidates in the senatorial and presidential races (Hsia interview). Even though its political donors were predominantly Chinese American businesspeople, the council used its financial leverage to lobby Congress not only for Chinese causes but for pan-Asian causes (e.g., immigration restrictions, trade sanctions against Asian countries, and anti-Asian violence). The council's co-chair comments on the strategic and constructed nature of pan-Asian ethnicity were:

> When we go to talk to Congresspeople, it is good to show that
> we have pan-Asian support. So we get letters of support from
> key Asian American organizations in the country. When we have
> everybody on board, the Congresspeople are impressed. They have
> to pay attention then. (Hsia interview)

Because of its involvement in pan-Asian issues, the council was able
to widen its fund-raising efforts to include other Asian American
groups, particularly Asian Indians (Hsia interview).

Outside Hawaii, Asian American candidates have not relied on
Asian American votes to win. But they have relied on Asian American money. For example, 75 percent of California Secretary of State
March Fong Eu's campaign money and 70 percent of Delaware Lieutenant Governor S. B. Woo's fund-raising coffer come from Asian contributors (Tachibana 1986a; Lew 1987).[10] To estimate the pan-Asian
support for Asian American candidates, I analyzed the campaign disclosure statements of Los Angeles City School Boardmember Warren
Furutani and Los Angeles City Councilman Michael Woo.[11] Pan-
Asian support means support from Asian American groups other
than Chinese Americans in Woo's case, and from Asian American
groups other than Japanese Americans in Furutani's case.[12]

The analysis of Warren Furutani's campaign contributions covers
the year immediately before his election in April 1987. As indicated
in Table 3.4, the financial support from the Japanese American community was substantial: Japanese Americans constituted over 61 percent of the contributors and accounted for close to 45 percent of the
money. Given Furutani's Japanese American background, this ethnic
support is to be expected. However, Furutani also received substantial support from other Asian American communities, suggesting
that he was viewed not only as a Japanese American candidate but
as an Asian American candidate. In all, Asian Americans comprised
approximately 83 percent of all the contributors and accounted for
61 percent of the approximately $89,000 raised. This proportion is
staggering considering that Asian Americans constitute less than 10
percent of the district's population. In contrast, in this same period,
John Greenwood, Furutani's opponent, received virtually no support
from the Asian American community: only four Asian Americans
contributed a total of $500 to his campaign.

Similarly, Michael Woo received substantial support from the
Asian American community in his June 1985 election. Woo's fund-

TABLE 3.4

Financial Contributors * *to Warren Furutani's Campaign*
by Ethnic Group, 1 July 1986–13 April 1987

Ethnic Group	Number of Contributors*	Percentage of Contributors	Total $	Percentage $ Contributions
Total	348	100.0	89,135	100.0
Japanese	214	61.5	39,850	44.7
Other Asian	74	21.3	14,630	16.4
Total Asian	288	82.8	54,480	61.1
Non-Asian	44	12.6	6,255	7.0
Unknown†	16	4.6	28,400	31.9

Source: Compiled by author from Warren Furutani's campaign disclosure statements on file at Los Angeles City Hall.

* Contributors include individuals, businesses, and organizations.

† This category includes persons with surnames identical to those of non-Asians and names with only initials, and businesses and organizations with unidentifiable ethnicity. Because this category includes many businesses and organizations, it accounts for a large percentage of the monetary contributions.

ing reports (for the six-month period prior to election day) indicate that Chinese Americans constituted 37 percent of the contributors and accounted for close to 27 percent of the funds; other Asian American groups comprised over 14 percent of all the contributors and accounted for approximately 9 percent of the money. These data indicate that Chinese and other Asian Americans donated funds disproportionate to their numbers: even though Asian Americans comprised only 5 percent of the district's population, Asian American donors constituted 51 percent of the contributors and accounted for 35 percent ($136,380) of the approximately $385,000 raised (see Table 3.5). In contrast, in this same period, Woo's opponent, Peggy Stevenson, received a total of $1,300 from twelve Asian Americans.

Asian American financial support for Asian American candidates also crosses geographic boundaries—a further indication that their political giving occurs primarily along ethnic and panethnic rather than political lines. For example, even though Furutani ran for a seat on the Los Angeles City School Board, he also held fund-raising

TABLE 3.5
Financial Contributors to Michael Woo's Campaign
by Ethnic Group, 1 January 1985–1 June 1985

Ethnic Group	Number of Contributors*	Percentage of Contributors	Total $	Percentage $ Contributions
Total	987	100.0	385,855	100.0
Chinese	365	37.0	102,560	26.6
Other Asian	142	14.4	33,820	8.8
Total Asian	507	51.4	136,380	35.4
Non-Asian	360	36.4	189,390	49.1
Unknown†	120	12.6	60,085	15.6

Source: Compiled by author from Michael Woo's campaign disclosure statements on file at Los Angeles City Hall.

* Contributors include individuals, businesses, and organizations.

† This category includes persons with surnames identical to those of non-Asians and names with only initials, and businesses and organizations with unidentifiable ethnicity.

events in New York, Seattle, and San Francisco (Furutani interview). Similarly, in his unsuccessful 1987 senatorial bid, Delaware's Lieutenant Governor S. B. Woo crisscrossed the country to solicit money from Asian Americans (Lew 1987). In 1989, when Dolores Sibonga, a Filipina American, ran for mayor of Seattle, Washington, she was the beneficiary of a $50-per-person fund-raising affair sponsored by Asian American supporters in Los Angeles.[13]

Asian American Political Advocacy Groups

Given their electoral weakness, Asian Americans have had to pay more attention to organizational strategies. While ethnic-specific advocacy groups remain important, pan-Asian organizations have also proliferated. Together, these two organizational structures mobilize a broad Asian American constituency in the service of both ethnic-specific and panethnic goals. Even organizations that originally served only one ethnic group have taken on broader constituencies. The Japanese American Citizens League (JACL) is the prime example.

Founded in 1930, JACL continues to be the most established and visible Japanese American organization. In 1989 JACL claimed 27,000 members in 115 chapters nationwide, making it the largest Asian American national organization (Morimoto 1989b). In contrast, in 1988 the national Chinese American Citizens Alliance (CACA) and Organization of Chinese Americans (OCA) counted 8,000 members in 16 chapters and 7,500 members in 40 chapters respectively (*East/West* 1988a; Siao 1988). For the most part, JACL's membership, purposes, and energies have been limited to its Japanese American constituency. On the other hand, because it is the only national Asian American organization with an established base, JACL has often represented all Asian Americans by default, particularly in Washington, D.C., where it has a legislative liaison office (Ignacio 1976: 101; Morimoto 1989b). For example, JACL played a major role in the passage of the 1952 McCarran–Walter Immigration and Naturalization Act and the 1990 immigration bill that ensures that the family will remain the cornerstone of U.S. immigration policy.

In the 1980s, faced with dwindling numbers, rising anti-Asian violence, and a lack of urgent political issues within their own community, JACL had to become more pan-Asian in scope. In a series of interviews with community leaders on the future of the Japanese American community, Joy Morimoto (1989a: 1) reported that "much of the current talk in the JA community centers on cultivating relationships with other Asian communities in order to build political clout as an 'Asian Pacific American' voice." Other single-ethnic organizations have similarly adopted a pan-Asian stance. For example, the nationwide Organization of Chinese Americans (OCA) and the San Francisco–based Chinese for Affirmative Action (CAA) are leading advocacy groups for both Chinese American and Asian American rights (*East/West* 1988a; *Asian Week* 1989a). In fact, the keynote speaker at CAA's twentieth-anniversary fund-raising banquet was U.S. Representative Robert Matsui, a Japanese American legislator (Lau 1989).

In addition to single-ethnic organizations, pan-Asian advocacy groups have also increased. A 1984 national roster of Asian American advocacy groups indicated that 52 percent (61 out of 117) were pan-Asian. These groups include bar associations, civil rights groups, educational organizations, political party clubs, and public employee organizations (Nakanishi and LaForteza 1984: 16–22). Unlike the Asian American movement of the late 1960s, these advocacy groups prefer lobbying, developing networks, and engaging in leadership training to political protest (Nakanishi 1985–86: 20). Their activities range from promoting Asian American political representation, to monitoring anti-Asian discrimination and violence, to advocating for their particular professional interests.

Because the 1990 census figures confirm the rapid growth of Asians in the United States, Asian American advocacy groups have sought increased political representation through redistricting. In the past, many Asian American communities have been fragmented into two or more electoral districts. For example, as a result of the 1981–82 redistricting, Koreatown in Los Angeles was divided up between three congressional, four senatorial, three assembly, and two city council districts (Azores and Ong 1991). Emboldened by their dramatic population growth, pan-Asian groups in major urban areas have pressed for voting districts that would not dilute Asian American representation. However, creating a district where Asian Americans comprise a majority of the population is no easy task (Ong, Espiritu, and Azores 1991). For the most part, supporters have had to settle for "Asian-plurality" rather than "Asian-majority" districts. For example, in the 1991 proposed "Asian" district in New York City, voting-age whites outnumber Asian Americans 41 to 38 percent (Ohnuma 1991). In Houston, the discrepancy is even higher: Asian Americans would constitute only 18 percent of the proposed "Asian" district population, not nearly enough to elect the first Asian American to the city council (J. Ng 1991b).

Although Asian American advocacy groups are expanding, they continue to represent only a limited segment of the Asian American community. First, members of these groups are primarily citizens. In their survey of California minorities, Cain and Kiewiet (1986: I-24) found that Asian American citizens were twice as likely as noncitizens to have worked within a group context to solve social and political problems. Furthermore, because the advocacy process has become professionalized in recent years, Asian American advocacy groups tend to be dominated by middle-class professionals who share narrow political and economic interests (Nakanishi 1985–86: 20). Some organizations also require exorbitant membership fees, thereby excluding the average person. For example, membership in the Pacific Leadership Council costs $5,000, and in the Leadership Circle, $25,000. This class bias undercuts the legitimacy of the advocacy groups and often weakens the very unity they seek (Espiritu and Ong 1991). And yet, these advocacy groups are the political voice of the Asian American community: "They usually speak for Asian American interests and are perceived as the representatives of organized ethnic concerns" (Nakanishi 1985–86: 20). In other words, given the low electoral participation rate of Asian Americans, the political views of the largely foreign-born mass are represented—adequately or inadequately—by American-born, middle-class professionals in well-organized and highly technical advocacy groups.

To maximize their political resources, Asian Americans have also allied themselves with other minority groups. For example, Asian and Latino American immigration activists united to fight the Kennedy–Simpson immigration bill,[14] and Jesse Jackson built his presidential campaign upon a "Rainbow Coalition" (S. Chen 1989b). In the fall of 1989, Asian Americans and other minority groups in New York City coalesced to elect David Dinkins, the city's first African American mayor (Chin and Chen 1990). In Los Angeles, where African Americans, Latino Americans, and Asian Americans together comprise the majority of the city's population, community leaders have advocated intergroup cooperation because economic revitalization "cannot be achieved if the new majority remains divided" (Ridley-Thomas, Pastor, and Kwoh 1989).

While occasionally effective, such interethnic alliances are often short-lived. They also tend to be inhibited by the groups' divergent political attitudes. A 1984 survey of minorities in California indicated that, on the whole, Asian American political attitudes were more like whites' than like Latinos' and blacks' (Cain and Kiewiet 1986: I-12). For example, Asian Americans were much less enthusiastic than Latinos and even less enthusiastic than blacks about bilingual education programs, and were less likely to favor increased welfare spending than blacks and Latinos. Such differences in political interests divide the three groups. Commenting on the lack of coalition building among the major minority groups, an *East/West* (1988b) editorial stated:

Most [Asian Americans] are united not by the struggles of the American civil rights movement, but by a nationalistic/racial pride that they shouldn't be discriminated against. This basis for unity translates well into issues like anti-Asian quotas in colleges and voting for and contributing to Asian candidates running for office, but fails miserably when it comes to coalition building with other minorities and "nuts and bolts" civil rights issues like voting rights.

The organizational structure of the Asian American population has become increasingly elaborate and dense, with links being forged within and among Asian American groups as well as with non-Asian constituencies. In the political arena, these advocacy groups have been the principal agents through which Asian Americans articulate their political interests. Although the various organizations hardly constitute a united front, together they form an elaborate network of organizational links and resources that can effectively facilitate political action.[15]

Asian American Political Representation

Although political power may be exercised without elected representatives, and officeholders may wield only minimal political power, the election and appointment of "one of their own" continue to be important for minority populations. Concretely, minority representatives are desirable because they can promote their groups' interests. For example, it is the small group of Hispanic American legislators who shepherded the legislation of the most interest to the Hispanic American population (Moore and Pachon 1985: 195). Symbolically, the election of one's own is an assurance that the system does not discriminate against one's group. Moreover, minority representation promotes group pride and encourages other members of the group to enter the political arena (Cain and Kiewiet 1986: I-25–26).

Elected Officials

In general, ethnic politicians come from areas where their compatriots are numerous. According to Lieberson (1980: 96), the racial and ethnic composition of the electorate appears to be the primary determinant of political success among black candidates and the most frequent factor for the South, Central, and Eastern European groups. In 1982, seven out of the ten Hispanic American members of Congress came from districts in which more than 50 percent of the population was Hispanic; fourteen out of the seventeen black representatives came from districts in which more than 40 percent of population was black (Moore and Pachon 1985: 172).

Asian American political influence, as measured by the number of Asian American elected officials, is greatest in Hawaii, where Asians constitute the majority of the population. In 1990, Asian Americans comprised the majority of the population in all of Hawaii's twenty-five largest cities except in Kailua, where they accounted for 40 percent of the population (J. Ng 1991a). The long-delayed grant of statehood to Hawaii in 1959 marked an important turning point in Asian American politics. In the state's subsequent election, Hiram Fong and Daniel Inouye became the first Asian Americans to be elected to the U.S. Congress by a largely Asian American constituency (Daniels 1988: 309–311).[16] Since then, election of Asian Pacific Americans to public office in Hawaii has become routine. In 1990, the state's governor, lieutenant governor, and fifty-four state senators and representatives were Asian Pacific Americans (Asian/Pacific American Municipal Officials 1990). The majority of Asian American representatives in Washington have come from Hawaii, not the mainland.

Unlike representation in Hawaii, Asian American elected officials are still relatively rare on the mainland. In the 1980s, the mainland states sent only two Asian Americans to the U.S. House of Representatives: Robert Matsui (D–Sacramento) and Norman Mineta (D–San Jose), both Japanese Americans and both from northern California. In California, with the largest Asian American population in the country, no Asian American has held a seat in the state legislature since the late 1970s. Moreover, although Asian Americans comprised close to 10 percent of the state population in 1990, they only held about 2 percent of the state's top three hundred elected offices and only 1 percent of the city council and school board seats (Efron 1990). New York, the state with the third largest Asian American population (after California and Hawaii), also has no Asian American in the state legislature. In 1990, New York had only seven elected Asian Americans in city government, five of whom were community school board members and two of whom were civil court judges (Wone 1990).

However, some progress has been made. Spurred by their post-1965 population growth, Asian Americans have become viable political participants in Asian-populated pockets. For example, in Los Angeles County, Asian Americans have won municipal offices in Monterey Park, Gardena, Cerritos, Torrance, and Carson (Nakanishi 1986: 14).[17] In contrast to the general dearth of Asian American political candidates in previous years, in 1991, in Houston, Seattle, and New York City, several Asian Americans competed with one another for different seats on the city council, and at times for the same seat. Some Asian American political insiders have cautioned that having several Asian American candidates running at the same time can split the Asian American votes and community resources, thus pulling all the candidates down.[18] This concern suggests that, as more Asian American candidates enter the political arena, pan-Asian support can become diluted—and even divided when the candidates are from different Asian subgroups.

Although the Asian American population is growing, in no district is it so large that any candidate could gain office simply by winning all the Asian American votes. In 1980, at the congressional district level, Asian Americans constituted a majority in only two districts— both in Hawaii. In just eight other districts did Asian Americans comprise as much as 10 percent. In contrast, the Hispanic American population predominated in nine districts and comprised at least 40 percent in ten others. Blacks were more numerous, constituting a majority of the population in fifteen congressional districts. They also comprised at least 40 percent of the population in twenty-five other districts, and at least 20 percent in seventy-eight other districts (U.S. Bureau of the Census 1983c: 3). Given the small numbers of compatriots in most voting districts, Asian American candidates appear to need panethnic coalitions the most, followed by Hispanic, and then black candidates.

To win, Asian American candidates must also rely on non-Asian votes. According to Cain and Kiewiet (1986), Asian American politicians in California are more likely than black or Latino candidates to be elected by voters of other ethnic groups. Using citywide data from the early 1970s to the early 1980s, Cain and Kiewiet (1986: I-28) found that over two-thirds (73 percent) of Asian American officeholders in California represented areas that were less than 10 percent Asian.[19] In contrast, only 27 percent of the black and 9 percent of the

Latino officeholders in California came from districts that were less than 10 percent black or Latino. Given the demographic composition of their districts, it would be political suicide for Asian American candidates to pursue solely Asian American votes. As a result, Asian American candidates have been less likely to run as representatives of their groups than black and Latino American candidates. At the state and federal legislative levels, several Asian American candidates have explicitly stated that they did not consider themselves to be minority candidates (Cain and Kiewiet 1986: I-28).

This is not to say that Asian American candidates can ignore their compatriots. Notwithstanding their small electorate, Asian American support continues to be important for Asian American candidates. As discussed earlier, Asian American candidates rely heavily on campaign contributions from their compatriots. They also rely on their votes. In a low voter turnout, common in local elections, Asian American voters can be decisive: they can skew the results if they vote at a high percentage—and as a pan-Asian bloc. Such was the case in Warren Furutani's 1987 election to the Los Angeles School Board. Furutani's victory rested primarily on the Asian American votes in Asian-populated precincts: "Although the incumbent beat me in many precincts, it did not make much difference because the turnout was so low. However, where I was strongest was in Gardena, Wilmington, and San Pedro. In these areas, Asian Americans voted in maximum force. They could and did skew the results" (Furutani interview). Furutani won by a mere 450 votes, or one vote per precinct.

Also, even when a candidate's compatriots are a numerical minority, they can provide the building blocks for a victorious campaign (Lieberson 1980: 61). Floyd Mori (1980: 24) described the contribution of the Japanese American community to his race for a California State Assembly seat: "In terms of voting strength, it did not play a major role, because it isn't very large; but it made a significant contribution in terms of personnel, manning my office, addressing letters and so on." In his bid for a seat on the Los Angeles city council, Michael Woo also benefited from a "huge Asian Pacific American volunteer force" (Miyamoto interview). Woo described the Asian American community as an "indispensable" base of support from which to spring his campaign (Tachibana 1986b).

Similarly, Judy Chu could not have won the 1988 city council race in Monterey Park, California, without coalition support. Although Chu received the strongest endorsement from the Chinese American community,[20] she also had substantial backing from the Japanese American community. According to an exit poll sponsored by the Southwest Voter Research Institute and the Asian Pacific Voter Registration Project, almost 90 percent of the Chinese Americans and 75 percent of the Japanese Americans in the sample voted for Chu. Chu also received 30 percent of the Anglo votes and 35 percent of the Latino American votes (Horton 1988).

Most important, regardless of the ethnic composition of their districts, Asian American politicians are de facto representatives of the wider Asian American community. Usually, elected officials represent the interests of their constituents, who may or may not be their compatriots. Minority officeholders, however, are obligated to serve an additional group—their compatriots, who may or may not be their constituents. As Moore and Pachon (1985: 195) observed, "Hispanic congressmen are thrust into two roles. Not only are they expected to represent their districts, but the larger Hispanic world expects them to be sympathetic and to understand Hispanic concerns far outside their constituencies."

Describing this added responsibility, former California State Assemblyman Floyd Mori (1980: 25) stated, "Although I represent an area that has very few Asians, I feel an obligation to do what I can to effectively involve Asian people in the political process." This obligation is yet another aspect of racial lumping: Asian American elected officials are expected (by Asians as well as non-Asians) to understand and respond to the needs of all Asian Americans.[21] This expectation is so strong that when Asian American legislators deviate, they are branded traitors by the larger Asian American community. Former U.S. Senator S. I. Hayakawa was one such offender. Often antagonistic toward Asian American concerns, Hayakawa was infamous for his hard line against the 1968 San Francisco State College student strike[22] and his endorsement of the internment of Japanese Americans in World War II. As columnist William Wong (1987: 4) opined, Hayakawa was "probably loved more by white Americans than yellow Americans for his peculiar and iconoclastic brand of conservative philosophy."

Because Asian American legislators are expected to promote Asian American causes, they often are the ones who spearhead policies and programs that affect the Asian American community. In 1978, when the Small Business Administration Act deleted "Asian and Pacific Americans" from the list of minorities eligible for government contracts, it was U.S. Representative Norman Mineta who introduced an amendment bill adding Asian and Pacific Americans to the list (*Los Angeles Times* 1979). In a similar case in 1985, U.S. Representatives Robert Matsui and Norman Mineta called attention to the omission of Asian Americans from the list of designated minorities in the Higher Education Reauthorization Act, which contains provisions that reserve funding for post-secondary institutions with the highest percentage of minority enrollment (*Pacific Citizen* 1985). It is important to note that by striking the "Asian and Pacific American" category from the designated list, the federal government had ignored differences among national subgroups, eliminating them all without distinction. Asian American congressional leaders also led the fight against anti-Asian violence, testifying at congressional hearings on hate crimes committed against Asian Americans and pushing for nationwide documentation of such crimes. Their attentiveness to the larger Asian American community helps to explain the widespread support they receive from Asian Americans outside their districts. Asian American elected officials are not the only individuals active in American politics; appointed Asian American officials are also becoming increasingly visible.

Appointed Officials

Because political appointments depend on political visibility, Asian Americans have had few appointments to high-level positions in the government. However, some gains have been made. From 1976 to 1980, more Asian Americans have been appointed to presidential commissions and advisory councils, administration and agency committees and posts, and federal judgeships than in all previous administrations (U.S.–Asia Institute 1980). Like elected representatives, Asian American appointed officials are concentrated in California and Hawaii, the states with the largest Asian American populations (Asian/Pacific American Municipal Officials 1990).

As late as the 1980s, many Asian American political appointments were still hailed as the "firsts" for the group. In 1988, President Ronald Reagan appointed the first Asian American, Sherwin Chan, to the U.S. Commission on Civil Rights. In 1989, President George Bush appointed Sichan Siv as the first Asian American community liaison to the White House and named Elaine Chao deputy secretary of transportation, the highest office ever reached by an Asian American in the executive branch. State and local appointments have also been rare. In 1986, Governor George Deukmejian appointed John Kashiwabara to the California State University Board of Trustees, making him the first Asian American to sit on the policy-making board. The same year, San Francisco Mayor Dianne Feinstein appointed Thomas Hsieh to the Board of Supervisors, the only Chinese American on the eleven-member board in a city with a population that is 12 percent Chinese American and about 25 percent Asian American. Like Asian American elected officials, these political appointees are often expected to represent not only their own ethnic group but the entire Asian American community.[23]

Japanese and Chinese Dominance

For the most part, Japanese and Chinese Americans have controlled Asian American electoral politics. As indicated in Table 3.6, in 1978, 1984, and 1990, Chinese and Japanese Americans in California dominated elected and appointed positions at the federal, state, and local levels. Chinese American representation is visible with Michael Woo in Los Angeles, Thomas Hsieh in San Francisco, and March Fong Eu at the state level. For their part, Japanese Americans sent two representatives to the U.S. Congress: Robert Matsui of Sacramento and Norman Mineta of San Jose. In Hawaii, Japanese Americans also dominated electoral politics in the early 1970s, when Japanese Americans comprised over 50 percent of the state's House of Representatives (Kitano 1976: 183). In 1990, they constituted over 60 percent of the state senators and representatives (Asian/Pacific American Municipal Officials 1990).

Demographic factors partially explain the dominance of Japanese Americans (and to a lesser extent, of Chinese Americans) in Asian American electoral politics. Japanese Americans have the largest proportion of native-born citizens among all Asian American groups, with Chinese Americans trailing second (see Tables 3.2 and 3.3). As a result, they tend to have a higher electoral participation rate. In Los Angeles County, Japanese and Chinese Americans have the

TABLE 3.6

Asian American Elected and Appointed Officials in California by Subgroup, 1978, 1984, 1990

Type of Office	Japanese	Chinese	Filipino	Korean	Other Asian*
FEDERAL OFFICIALS					
1978	2	0	0	0	0
1984	4	0	0	0	0
1990	2	0	0	0	0
STATE OFFICIALS					
1978	3	1	1	1	0
1984	2	1	0	0	0
1990	36	48	17	3	7
COUNTY OFFICIALS					
1978	1	2	1	0	0
1984	21	6	3	0	0
1990	8	6	1	1	0
CITY OFFICIALS					
1978	28	6	1	0	0
1984	6	9	2	0	0
1990	47	43	19	6	5
EDUCATION OFFICIALS					
1978	7	3	0	0	0
1984	12	5	3	0	0
1990	26	23	7	3	6
JUDICIAL OFFICIALS					
1978	14	3	0	2	0
1984	19	7	2	1	0
1990	25	10	4	5	1
Total	263	173	61	22	19

Source: The 1979 and 1984 data were compiled from Nakanishi (1980) and Nakanishi and LaForteza (1984) respectively, and the 1990 data from Asian/Pacific American Municipal Officials (1990). Because these three directories are not comprehensive, it

TABLE 3.6 (*Continued*)

is not possible to determine if the number of Asian American officials has increased or decreased over the years. On the other hand, the pattern of Japanese and Chinese dominance appears to be consistent over time.

* This category also includes officials with surnames not readily attributable to any Asian subgroup.

TABLE 3.7
Voter Registration Rates of Asian American Groups
in Los Angeles County, 1984

Ethnic Group	Registration Rate (%)
Asian Indians	28.5
Chinese	35.5
Filipinos	27.0
Koreans	13.0
Japanese	43.0
Samoans	28.5
Vietnamese	4.1
Overall Asian rate	29.4
Overall county rate	60.0

Source: Nakanishi (1986: 21).

highest voter registration rates of all Asian American groups (see Table 3.7). Similarly, Japanese American electoral success in Hawaii is due largely to a sizeable voting population and to its tendency to vote as a bloc (Haas 1987: 659).[24] According to Fugita and O'Brien (1991: 151–152), the proportion of Japanese Americans that vote in local elections is larger than that of the general population (70 to 47 percent).

More important, Japanese and Chinese Americans reap more political benefits because they are more established and organized than other Asian groups in the United States. For example, Japanese

Americans have a larger political base than newly arrived Asian immigrants because they have "numerous organizational links with both their ethnic and mainstream communities" (Fugita and O'Brien 1991: 164). In March 1990, Chinese and Japanese American advocacy organizations such as the Chinese American Citizens Alliance, Organization of Chinese Americans, and Japanese American Citizens League were the primary sponsors of the first national conference on Asian Americans in politics. This organizational resource allows Japanese and Chinese Americans to take advantage of the demographic strength provided by the post-1965 influx of Asian immigrants. In American politics the politically sophisticated and professional segments are historically the ones to benefit from their group's demographic advantage. Examples are plentiful: West Indians achieved important political positions as representatives of black Americans; Spaniards and Latin Americans became the representatives of Puerto Ricans; and German Jews rose to Congress in districts dominated by Eastern European Jews (Glazer and Moynihan 1963: 16–17; Lieberson 1980: 88–89). According to Lieberson (1980: 86), the relatively early entry of Jewish Americans into the political arena "is to be explained by the German Jews who had preceded the Eastern European wave. The pre-1880 migration of Jews meant that politically sophisticated, wealthy, and professional segments were available at an earlier date to take advantage of the demographic strength provided by the incoming waves of Eastern European Jews." In other words, the issue is not one of Japanese and Chinese Americans versus other Asian Americans groups, but rather one of established groups versus new immigrants.

In contrast to the established Chinese and Japanese American communities, new Asian groups often have no single dominant organization or spokesperson to represent their interests. However, progress has been made. New immigrants, particularly Korean Americans, have begun to organize politically. Though their impact has been limited thus far, Korean immigrants have become increasingly involved in politics, particularly in Los Angeles, home to the largest Korean population outside Asia. In 1985, the Korean American Coalition began a ten-year voter registration drive (Tachibana 1986a). In 1988, the Korean American Democratic Committee was formed in Los Angeles to raise money from Koreans nationwide to contribute to Democratic candidates (Miller 1988). In 1990, the five-year-old Korean American National Political Action Committee (KANPAC) registered some seven thousand new Korean American voters in the Los Angeles area in just six weeks (Andersen 1990c).

For our purposes here, it is not necessary to pinpoint the causes of the unequal distribution of political power among Asian American subgroups. It is more important to recognize that such inequity often leads to factionalism and infighting, as less successful groups publicly question the legitimacy of a pan-Asian front. As a Korean American community leader complained:

> There's a perception that Asian coalitions are used primarily by Japanese and Chinese Americans to their own benefit and not to benefit the other members of the coalition. To some extent this is understandable because there are more of them and more of them are better trained to take the plums offered to the Asian community. But to keep the coalition, you've got to spread the plums around. (Cited in Tachibana 1986a)

Similarly, a Filipino American legislative aide explained:

> There is a sense of feeling that Japanese and Chinese have gotten a piece of the pie and that Filipinos are not getting enough of the pie. The issues being addressed have always been Japanese and Chinese issues. Filipinos believe in coalition building with other Asian Americans. They understand its strength. At the same time, they don't feel that the coalition is benefiting them. (Ricasa interview)

Asian Pacific Americans in Hawaii also have publicly complained of the "inordinate amount of 'Japanese influence' in the islands" (F. Ng 1980). In 1971, Hawaiians protested the appointment of a Japanese man (instead of a Hawaiian) to the board of the Bishop Estate, which administers the Kamehameha Schools for Hawaiian students (Wright 1972: 257). Since this protest, "countless intimations were made that the Japanese-Americans controlled the city and county governments and dominated the Department of Education" (F. Ng 1980: 96). It is important to note the material basis of this ethnic resentment: political representation is important because it can affect the allocation of resources to various constituent groups. For example, under the governorship of George Ariyoshi (1974–86),

Japanese Americans were overrepresented in civil service jobs; in contrast, Filipino Americans did not advance in government employment throughout Ariyoshi's twelve years in office (Haas 1987: 663–664). Resentful Filipinos have maintained that "their lack of upward social mobility was frustrated by ethnic favoritism by the Japanese-controlled political system" (Haas 1987: 663). This class-based ethnic resentment is yet another strike against the pan-Asian voting bloc.

Conclusion

Due to their small numbers among the voting population, divergent political attitudes, and limited political participation, Asian Americans have not been a powerful electoral force. Despite their growing numbers since 1965, Asian Americans are still a small group. Therefore, their votes are decisive only in close elections in Asian-populated pockets. But swing votes cannot be counted on to advance the Asian American political agenda. Furthermore, the Asian American national contingents still lack the numbers to mount a strong political campaign by themselves. For this reason, politically minded Asian Americans find it necessary to aggregate Asian American nationalities when seeking political recognition.

Such pan-Asian efforts have had mixed results. At the mass level, unity has been achieved on only a few issues such as education and immigration. More often, internal diversity—of national origins, generations, social classes, and political orientations—has prevented Asian Americans from uniting at the polls. Ironically, the very force that has boosted the numerical strength of Asian Americans—immigration—has also exacerbated intergroup divisions, making it difficult to maintain pan-Asian political unity. On the other hand, at the organizational level, Asian American advocacy groups recognize that pan-Asian organization is important—and at times essential—for the maintenance and expansion of Asian political and economic interests. Due to political necessity and public expectation, Asian American political officials—whatever their specific ethnic backgrounds—recognize the benefits of touting the pan-Asian line.

Thus, in their political roles, Asian American advocacy groups and elected officials actively promote pan-Asian consciousness. As visible representatives of organized group interests, *their* Asian American agenda becomes the agenda of all Asian Americans. While it may conflict with the views of Asian subgroups or individuals, the public agenda is often the one upon which policies and programs are built.

Chapter 4

The Politics of
Social Service Funding

The lack of unity among Asian Americans at the polls does not nec-
essarily mean that they never organize along a pan-Asian line, but
only that they do not always do so. Calling attention to the situation-
ality of panethnicity, this chapter and the next two show that when
an appropriate issue emerges, and when political and economic conditions favor—or demand—an inclusive identity over a splintered
one, Asian Americans can and do mobilize as a collective group to
protect and promote their common interests.

The urban uprisings of the 1960s forced governments to redefine
and expand the rights of minorities, leading to increased funding of
minority social welfare programs. While outside funding provided
needed services to the Asian American poor, it also disrupted long-
established community power structures and group boundaries. As
government-funded agencies took over the welfare services once provided by traditional associations, the latter declined in power and
influence (Kwong 1987: 6), while outside funding led to the consolidation of previously vying subgroups. To compete more efficiently
for the pool of government monies, social workers from various
Asian American groups began to work together. In so doing, they
unwittingly reified and legitimized the category *Asian American*.
Asian American social service providers coalesced because numbers

count in the American political structure and because funding agencies often treat Asians as a largely undifferentiated racial category. In other words, pan-Asian organization was a tactical reaction to American political policies and rules of access. These early pan-Asian groups were the spawning ground for many social service agencies that are today institutionalized in the Asian American community. This process of organizational consolidation, however, was at times interrupted, as competing factions fought for their shares of available jobs, money, and power.

From Private to Public Welfare

Before the 1960s, traditional associations were the principal welfare institutions among Chinese and Japanese Americans. Destitute Chinese could rely on family and district associations for relief; needy Japanese could secure assistance from the *kenjinkai,* or prefectural clubs. Because of this private assistance, few Chinese and Japanese in the United States became public welfare clients. As the principal agents for the disbursement of mutual aid, the established leaders of territorial and clan organizations wielded decisive control over their people (Light 1972: chs. 4–5; Ichioka 1977; Lai 1987).

In the late 1960s, young Asian American dissidents challenged this power hegemony, charging that traditional organizations were leaving human needs unmet (Weiss 1974: 238). A former director of the San Francisco's Youth Services Center recalled:

> When we came into Chinatown, we criticized the Chinese establishment, the Chinese Chamber of Commerce, all the family associations, and the Chinese American Citizens Alliance for not being able to do anything in the community, for suppressing the problems in Chinatown, and for exploiting the people of Chinatown. (Editorial Board 1971: 278)

Exacerbating this indigenous opposition was the post-1965 influx of Asian immigrants. By 1970, the population of San Francisco's overcrowded Chinatown had doubled. In 1968, the San Francisco Department of Social Services detailed the burgeoning problems in the city's Chinatown: one-third of the families in Chinatown census tracts earned incomes below the federal poverty level; 27 percent of Chinatown housing was substandard; tuberculosis was endemic; and the district contained a high proportion of persons sixty-five years of age and older, among whom suicide rates were unusually high (Light 1972: 181). Also, New York's Chinatown bulged, as the Chinese population in New York City increased from approximately 18,000 in 1950 to over 69,000 in 1970 (B. Wong 1977: 19). In the face of these urgent community needs, the resources of the "existing community institutions were either irrelevant, antiquated or impotent" (Chin 1971b: 287).

Responding to the growing and neglected needs of their people, young Asian American activists directed their energy toward community work. "Serve the People" programs sprouted in large Asian American communities, especially in San Francisco, Los Angeles, and New York (P. Wong 1972: 38).[1] Many of the self-help organizations devoted themselves to combating rising gang violence, parental problems, and drug abuse among Asian American youth (Ignacio 1976: 125).[2] Some of these self-help programs were ethnic-specific, such as Pagkakaisa (Unity) and Omai Fa'atasai, which worked with Filipino and Samoan youths, respectively (Coalition for Asian Mental Health 1976: 20–22). Others were more inclusive, such as Yellow Brotherhood and Asian American Hard Core—two Los Angeles organizations that tried to help all Asian youths "stay clean of gang banging and dope" (E. Wong 1971: 248; Asamura 1989: 157). As a counterpart to Yellow Brotherhood, Asian American women formed Asian Sisters to deal specifically with the drug problems of Asian women (Ling 1989). For the most part, these self-help organizations were founded by "community activists, ex-cons, and dope fiends" to help themselves and others in similar situations (Gotanda 1970).[3]

In the early 1970s, college students descended on poor urban Asian American communities to work with "the masses." There, they collided with grass-roots activists who referred to them as "educated youth who were 'do-gooding' in their off-time" (Nishida 1989). Although energetic and committed, these student activists were divorced from the reality confronting most community residents. A Chinese community activist described the students' alienation from the community:

> A lot of college students are still not aware of what is going on in the community even though they're physically down here in the

> Asian community center. . . . They still have this outsider's men-
> tality. I really can't blame them because a lot of them are brought
> up in the suburbs and white middle class areas. And when they
> come here, they feel a gap. (Editorial Board 1971: 281)

Because of their middle-class background, suburban values, and outsider's mentality, most student activists occupied only a marginal
position in the communities (Nishio 1982: 37). Their relationship
to the community residents "was analogous to that between third-
world intellectuals who were trained in the West and the masses in
their countries" (P. Wong 1972: 38).

Both community- and student-initiated "Serve the People" programs were short-lived. Some programs folded because they ran short
of staff (Coalition for Asian Mental Health 1976: 20–22). As a former
Yellow Brotherhood organizer related, "Many of our members abandoned the group to pursue more lucrative goals" (Asamura 1989:
157). Often inexperienced, volunteer staff were also ill equipped to
deal with social ills. A former volunteer reflected on her fledgling
attempts to assist Asian American women from the "streets":

> We didn't realize it was dangerous until afterwards [laughs]. We'd
> get calls from mothers, sometimes at 3:00 A.M. They'd say, "My
> daughter hasn't come home yet. I think she's at this hotel." So the
> two of us would go out at four in the morning into these sleazy
> hotels to find these young girls. We could have just as easily been
> hurt. We didn't think about that [laughs]. We were probably too
> naive [then]. (Cited in Ling 1989: 57)

Most important, these self-help organizations lacked the money to
continue their welfare activities. As their financial needs increased,
these organizations could no longer rely on the Asian American
community as their primary means of support. Outside funding was
needed. As a result, government-funded agencies began to take over
many of the Asian American services and programs initiated by volunteer groups. The availability of outside funding caused confusion
and shifts in strategies, further changing the power and organizational structure of the Asian American community (Sung 1967: 139;
Nishio 1982: 37–38).

The Funding Game

In the mid-1960s, energized by economic growth and the relaxation of international tension, Americans shifted their attention to domestic problems and became increasingly receptive to social welfare issues. The urban uprisings of the 1960s and their popular support forced government authorities to respond—however inadequately—to the needs and demands of the destitute. In 1964, President Johnson signed the Economic Opportunity Act, forwarding aid to impoverished young people, hard-pressed small businesspersons, marginal farmers, and welfare recipients. In 1965, Congress passed Great Society legislation in the fields of medical care, education, housing, civil rights, poverty, and immigration (Polenberg 1980: ch. 5).

Dominated by social welfare programs, federal assistance programs experienced their most extensive growth during the 1960s (Library of Congress 1975: 16). Between 1960 and 1968, the number of federal grant programs nearly tripled, from 132 to 379, and federal aid dollars more than tripled, from $7 billion in 1960 to $24 billion in 1970 (Conlan 1988: 6). These programs brought increased public services to many people who had never known them. More important, the social policies of the Johnson years legitimized the claims of the disadvantaged by placing them on the national agenda. Administratively, blacks, Chicanos, Puerto Ricans, Native Americans, and Asian Americans became "disadvantaged" groups, deserving of assistance to correct past discrimination (Kwong 1987: 20; Cornell 1988a: 192). Taking advantage of these liberal social welfare policies, Asian American social workers began to seek community change through participation in government-funded programs. Government funds provided start-up money for numerous Asian American agencies, the majority of which serve multiethnic groups (Spector-Leech 1988).[4]

Despite cutbacks in public funding in recent years, government continues to be the key source of financial support for Asian American social service agencies. In contrast, private foundation funding has been inconsequential. According to the deputy director of a national pan-Asian advocacy organization, "There is a real exclusion of Asian Americans by private funding organizations. They do not consider us a 'high target' group. We are mostly funded by federal money" (Ponce interview). A study of the funding patterns of major private foundations indicates that nationally, for the years 1984–87 inclusive, only $4.2 million of the $2.42 billion awarded annually went to the Asian Pacific Islander[5] community. In other words, less than two-tenths of 1 percent (0.17 percent) of total foundation grant monies was allocated to Asian Pacific Islander community organizations and programs. Similarly, in Los Angeles County foundation grants constitute on the average only 4 percent of an agency's total budget; in contrast, public funding (federal, state, county, and city funding) accounts for 64 percent. The remaining portions of the budget come from individual donations, fees, and other private grant-makers such as the United Way (Kimura 1990: 4–6).

Professionalization of Social Work

Because the funding system requires professionalism, to procure outside funding Asian American social workers need to be trained and credentialed. Since World War II, individual Asian Americans have pursued the profession of social work, but they were invisible as a political force until the Asian American movement gave them prominence (Kushida, Montenegro, Chikahisha, and Morales 1976: 186). In the 1960s, prompted by the political activism of the time, Asian American social service providers united to lobby for Asian American welfare, demanding not only equal access to services but also equal opportunity to administer those services. One of their principal goals was to increase the number of certified Asian American social workers. In 1965, only twelve Asian American students were enrolled in seven West Coast graduate schools of social welfare. Due largely to the recruitment drive of the Los Angeles–based Asian American Social Workers (AASW), the number of Asian American students in these social welfare schools increased to 67 by 1970 and to 108 by 1974 (Kushida et al. 1976: 186–187).

In 1972, with funding from the National Institute of Mental Health, AASW established the Asian American Community Mental Health Training Center (AACMHTC), one of the first institutions to provide social work training relevant to the Asian American experience (Choi et al. 1975: 197–200). Recognizing the heterogeneity of the Asian population in the United States, AACMHTC organizers strived to build a multiethnic base. The training consultants, training sites, and advisory boards were selected from the Chinese, Korean, Guama-

TABLE 4.1

Ethnic Representation and Educational Level of Participating Students in the Asian American Mental Health Training Center, 1972–75

Ethnic Group	1972–73 Under-graduate	Graduate	1973–74 Under-graduate	Graduate	1974–75 Under-graduate	Graduate	Total
Chinese	1	2	3	2	1	4	13
Filipino	1	2	2	2	5	3	15
Guamanian	0	0	1	0	2	0	3
Iranian	0	0	1	0	0	0	1
Japanese	3	4	2	4	2	7	22
Korean	1	0	2	0	5	1	9
Samoan	2	0	2	0	5	1	10
Total	8	8	13	8	20	16	73

Source: Kushida et al. (1976: 189).

nian, Filipino, Japanese, and Samoan communities. Although student selection was based on competence and commitment, special effort was made to ensure that the student population would reflect the multiethnicity of the total Asian American population. As indicated in Table 4.1, students were selected at both the graduate and undergraduate levels. Undergraduates were included primarily to increase the proportion of underrepresented groups such as the Samoans and Guamanians in the job pool (Kushida et al. 1976: 187–189). Notwithstanding these affirmative action efforts, Table 4.1 reveals the dominance of Japanese Americans, particularly at the graduate level. This early dominance foretold the prominent role that Japanese Americans would play in the Asian American social service arena.

The professionalization of social work eroded the power of the traditional elites as well as that of the grass-roots activists (B. Wong 1977: 7). Because of the political nature of the funding process, the ability to deal effectively with government officials became a desirable qualification for leadership—a development that favored more acculturated and professional persons. Most traditional elites and grass-roots activists were unfamiliar with or hostile to U.S. politics and the funding structure; hence, their effectiveness and credentials gradually diminished (Light 1972: 182–183; Ling 1984: 76–78). For example, since its establishment in the nineteenth century, the Chinese Six Companies often hired white lawyers to serve as their spokespersons before national, state, and local governing bodies and courts (Kitano and Daniels 1988: 26). In contrast, from the 1960s on, professional social workers themselves administered welfare services and procured government funding. Articulate and politically sophisticated, these professionals became de facto representatives of Asian American interests—even though their competence was often limited to social services.

As Asian American professional social workers and administrators were hired from the outside to head government-funded agencies, they collided with community activists who regarded them "as latecomers into the Asian American and Pacific Islander scene . . . who have no experience or understanding of the real dynamics of the authentic Asian Pacific ethnic communities in the U.S." (Ignacio 1976: 219). According to Bernard Wong (1977: 4–5), the Chinese American social workers in New York's Chinatown were American-born, college-educated, and more familiar with the English language and American society than with Chinese traditions. Although they worked in Chinatown, they lived in suburban neighborhoods.

Professionalism is important in the funding game because the funding system places a premium on grantsmanship. According to the chief deputy of a Los Angeles county supervisor, "If the agencies don't write a good proposal, they are not going to get any money" (Fukai interview). Therefore, organizations that have the best professional staffs are likely to prepare the best proposals and thus receive the most funding (Yip interview). Yet these organizations are also likely to be the ones that already have the best financial bases. Such a system favors professional applicants over less capable ones, regardless of their relative objective needs. A study of Asian American social service agencies in Los Angeles County indicates that large agencies (with an operating budget of more than $1 million) receive the most funding from the government, with public funding accounting for 80 percent of their operating budgets. In contrast, smaller, relatively new agencies (with an operating budget of less than $300,000) are often overlooked by funding sources that favor the more established organizations (Kimura 1990: 42–48).

Ironically, it is the smaller agencies that are most in need of financial support; yet their limited staff and lack of technical expertise and familiarity with government operations bar them from ready access to funding sources. This is especially true for ethnic-specific agencies serving the Asian immigrant communities (Kimura 1990: 28–29). In order to receive funding, less established Asian groups often have to depend on the technical assistance of older, more experienced organizations. As the director of the Samoan Service Center in Los Angeles explained, "Other Asians have the know-how and the education. We don't have enough resources on our own. They assist us with proposal-writing. I haven't met a Samoan that is good at writing proposal. Most of our proposals are written by Chinese or Japanese" (Mann interview).[6]

Funding administrators are also reluctant to finance organizations with no track records, making it difficult for new agencies to establish themselves (Kimura 1990: 43). For example, in the early 1970s, the federal government refused to give the $200,000 earmarked for the Asian American and Native American populations in Los Angeles to Asian American agencies because these organizations had no track record. Instead, the money was given to a Mexican American foundation, which then hired an Asian American staff to serve the Asian American clientele (Coalition for Asian Mental Health 1976: 33). To circumvent this restriction, a new service center can name as its fiscal agent another agency with an established track record. In exchange, the established agency retains ultimate fiscal responsibility and extracts a percentage of the money for its service.[7] The founding director of an established pan-Asian agency in San Diego expounded on the difficulties faced by new agencies:

> To get public funding, you have to follow this Request For Proposal (RFP) process, which is very difficult: you've got to have a track record, you've got to be established, you've got to show that you can manage money. And if you're starting as a new organization, you generally don't stand a chance when you're up against the established organizations. So if the new immigrants really looked at the obstacles and barriers, the easiest way for them to get a track record and to develop programs is to ally with an established organization (Yip interview).

Thus, in the present funding system, grantsmanship, profession-alism, and an established track record can be more important than relative objective needs in determining which agencies receive the most financial assistance. Such a system favors accredited individu-als and established organizations over untrained and inexperienced ones. As a result, new Asian immigrants and refugees often have to rely on the technical expertise and experience of the more established Asian American groups, and in so doing yield to the leadership of the old-timers. Because this arrangement shifts the fiscal and program management responsibility to the more established Asian American groups, it invariably fosters dependency, making it difficult for new-comers to pursue their interests outside the pan-Asian framework, while simultaneously engendering a pan-Asian funding strategy.

Consolidation of Group Boundaries

In the late 1960s, to be competitive in the funding game, social workers from various Asian backgrounds began to combine forces. Founded in 1973, the Pacific/Asian Coalition (PAC) became the first national Asian American organization of mental health pro-fessionals with representatives from every region in the country (Coalition for Asian Mental Health 1976: 24–25). Pan-Asian social service agencies sprouted in major U.S. urban centers. Established in 1968, the Council of Oriental Organizations (COO) was the first federation of Asian American social service agencies in Los Angeles County. From COO's inception, "there has been a unanimous convic-tion that the separate Oriental communities could be more effective in dealing with common concerns if that concern could be voiced through a coalition or council" (Saito 1968: 2). In 1974, leaders from the Japanese, Filipino, Chinese, Korean, Samoan, and Guamanian communities in San Diego established the Union of Pan Asian Com-munities (UPAC) to serve the needs of the city's small but diverse Asian American population (Yip interview). In Chicago, the first multilingual and multicultural shelter was formed in 1990 to care for victims of domestic violence in the Asian Indian, Pakistani, and Korean communities. Reflecting the city's large South Asian popula-tion, the shelter's name is "Apna Ghar," a Hindi–Urdu phrase which means "our home." Pan-Asian social service agencies also exist in Oakland, San Francisco, Boston, Seattle, and Honolulu.[8]

At one level, pan-Asianism is an efficacious organizational strategy. Competing with other ethno-racial groups for influence with government officials, Asian Americans benefit from the greater ability of large-scale organization to command attention. In 1970, the combined Asian American[9] population in the United States accounted for less than 1 percent of the total population. In contrast, blacks and persons of Spanish heritage comprised approximately 11 and 5 percent of the nation's population respectively (U.S. Bureau of the Census 1973a: tables 189–190). Since numbers count in the American political structure, Asian American groups have to combine to enlarge their relative share of the population. A Filipino American administrator explained the politics of numbers: "We decided that if we didn't go Asian, we wouldn't be big enough to compete against blacks and Latinos. We had to have a broader constituency" (de la Cruz interview). Reflecting on the pan-Asian strategy of the late 1960s, an Asian American community leader recounted that various Asian American groups joined forces because "each of the groups individually found that social institutions were unresponsive until they united" (F. Kuramoto 1976: 213).

But political efficacy is only one reason that Asian American groups coalesce. Asian Americans also come together because the funding structure encourages—and even demands—that they act on a pan-Asian basis. Some funding agencies specify in their requests for proposal a preference for multiethnic projects.[10] More often, the preference for multi-Asian projects is an unstated policy, understood by experienced social service providers. According to a long-time administrator, "From my experience as deputy director of PACE [Pacific Asian Consortium on Employment] for the last thirteen years, I find that your chances of getting funded increase if you are a pan-Asian group. You want to be able to say that you are representing the entire Asian American community" (de la Cruz interview). Naomi Kimura (1990: 42–48) reported that in Los Angeles County, agencies serving multiple Asian Pacific Islander groups were more financially stable than agencies with a primarily single-ethnic focus. Similarly, when public funding dwindled in the early 1980s, San Diego County defunded all of the Asian community-based agencies, except for the Union of Pan Asian Communities (UPAC). The founding director of UPAC explained the organization's longevity:

The reason why we have been able to get funding is because we serve more than one Asian group. It's very hard to get a grant when you are serving only one ethnic group, especially in San Diego, where the number of Asians is not that great. In fact, when the county defunded everybody, they wanted us to be the umbrella group dispensing the money to the different Asian communities. (Yip interview)

Funding administrators prefer to fund coalitions because politically it is the safest decision, freeing them from having to choose one Asian ethnic group over another. According to the executive director of a large service agency in Los Angeles, "I have heard this from the Feds, state, and county. They say that there is no way they are going to fund just one group because of the political ramifications of that decision. The other Asian groups will be up in arms. That's how bureaucrats have to think" (Hatanaka interview). This is especially true in localities where multiple Asian-origin groups reside. For example, the Federal Public Housing Service (FPHS) has shied away from Los Angeles because of the ethnic diversity of the county's Asian American population. In contrast, FPHS has funded several projects in the Chinatowns in New York, Boston, and San Francisco, because in these urban areas agency administrators have to deal with only one Asian American group. Because FPHS prefers to fund one rather than several Asian American groups, ten Asian Pacific agencies in Los Angeles County incorporated the Asian Pacific Health Care Venture and applied for funding as one entity. The Venture became the first Asian American outfit in the county to receive funding from FPHS (Hatanaka interview).[11]

The FPHS example suggests that geographical overlap and concentration make panethnic cooperation possible and sometimes necessary. When multiple Asian American groups are concentrated in the same urban area, as in Los Angeles, they have more opportunities to interact; they also tend to share similar political and economic interests, making it necessary to coalesce (Lopez and Espiritu 1990: 207). In contrast, in New York City, where Chinese Americans predominate, pan-Asian efforts have been rare.[12] The city's largest Asian American social service agency is the Chinese-American Planning Council, a $21 million umbrella agency serving principally Chinese clientele (over 90 percent). As the city's Asian American population becomes more ethnically diverse, particularly with the arrival of Koreans and Asian Indians, pan-Asian organization may become more feasible and even necessary.

Funding agencies also encourage pan-Asian projects because of their fiscal soundness: it is cheaper to fund one multiethnic project than several single-ethnic ones. According to a United Way planner, "Although there is no policy stating that we prefer to fund an Asian coalition, an Asian coalition does have a better chance of getting funded than an ethnic-specific one. In general, funding agencies like to see that their money goes as far as it can" (Nakamura interview). As an executive director of a drug abuse agency (who declined to be named) expounded on this funding logic: "We know damn well that we should have a drug program for each Asian ethnic group. But you're not going to get that much money. So when we advocate for funding, we use the unity line. The Asian line works because it is cheaper for the funding agencies." The need to coalesce is even greater when there is limited funding. As the executive director of an established social service agency explained: "In a competitive situation, when the amount of money is fixed and small, it is better to band together rather than open competition. If we compete among ourselves, we cancel each other out. If we coalesce, we have much greater clout to fight for a larger share" (Hatanaka interview). In essence, being part of a coalition assists individual Asian groups in getting funded.

Conflict and Competition

Whatever the reason, implicit in the funders' preference for multiethnic projects is the assumption that there is a generalized Asian group that can best be served by a generalized Asian policy. As a Department of Health, Education, and Welfare (1974: 1–2) report stated, "Historical precedent indicates that these [Asian] groups may be treated as a whole, particularly in addressing their social service needs." This racialist construction of Asian Americans as homogeneous imposes a pan-Asian structure on persons and communities dependent on public monies.

But the pan-Asian boundary encloses communities with genuinely different needs and goals. Within the larger community, constituent members compete for the same limited resources; the determination of what and whose interests will be funded can lead to intense internal conflict. As a community leader stated, "Once an effort succeeds in stimulating outside funds, the more established members of the community and others tend to compete for a 'piece of the action' and recognition" (F. Kuramoto 1976: 214). For this reason, some Asian American activists oppose all government funding. For example, Shin'ya Ono (1973) claimed that the government is using federal resources "to create and maintain a leverage to pit one Asian community against another." Moreover, because the process of consolidation inevitably reduces the influence of some individuals and groups and increases the power of others, the "losers" may wish to pursue their goals outside the pan-Asian framework. Such defection weakens the coalition and reduces its legitimacy in the eyes of the larger society.

The post-1965 wave of Asian immigration has exacerbated intergroup conflict and competition. The newcomers have recomposed the Asian American population. In 1960, Japanese, Chinese, and Filipinos made up 90 percent of all Asians. By 1980, with the immigration of Koreans, Vietnamese, Cambodians, Laotians, and Asian Indians, that share had dropped to 65 percent. Chinese and Filipinos maintained their shares with immigration of their own, but the Japanese share plummeted from 47 percent to 20 percent in the same period (Xenos et al. 1987: 256–257). With their increasing numerical strength, some of the newer groups have begun to challenge the established leadership of the Asian American community. The new immigration has also brought new constituencies into the pan-Asian fold. Joining Chinese, Japanese, Koreans, and Filipinos are Asian Indians, refugees from Southeast Asia, and immigrants from the Pacific Islands—many of whom are unfamiliar with or indifferent to the Asian American concept upon arrival. As a consequence, some social service providers have questioned the effectiveness of a pan-Asian framework—both as a service-delivery model and as an advocacy coalition model. An Asian American leader commented on the irony of the new Asian immigration: "The success of one thing that we have fought for, namely, fair and equal immigration policies, has institutionalized a system which keeps us in constant flux" (B. O. Hing 1986: 14).

Pan-Asian Service-Delivery Model

Although the pan-Asian service-delivery model purports to serve the needs of all Asian American groups via the same agency, the effectiveness of these agencies is often mitigated by the cultural and linguistic differences among the heterogeneous Asian American clienteles. Ideally, the ethnic composition of an agency's personnel should match that of its clients. But due to limited human and financial resources, such a perfect correspondence is not always possible. The new Asian immigration has made an imperfect situation worse. With so many new Asian groups, it is often not feasible to have staff members from every single group. The growing number of Asian immigrants and refugees also strains the already limited social services and funding, making it even more difficult to cater to the specific needs of the individual communities.

As jobs and funding become more scarce, competition increases. Under these conditions, the determination of who gets served—or more aptly, who gets the jobs—often leads to factionalism. Although the conflict is often over the few jobs that are available through funded programs, the fight is often waged in ethnic terms, with some Asian American groups accusing the more established Japanese and Chinese Americans of monopolizing the staffing and governing body of pan-Asian agencies (P. Wong 1972: 35; Ignacio 1976: 106; Bagasao 1989). Because data on Asian American subgroups are not required by funding agencies, it is often impossible to validate the claim of Japanese and Chinese American dominance. Although agencies receiving government funding are required to submit data on the ethnicity of their personnel, the legally relevant category is "Asian or Pacific Islander," not the individual subgroup (Office of the Secretary 1978). However, interviews with agency administrators indicated that most Asian American agencies have a bicultural and bilingual staff—primarily to attract a multiethnic clientele (Watanabe, de la Cruz, Hatanaka, and Yip interviews). For example, when a drug abuse program in Los Angeles County added two Vietnamese-speaking staff members to its Prevention Unit in 1987, the number of Vietnamese participants increased substantially.

But even when agency directors strive for a multiethnic staff, they reserve the management positions for those they deem to be most qualified. As a result, American-born Japanese and Chinese professionals tend to be higher in the job hierarchy than newly arrived Asian immigrants and refugees. A former deputy director in Los Angeles described his hiring philosophy: "In staffing patterns, we have a good mix because if you want to serve a certain community, you have to get staff in that community. But it is different with the upper echelons. We have to get the best person for the job. So, the top echelons are primarily Japanese and Chinese Americans" (de la Cruz interview). One of the few Filipino Americans in management positions, de la Cruz has a doctorate in philosophy. Another experienced executive director echoed this sentiment: "Our staff are bilingual and bicultural. We hire them off the street. They don't have to have any experience. But most of our program managers are people with master's degrees. And they generally are Chinese and Japanese" (Yip interview). In Los Angeles County in 1990, of the executive directors of the five largest and oldest pan-Asian agencies—Asian Service Center, Asian Rehabilitation Services, Asian American Drug Abuse Program, Pacific Asian Consortium on Employment, and Special Services for Groups—four were Japanese Americans and one was Chinese American. Although this ethnic bias may not affect the delivery of services to various subgroups, it does mean that some Asian American groups are able to exercise greater power over the pan-Asian agencies than can other groups (Espiritu and Ong 1991).

As a result, some community advocates have claimed that the pan-Asian model allows the more established groups to dominate the funding meant for all Asian Americans; newer and less powerful groups are simply used as window displays. For example, Korean American leaders have questioned pan-Asian projects that included Korean Americans in the proposal, but ignored them in the implementation. At the 1974 Northern California Pacific Asian Coalition Regional Conference, the Korean caucus charged that they were left out of pan-Asian programs and called for an end to this neglect (Ignacio 1976: 106). A disenchanted Filipino American community advocate described the power hierarchy of a pan-Asian agency in Sacramento:

> The funding is dominated by Chinese and Japanese. The director is Japanese and the next person down is Chinese. They hire Filipinos but only for the lower jobs, as community workers—way down the organizational chart. The Japanese are full-time and the Filipinos are only half-time. The governing board is also dominated by Chinese and Japanese. (Jacaban interview)

Ironically, justification for government funding is often based on the low socioeconomic status and social service needs of the very Asian groups that have the least power within the pan-Asian structure. In general, agencies that target needy immigrants, particularly Southeast Asian refugees, have a better chance of being funded than those that do not. This practice is possible because of government funding policies that lump diverse Asian American groups together. When new Asian immigrants and refugees arrive, they are placed under the "Asian American" rubric—whether or not they see themselves in such terms. For example, in the early stages of resettling Southeast Asians, refugee officials turned to Asian American associations for assistance. In 1981, Asian American agencies accounted for 43 percent of all nonprofit organizations in California that received refugee social service funding. In funding Asian American agencies to resettle the refugees, refugee officials linked newly arrived Southeast Asians with the established Asian American community. These officials even went so far as to distribute a publication entitled "We, the Asian American" to Southeast Asians in the refugee camps (Hein 1989). Given the availability of government funding, many Asian American agencies eagerly welcomed the refugees into the pan-Asian fold. According to a former director of the Pacific/Asian Coalition, "There were many bandwagon hoppers into the Asian scene because of the novelty of the Vietnamese/Cambodian issue and the glitter of the monies appropriated by U.S. Congress to resettle the new Vietnamese immigrants" (Ignacio 1976: 208–209). In so accepting them, the established Asian American communities reified the pan-Asian concept and provided additional pressure on the refugees to consider themselves in pan-Asian terms.

There are several explanations for the dominance of Japanese and Chinese American administrators. As stated earlier, the social work system rewards articulate, credentialed, and politically sophisticated individuals. In such a system, established Japanese and Chinese Americans benefit more than newly arrived Asian immigrants. There is also a historical dimension to the Japanese and Chinese American dominance: they were here first. In the late 1960s, Japanese and Chinese Americans played a prominent role in the Asian American movement: they were the first advocates and thus the first directors of social service agencies (Chun-Hoon, Hirata, and Moriyama 1973: 85; Spector-Leech 1988: 12–13). Chinese and Japanese

Americans also profited from the liberal affirmative action programs of the time. Because they got the jobs first, they now tend to be more highly placed than newly arrived Asian groups. According to a survey conducted by the Asian American Mental Health Research Center, in 1977 Chinese and Japanese Americans constituted over 60 percent of all Asian Pacific American mental health workers in the United States. In contrast, Guamanian, Hawaiian, Samoan, and Thai mental health workers together comprised less than 2 percent of the total (Asian American Mental Health Research Center 1977: viii). An agency director explained the Japanese and Chinese American advantage: "There are more MSWs [Master of Social Work] among the Japanese and Chinese. Until the other Asian groups start going into the colleges, and graduate with professional degrees, they will never be able to get the top positions" (Yip interview).

Whatever the reason for the dominance of Japanese and Chinese Americans, skeptics have charged that these two groups, in their administrative capacity, favor their own groups over other groups in the hiring process (Jacaban 1988a). Undoubtedly, favoritism exists primarily because "every ethnic group has their network within their own group. When an opportunity comes for them to hire someone, they usually hire someone within their own network" (de la Cruz interview). But newly arrived Asian refugees and immigrants are also disadvantaged because they "lack the leadership and the training in social service delivery" (Demonteverde interview). Commenting on the dearth of Filipino Americans in management positions, a Japanese American director who wished to remain anonymous stated, "I am not defending the hiring records of Filipinos. On a pure statistical basis, they have a case because not that many Filipinos have been hired. But the Filipinos have not developed that capacity yet." In other words, they do not get the jobs because they are not qualified. Ironically, this logic is the same as that used by the larger society to explain the dearth of minorities in management positions and to discredit affirmative action practices, particularly during Republican administrations.

Pan-Asian Advocacy Coalition

The election of Nixon in 1972 ushered in an era of fiscal constraints and weakening federal support for social service programs. It was the beginning of the restrictive federal reactions to the liberal social welfare policy of the 1960s (Conlan 1988). Plagued by rising unemployment and the Vietnam war, the 1970s marked the end of the War on Poverty. During this decade, the establishment of new grant programs slowed considerably (Library of Congress 1975: 16; California 1989: 11–12). To be more competitive in the funding game, Asian American social service groups formed pan-Asian advocacy organizations to lobby on their behalf. These organizations monitor government policies and programs, lobby private foundations and public officials for increased social service funding, and educate the public and government entities on the unique social service needs of Asian Americans. In addition to these formal functions, advocacy organizations provide an indispensable forum for social service professionals, organizations, and interested individuals to link resources, to share information, and to advance one another's interests—and, in so doing, to further promote the pan-Asian concept.

The pan-Asian strategy has led to some political victories. Pan-ethnic advocacy organizations are most effective when they present a united front against the dominant society. Thus, in the interest of survival, these federations have to continue to expand their support base by retaining existing members and attracting new ones. Panethnic advocacy organizations are most attractive when they provide thorough and equal representation for all constituent members. When this is not the case, members can threaten to secede and would-be members can refuse to join, thereby reducing the federation's legitimacy and effectiveness. In other words, panethnic organizations have the best chance of survival when they are willing to include and share power with the constituent groups. Two examples illustrate this point.

In 1990, representatives from two national health advocacy groups —the Asian American Health Forum (AAHF) and the Association of Asian/Pacific Community Health Organizations (AAPCHO)—pressed members of Congress to introduce and pass the Asian Pacific Islander Health Act of 1990 (HR 4992).[13] Sponsored by U.S. Representative Norman Mineta, the bill allocated $1 million for the improvement of data collection on the health needs of Asian Americans. Maintaining that aggregated data mask the bipolarity of the Asian Pacific population and the needs of high-risk groups, Asian American advocates pushed for the collection of *separate* health data on individual Asian subgroups (Ponce and Strobel interviews). It is important to note that this demand for a separate count was made by a pan-Asian coalition. Asian American advocates involved in this effort saw no contradiction between a pan-Asian stand and the goal of separate counts. The deputy director of Asian American Health Forum elaborated on the group's strategy:

> We couched the needs of the subgroups within the larger Asian Pacific framework. We always approach policymakers as a united Asian Pacific group. The reason is that we are much more formidable when there are more of us. If we're looking to affect policy nationwide, then we have to be pan-Asian. We'll be wiped out if we lobby as separate ethnic groups. (Ponce interview)

In other words, the organizational dialectic of Asian American ethnicity is a response to the often conflicting demands of the American political structure and of the Asian American communities.

The Asian Pacific Planning Council (APPCON) in Los Angeles County provides a second example. Founded in 1976, APPCON has become the largest federation of Asian Pacific social agencies in Southern California. In 1989, APPCON numbered more than forty agencies and agency representatives. As an advocacy organization, APPCON does not receive funding. However, it intervenes in the funding process by lobbying for grant proposals from its member agencies. The organization is an effective lobbyist because its members are tied to multiple levels of funding in the county. Moreover, the Los Angeles County Board of Supervisors, city officials, and private funding sources consult primarily with APPCON on matters affecting community funds for Asian American programs (Pagdan 1989; Fukai and Watanabe interviews). Because APPCON is the recognized representative of the county's Asian American community, "being a part of APPCON makes you more acceptable to the funding people" (Kokubun interview). Its political clout thus benefits all constituent members.

In the late 1980s, some Asian American groups charged that, although APPCON purported to represent the needs of all Asian Americans, in fact it represented only the needs of member agencies. For example, newly established Asian communities criticized APPCON for failing to respond to the demographic and geographic changes of the Asian American population. When APPCON was first established in the 1970s, the Asian American population basically consisted of Chinese and Japanese Americans who congregated in the central Los

Angeles area. In the 1980s, new Asian communities sprang up in suburban areas such as the San Gabriel Valley and Long Beach; however, APPCON has been slow in reaching out to them. As a result, these groups have steered away from APPCON and founded their own advocacy organizations. For example, Asian Americans in Long Beach started the Asian Services Coalition and Asian Americans in the San Gabriel Valley formed the Asian Task Force to lobby on their behalf. It is noteworthy that both of these new organizations are pan-Asian.

Other community activists have also accused APPCON of unequal representation, alleging that the council ignores the needs of newer Asian Pacific groups, especially Southeast Asian and Pacific Islander communities. A former APPCON member who wished to remain anonymous charged that APPCON "does not heartily push for programs from the Filipino and Indochinese agencies." After a dispute over funding, Filipino American Service Group, Inc. (FASGI) seceded from APPCON in 1988, declaring that the council does not represent the interests of the Filipino American community. The director of FASGI explained her decision to leave APPCON:

> In 1988, FASGI submitted a grant proposal for elderly abuse to California Foundation. The Asian Pacific Older Adult Task Force [an APPCON committee] also submitted their proposal to the same foundation. APPCON people got mad, saying that FASGI had no business doing their own thing. They invited the vice president of California Foundation to an APPCON meeting. At that time, the vice president of APPCON was the program director of California Foundation. Do you see the conflict of interests? Their proposal got approved. Ours didn't. Our proposal was denied because we served only one group, the Filipinos. I was fighting like mad to get the program going. I felt like a little Filipino horse running against the big Asian horse. APPCON was trying to kill us. After that, I felt that FASGI should have nothing more to do with APPCON. (Guerrero interview)

This episode highlights the importance of networking and the advantage that pan-Asian projects have over single-ethnic ones in the funding process. More important, it indicates that, in addition to their political lobbying efforts, advocacy groups also reduce competition for funds and duplication of services among their members. From APPCON's point of view, FASGI violated the agreement to work cooperatively—instead of competitively—with other agency members. From FASGI's perspective, APPCON was trying "to build power at the expense of the less powerful groups" (Guerrero interview). Because FASGI organizers found it difficult to pursue their group interests within a pan-Asian structure, they opted for secession. The special projects director of FASGI defended the agency's decision: "APPCON people used the Marxist line saying that we're being separatists. I just turned around and said that it is an equity issue" (Bagasao interview). This episode notwithstanding, both Guerrero and Bagasao stated that they would coalesce with other Asian American groups as long as Filipino Americans received their fair share of resources.

Responding to charges of favoritism and limited representation, APPCON formed a committee to reach out to the underserved Asian Pacific communities and the underserved geographical areas. Through its newsletter, outreach visits to nonmembers, and organization mentoring program, APPCON hopes to recruit new members into its fold. Undoubtedly, APPCON reached out to new communities because it wanted to assist heretofore underrepresented Asian groups. But altruism is not the only reason. The group also instituted outreach measures for a practical reason: "If APPCON doesn't recruit new communities, its credibility will suffer. If APPCON falls apart, we're going to be manipulated, overlooked. Then none of us will get anything" (Watanabe interview). In other words, APPCON's political effectiveness hinges on the cooperation and support of the constituent groups. But the latter also are in a very real sense captives of the rules of the funding game.

"Dropping Out": Filipino Americans and the Politics of Numbers

The perceived or real inequity within pan-Asian social service organizations has caused participants from the less dominant groups to feel shortchanged and marginalized and has led them to attempt to go outside the coalition framework to pursue their goals. But dropping out is not a viable option for all subgroups. Only established groups that have the numbers, human and organizational resources, and political experience can operate independently of the panethnic framework. Even then, they are often constrained by "the dominant discursive construction and determination of Asian Americans as a homogeneous group" (Lowe 1991: 29).

Filipino Americans have been the group most outspoken against the pan-Asian framework. Although they are willing to caucus with other Asian American organizations, Filipino Americans often prefer their own advocacy groups. For example, at the first Asian American national conference in San Francisco in 1972, Filipino Americans separated themselves from the larger Asian American body and organized their own "Brown" Asian caucus (Ignacio 1976: 139). Recently, at the 1989 national conference on HIV infection and AIDS in minority and ethnic populations in Washington, D.C., there was an Asian Pacific caucus as well as a Filipino caucus.

The post-1965 influx of Filipino immigrants has increased their population base, making it more feasible for Filipino Americans to secede from the pan-Asian framework. In 1980, Filipino Americans were the largest Asian American group in the United States as well as in California. In 1990, they narrowly trailed Chinese Americans at the national level, but were still the largest Asian American group in California (see Table 4.2). Numerical superiority has given them superior clout. Consequently, some Filipino Americans contend that they no longer need to coalesce with other Asian American groups. As one Filipino American leader who declined to be named asserted, "We felt disfranchised and deprived before. But now, we do not need to unite with other Asian groups. We do not need the numbers; we have the numbers."

In Los Angeles County, Filipino American social service workers have claimed that their large numbers entitle them to a larger share of the available social service monies. A Filipino American community activist complained of the unequal distribution of funding: "Even though we're the fastest growing Asian community, we're still getting crumbs" (Bagasao interview). Similarly, a harshly worded editorial in the San Francisco–based *Philippine News* argued that Filipino Americans need to be separated from the Asian Pacific classification because "the Japanese and Chinese . . . dominate every outreach funding meant for Asian and Pacific Islanders combined" and that "[they] are only using the numerical strength of the Filipinos to attract larger fundings for the Asian and Pacific Islanders" (Jaca-

TABLE 4.2

Asian American Population in the United States and California,
1980, 1990, and Projected for 2000

Ethnic Group	California	United States
JAPANESE		
1980	261,822	716,331
1990	312,989	847,562
2000	352,161	856,619
CHINESE		
1980	322,309	812,178
1990	704,850	1,645,472
2000	775,738	1,683,537
FILIPINO		
1980	357,492	781,894
1990	731,685	1,406,770
2000	938,662	2,070,571
KOREAN		
1980	106,476	357,393
1990	259,941	798,849
2000	371,715	1,320,759
SOUTHEAST ASIAN		
1980	99,533	245,425 *
1990	485,427	1,092,329
2000	613,372	1,574,385 *

Sources: California data for 1980 and 2000 from Ong (1989: table 5); United States data for 1980 and 2000 from Gardner et al. (1985: table 16); California and United States data for 1990 from U.S. Census Bureau as reported in various issues of *Asian Week* in June and July.

* Data for Vietnamese only.

ban 1988*a*). In a telephone interview, Melecio Jacaban argued that, since affirmative action laws are based on numbers, Filipino Americans should be receiving a larger share than the Japanese and Chinese Americans: "If numbers count, then why should the Filipinos take a back seat? Because there are more Filipinos than Chinese or Japanese, we are the ones who should be dominating the outreach programs for Asian Pacific groups. We should be getting the directorship and the funding" (Jacaban interview). In other words, as the largest Asian American group, Filipino Americans expect to lead pan-Asian coalitions. But as discussed above, leadership positions are reserved for persons with credentials and experience—not necessarily for persons from the largest group.

The growing political strength of Filipino Americans is evident in their successful lobbying for the 1988 passage of California Senate Bill 1813, which requires state personnel surveys or statistical tabulations to classify persons of Filipino ancestry as Filipino rather than as Asian or Hispanic. With this bill, Filipino Americans can reap affirmative action benefits independent of the Asian American grouping because these outreach programs or funds "shall include equitable allocations based on the percentages of Filipinos in local governments in the State of California." The numerical strength of Filipino Americans was indeed a factor in the passage of California Senate Bill 1813. In a letter to State Assemblyman Peter Chacon, United States Congressman Jim Bates (1988) urged the passage of the bill stating that "there are more Filipinos in California than Japanese or Chinese and they are the fastest growing ethnic group in the state. The Filipinos should be separately categorized and given separate funding for outreach programs to serve their own people." The sponsor of the bill, Melecio Jacaban, also made use of the politics of numbers. In a memo to the bill committee, he wrote:

> As you are all aware of, the Filipinos are the third largest ethnic group in the state. . . . We estimate that there are about 850,000 Filipinos in California at this writing. And out of that number, there are approximately half a million Filipino American registered voters. This is quite a sizeable number of voters, and they could prove to be the margin of election victory for some of the legislators who have a heavy Filipino population in their district. (Jacaban 1988*b*)

The cultural distance between Filipinos and other East Asian groups partly explains the Filipino–Asian split. As a result first of Spanish and then of U.S. colonial rule, the cultural orientations of the Filipinos differ markedly from those of the two dominant Asian groups in the United States—Chinese and Japanese Americans (Rabaya 1971: 110; Min 1986–87: 58). Carey McWilliams (1964: 233) observed, "As an Oriental people, geographically and racially close to the great cultures of the East, yet Westernized to a large degree through familiarity with Western language, law, custom, religion, the Filipinos were the hybrid orphans of the Far East." Reflecting on the cultural differences between Filipinos and other Asian groups in the United States, a Filipina American stated, "Culturally, the East Asians share similarities. We don't share them. But when we get to this country, we are told that we are Asians. We are lumped together with Asians because of a geographical accident" (Yap interview). Although it is debatable how important these cultural differences are, especially among the American born, they are nevertheless used selectively to justify the Filipino–Asian division (Espiritu and Ong 1991).

Often overlooked is the class dimension of the Filipino-Asian conflict. For the most part, Filipino Americans are more disadvantaged in the labor market than are Japanese and Chinese Americans.[14] For example, college-educated Japanese Americans on the average earned $23,000 and Chinese Americans $21,000 in 1979. The same year, similarly educated Filipinos averaged just over $16,000. Moreover, compared to Chinese and Japanese Americans, Filipino Americans "appear to be more of a working-class ethnic group, with greater occupational concentrations in semi-skilled jobs" (Nee and Sanders 1985: 82–85; Cabezas, Shinagawa, and Kawaguchi 1986–87). Filipino Americans also fare less well in higher education: few graduate from colleges and fewer still enroll in graduate schools (Azores and Espiritu 1990: 24). Because of their relatively disadvantaged position in the labor market and their underrepresentation in higher education, Filipino Americans have a strong claim for protection from the state. However, when Filipino Americans are lumped together with other Asian American groups, their claim on the state is diluted due to the relatively high economic and educational levels of the Asian American aggregate. Therefore, in addition to the cultural gap, Filipino

Americans have an economic incentive to separate themselves from the Asian American rubric (Espiritu and Ong 1991). Citing similar economic disparities between themselves and other Asian American groups, Southeast Asian refugees and Pacific Islanders have also wanted out from under the "Asian Pacific American" umbrella.[15]

However, Filipino Americans face several constraints in their quest to secede from the pan-Asian framework. Their major disadvantage is their limited numbers. Even though Filipino Americans are the largest Asian American group in the United States, they remain a very small group outside this coalition—particularly when they have to compete against other coalitions such as Hispanics and blacks. Because of their limited numbers, dropping out of the pan-Asian framework is not a viable option for Filipino Americans as a group. Moreover, being a member of the Asian American coalition brings them instant political visibility—if not always benefits. Given the pitfalls of withdrawing from the pan-Asian rubric, many Filipino Americans have opted to stay with the coalition (Morales interview).

It is true that dissenting Filipino Americans are in the minority. On the other hand, the dissension has become public, with some Filipino Americans airing their grievances in mainstream newspapers and to government officials (Jacaban 1988a; Bagasao 1989). For example, in a letter to California Senator David Roberti, the Filipino-American Public Affairs Council in Southern California requested that the Filipino American community be treated independently from other Asian Americans because "Filipinos had not been receiving culture and language sensitive programs from both Japanese and Chinese service centers" (Padgan 1989). Such public exposure threatens the foundation of the pan-Asian framework, reducing its effectiveness. As a Japanese American director who declined to be named stated:

> We have always had internal conflict. But now for the first time, this conflict has gone beyond the community into the media, and to government officials. We have always advocated a strong principle of unity: conflict should be handled within the community. Otherwise, folks who control the funding will use that against us. They are going to manipulate it.

It is likely that, at a certain level, these ethnic fights are waged to advance the careers of individuals. If the directorships of most pan-Asian agencies are dominated by Chinese and Japanese Americans, then a Filipino American who wishes to be an agency director would have to start a separate agency. However, these fights are waged in ethnic terms. Opponents of the pan-Asian model are labeled "anti-Japanese" or "anti-Chinese" (Bagasao interview), and supporters of the model are judged to be "anti-Filipino" (Morales interview). As a Filipino American supporter of the coalition model related, "Some Filipinos thought that the other Asians did them in. Now, they're making it into an ethnic argument. They say I am less of a Filipino than they are" (Morales interview). This "more Filipino than thou" argument tells only half of the story: by accentuating the ethnic schism between Asian American groups, it conceals the class cleavages that continue to separate Filipino Americans (and other nondominant Asian groups) from the more established Asian American groups.

Community-Based Funding Sources

Given the recent cutbacks in public resources and the scarcity of private funding, Asian American agencies have had to institute new forms of "self-help." In addition to fund-raisers (e.g., banquets, beauty pageants), Asian American service providers have established community funding to finance Asian American programs. Founded in 1984, the Asian Foundation for Community Development (AFCD) in Oakland dispenses grants and loans to Asian American projects in Northern California. As the nation's first Asian American foundation, AFCD provides a community alternative to mainstream funding, often targeting programs that receive minimal or no public funding (J. Ng 1989). Formed in 1987 by a coalition of thirteen Asian Pacific agencies, the Asian Pacific Community Fund (APCF) in Los Angeles is another community effort to "provide a vehicle for Asians to give to Asian communities" (Woo interview). Modeled after the United Way and the Brotherhood Crusade, APCF allows Asian American employees, through payroll deductions, to donate funds directly to Asian American service providers. This donor option program was established, in part, to pressure the United Way of Los Angeles to allocate more of its funding resources to Asian American programs (R. Kuramoto 1987: 2–3).

Although important, these community efforts cannot rival mainstream funding. With a "shoestring staff of two, a few interns, and a core of about 15 volunteers," the Asian Foundation's modest budget allows it to award only small grants (averaging between $1,000 and $5,000) to Asian American programs (J. Ng 1989). Similarly, faced with resistance from United Way supporters,[16] the Asian Pacific Community Fund collected only $30,000 after four years of hard work, a meager sum in light of the abundant needs of the Asian American clientele in Los Angeles (Woo interview). Fund-raisers also bring little revenue. According to an experienced agency director, "In a good year, the Chinese community in San Diego raised only about $20,000. You can't support a professional staff with that kind of money" (Yip interview). Given the modest scope of community-based funding sources at present, public funding remains the major source of revenue for Asian American social service agencies (Kimura 1990: 4–6).

Conclusion

A community that relies upon outside funding must define its problems and needs in terms its sources can understand and with which they can concur. In the wake of the War on Poverty, government-funded social service agencies took over the welfare activities once provided by traditional Asian American associations. Despite cutbacks in public funding in recent years, government continues to be the key source of financial support for Asian American agencies. Because the funding system rewards professionalism, it reduces the influence of traditional elites and grass-roots activists, and increases the power of articulate, credentialed, and politically sophisticated persons. In such a system, established, professional Asian Americans are the executive directors and program managers of social service agencies, and the impoverished, newly arrived Asian immigrants their clientele.

Outside funding has also merged subgroup boundaries. Because funding sources often expect people of various ethnic origins to speak with a common voice, Asian American groups have had to unite to be competitive in the funding game. Thus, whereas pan-Asian cooperation is infrequent in the electoral arena, it has had to be entrenched in the social service arena. However, the pan-Asian boundary is also fragile here, enclosing individuals and groups with different class, cultural, and ethnic backgrounds. The determination of whose interests will be defended often leads to intense internal conflict. The post-1965 Asian immigration has exacerbated the competition for jobs, money, and power, with some groups choosing to pursue their goals outside the pan-Asian framework. The cases cited in this chapter suggest that, in accordance with the benefits and drawbacks of panethnicity, the organization of ethnicity among Asian Americans has occurred at multiple levels—not only at the extremes of consolidation or fragmentation.

Chapter 5

Census Classification: The Politics of Ethnic Enumeration

The disputes over the classification of Asian Americans in the 1980 and 1990 censuses epitomize this book's argument that Asian American ethnic organization is multitiered and situationally determined. Focusing on the demand for separate counts of Asian American subgroups waged by a pan-Asian coalition, this chapter calls attention to the linkages between these multiple levels and the conditions under which ethnic and panethnic goals are complementary and ethnic politics necessarily becomes panethnic politics.

Census Schedules and Ethnic Classification

The U.S. Constitution requires a decennial enumeration of the country's population as the basis for representation and taxation. From the inception of the census in 1790 to the mid-nineteenth century, few items pertained to ethnicity. Until 1820, the ethnic data were essentially by-products of the distinction between white citizens and groups with fewer civil rights and liberties, such as nonnaturalized foreigners, slaves, and tribal Indians. In 1830, the first nationally uniform printed schedule distinguished free white persons from free colored persons. In 1850, the concept of color, institutionalized as white, black, or mulatto, was first specified for free inhabitants, and black or mulatto for slave inhabitants (U.S. Bureau of the Census 1979; Lowry 1982: 47).

During the era of "melting pot" ideology, the census schedules greatly increased their coverage of ethnic minorities. Reflecting popular concern about newcomers' characteristics and their rate of Americanization, the 1870 census added two questions to determine whether either of the respondent's parents had been born abroad. The 1880 census recorded the specific country of birth for each parent and conducted a special census of the American Indian population. In the 1890 schedule, foreign-born males were asked their length of residence in the United States and their naturalization status. Additionally, all respondents were asked whether or not they were able to speak English and, if not, what language or dialect they spoke (Lowry 1982: 47; Petersen 1987: 196).

Responding to the social and political issues raised by the swelling tide of immigration, the census schedules from 1890 through 1930 increasingly attended to the complexities of ethnic identification. The 1910 census recognized forty-two principal foreign languages spoken in the nation. In 1930, the list of categories for "Race and Color" expanded to include "White, Negro, Mexican, Indian, Chinese, Japanese, Filipino, Hindu, and Korean," plus a space for other write-in choices. However, after the passage of the restrictive immigration laws of the 1920s, interest in ethnic composition waned. From the depression of the 1930s onward, the census schedules focused primarily on the economic well-being of the country. The number and complexity of questions dealing with immigration and the foreign born were reduced (Lowry 1982: 47; Petersen 1987: 196).

The census classification of ethno-racial groups has been problematic; the categories have been arbitrary and inconsistent—often reflecting the Census Bureau's administrative needs rather than the population's perceptions of meaningful cultural and racial differentiations. For example, the 1920 census stipulated that "any mixture of White and some other race was to be reported according to the race of the person who was not White" (U.S. Bureau of the Census 1979: 52).[1] In so doing, the census imposed an arbitrary racial identity on individuals of mixed parentage. Prior to the 1960 census, racial classification was obtained by the enumerator on the basis of observation. Although reasonably adequate identification could be made of the dominant and relatively large groups, smaller groups were often misclassified.[2] The 1960 census was the first in which respondents had an opportunity to classify their own race. Even then, the enumerator was instructed to reclassify those entries that diverged from the prescribed census racial categories. For example, "Puerto Ricans" and "Mexicans" were to be reclassified as "White" unless the respondents were definitely Negro, Indian, or some other race. Where the enumerator failed to do so, the reclassification was made in the editing process (U.S. Bureau of the Census 1964: xli; 1979: 70). Not until the 1980 census were enumerators no longer allowed to enter race by observation.

The census has been most inconsistent in its handling of persons of Mexican origin or descent. Even though there was no significant change in the population itself, the classification of Mexicans in the United States has changed from one census to the next. Mexicans were moved from a racial category ("other nonwhite") in 1930 to an ethnic category ("persons of Spanish mother tongue") in 1940. In 1950 and 1960, an even more ambiguous classification, "White persons of Spanish surname" was used, but only in five states of the "Mexican" Southwest. In 1970, the census category was "persons of both Spanish surname and Spanish mother tongue." Finally, in 1980, Mexican Americans, along with Puerto Ricans and other groups of Spanish origin or descent, were classified as a "super" ethnic group: Spanish/Hispanic (Moore and Pachon 1985: 3; Choldin 1986: 406).

The Politics of Ethnic Enumeration

A second problem related to ethnicity in the census enumeration process is the undercounting of certain groups. A census undercount is that fraction of the "real total population" that a census fails to include (Choldin 1986: 404). Since at least 1940, the Census Bureau has acknowledged the incompleteness of census counts; however, neither the executive nor the legislative branches required that these counts be adjusted. Initially, the census undercount was of interest only to academics and census officials. In the late 1960s, however, as Congress, federal court judges, and public officials turned to census statistics to administer civil rights laws, concern about the undercount intensified (Anderson 1988: 213).[3]

Civil rights legislation requires federal authorities to look for patterns of discrimination as evidenced by the underrepresentation of disadvantaged minorities; where such underrepresentation is found, affirmative action by the responsible party must be undertaken to correct it. Disadvantaged minorities are defined as those who have been historically subject to racial discrimination and economic oppression in the United States. By 1970, the courts allowed a limited use of mathematical ratios to determine the racial balance of a school system. In 1971, the Office of Federal Contract Compliance instructed firms with federal contracts to establish numerical goals and timetables for minority hiring. In 1977, Congress passed a $4 billion public works law that required 10 percent of the money for each construction project to be spent on purchases from minority contractors.[4] Designed to assist disadvantaged minority groups, these federal programs "created a need for statistical documentation of each group's disadvantages" (Choldin 1986: 406; Anderson 1988: 218). As a result, basic census information, such as the count of a minority population and its regional distribution, became essential, providing the framework for legislative approval of government projects and allocation of funds.

Congress also used census population statistics to ensure equal access to the electoral process. The 1975 Voting Rights Act requires bilingual voting materials for Spanish, Asian, American Indian, and Alaskan Native voters. Relying on census data, this law specifies that bilingual assistance must be available in voting districts in which more than 5 percent of the citizens are members of the affected language minority group. Because the 1970 census did not include language questions, the 1975 amendment used group identity as a surrogate for linguistic needs (Melnick 1981: 50; Keane 1985: 343–344). A census undercount of minority groups can thus affect their voting rights.

Because the census tabulations of ethnic groups form the benchmark for many legal tests of ethnic underrepresentation, census undercount—or more accurately, *differential undercount*—became an explosive political controversy. A differential undercount exists when "the census misses more of one segment of the population than of another" (Choldin 1986: 404). Traditionally, decennial census coverage has missed more nonwhites than whites. For example, it is estimated that the 1950 census missed 2.6 percent of all whites compared to 11.5 percent of nonwhites. In 1960, 2.2 percent of whites but 9.5 percent of nonwhites were missed. The Census Bureau improved coverage in the 1970 and 1980 censuses, but it still missed 8 and 9 percent of the black population respectively. The undercount rate was worst for black males. For the 1970 census, the undercount rate was 2.5 percent for the general population, but over 18 percent for black males twenty to thirty-four years old (U.S. Bureau of the Census 1989b). The 1990 census also missed more minorities than whites, undercounting about 5 percent of blacks and Latinos while overlooking fewer than 2 percent of whites. In July 1991, much to the dismay of local officials and minority groups, Commerce Secretary Robert A. Mosbacher refused to adjust the 1990 census population figures to reflect the more than five million persons estimated to have been missed (Fulwood III 1991). Because census figures stand for the decade, the potential damage of an undercount is not short term.

Influenced by protests from the black community, new ethnic constituencies mobilized and demanded better statistics of their groups. In the early 1970s, Latino and Asian Americans pressed the Census Bureau for better coverage of their respective communities, which included a significant proportion of new immigrants (Anderson 1988: 221–226).[5] Mexican American leaders "sued the census officials, complained to their senators and congressmen, and insulted the Census Bureau in letters, reports, and newspapers" (Choldin 1986: 409). Although actual affirmative action benefits are vague, ethnic activists believe that the larger the official count of their group's members, the greater the advantage the members have in these programs (Lowry 1982: 54).

Local public officials also entered into the undercount controversy. Besides affecting the apportionment of seats in Congress, seats in state legislatures, and even city council districts, census population counts bear directly on the distribution of federal monies to states, counties, and cities for everything from feeding the poor to running mass transit systems. From 1970 to 1979, the total direct federal grant to cities rose by more than 800 percent to nearly $11 billion (Maurice and Nathan 1982: 262).

Census statistics are also used to support applications for project grants. In 1988, sixty federal programs distributed an estimated $73 billion in formula grants based all or in part on population. About $40 billion was tied directly to population figures (Kirschten 1989).

Even when the population count does not determine the amount of funding, it may determine eligibility. For example, the Comprehensive Employment and Training Act (CETA) stipulates that, to be a prime sponsor, a city must have a population of at least 100,000 persons (Melnick 1981: 48–49).

Incomplete census counts translate into financial losses. In 1980, New York City claimed that it lost more than $50 million a year in federal aid because its black and Latino populations were undercounted (Clifford 1989). According to a California Senate subcommittee on minorities, women, and the 1990 reapportionment, the state would lose an estimated $683 million over the next ten years if the 1980 census undercount were repeated in 1990. Los Angeles alone would lose tens of millions of dollars in federal aid. Armed with a $1 million budget, the Los Angeles City Council and local agencies launched a full-blown outreach effort to ensure an accurate census count of the city's residents in the 1990 census (Stewart 1989).

Because undercounting occurs primarily in low-income, inner-city neighborhoods with significant minority populations, local governments and ethnic groups both desire accurate enumeration. A higher count of minorities in a particular locality raises the count of the area's total population, thus drawing more federal monies. With more federal monies, ethnic agencies have a better chance of being funded. More important, with a higher count of their members, ethnic leaders can exert more political pressure when they apply for local grants.

In sum, civil rights legislation and expanded grants-in-aid programs fueled new interest in the accuracy, adequacy, precision, and utility of census statistics. By the end of 1980, the census had become a major focus of ongoing political debate. Asian Americans who understand the importance of the census have therefore become involved in the politics of census enumeration.

Playing the Numbers Game: The Asian American Case

In 1870, Asian Americans first appeared in the census schedules when "Chinese" was given as an answer to the "Color" question. Anti-Chinese sentiment grew during this same decade and culminated in the 1882 Chinese Exclusion Act. One result of the Exclusion Act was the substitution of Japanese workers for Chinese workers in

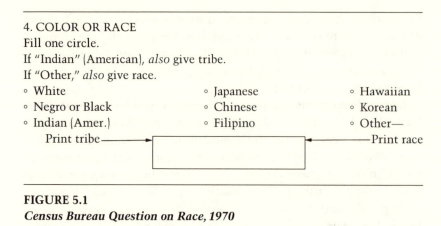

FIGURE 5.1
Census Bureau Question on Race, 1970

some economic sectors. The Japanese category appeared for the first time in the 1890 census. With the arrival of Filipino farm workers in the 1920s and 1930s, the 1930 census also included Filipinos in its "Color or Race" question. Koreans also had their own category in this census. Before then, they were classified in the "Other" category. However, because of their small numbers, Koreans were again relegated to the expedient heading "Other" in the 1950 and 1960 censuses.[6] In the 1970 census, five Asian Pacific groups were identified in the "Color or Race" question: Japanese, Chinese, Filipino, Hawaiian, and Korean (U.S. Bureau of the Census 1979) (see Figure 5.1). As detailed below, largely due to political lobbying, the number of Asian Pacific groups increased from five in the 1970 census to nine in the 1980 and 1990 censuses.

The 1980 Census

As the basis for determining representation and taxation, the census has always been a part of American politics (Melnick 1981: 64; Conk 1984: 102). Yet the 1980 census was unique in the intensity of the disputes it raised in the courts, legislatures, and communities. In 1980, the federal census received more political attention than it had since the 1920s. During the two years preceding the census, congressional committees held more than forty hearings on the subject (Melnick 1981: 64). More than fifty lawsuits were filed to challenge the undercount of the 1980 census. Predictably, the plaintiffs included jurisdictions with significant minority populations such as New York City, Los Angeles, Chicago, Houston, and Miami (Kirschten 1989; Roderick 1989b). The 1980 census cost approximately $1 billion, of which $406 million was spent on upgrading the census. Of this amount, $203 million was devoted to obtaining a better population count (Anderson 1988: 226).

The undercount of minority groups in the 1970 census figured prominently in the planning of the 1980 census. Departing from previous decades, the planning effort did not take place in the offices of the Census Bureau. For the first time since the Census Bureau was organized as a government agency, "a broad-based coalition of local officials, civil rights activists, academics, and congressmen demanded to be included in the planning process" (Anderson 1988: 221). Responding to pressures from ethnic constituencies, the Census Bureau established minority advisory committees to make recommendations on the content and conduct of the census (Anderson 1988: 226). These committees differed radically from previous advisory committees in that they included community people with no scientific or technical expertise (Choldin 1986: 410).

The Asian Pacific American Advisory Committee was created only after considerable pressure was exerted on the Census Bureau. In early 1975, Asian American advocacy groups (the Japanese American Citizens League, the Pacific/Asian Coalition, and the Asian and Pacific American Federal Employees Caucus) and Asian American legislators (U.S. Representatives Patsy Mink and Norman Mineta and U.S. Senator Spark Matsunaga) prodded the Census Bureau to form an Asian Pacific American Advisory Committee for the 1980 census (Census Advisory Committee 1979: 1). In a joint resolution with U.S. Senator Daniel Inouye to the Committee on Government Affairs, Senator Matsunaga outlined the fiscal impact of census undercoverage: "Asian and Pacific Island American ethnic groups are unable to obtain adequate assistance from Federal, State, and local social service programs due to the absence or incompleteness of planning data on which they must base their request for such services" (Census Advisory Committee 1979: 30).[7]

In March of 1976, the Census Bureau invited twenty-one Asian and Pacific Americans to an ad hoc meeting. The Bureau offered the group two options: to establish a formal advisory committee or to deal with representatives of the respective communities on a continuing basis. The group opted unanimously for the establishment of an advisory committee. In other words, they chose to organize at the pan-Asian level rather than at the ethnic-specific level. There were several reasons for this decision. One was enhanced group status: the establishment of an official advisory committee gave formal recognition to the Asian Pacific American population—alongside the African American and Latino American populations. The other was political effectiveness: because the committee was a congressionally mandated body, the Census Bureau was required to respond to its recommendations (Census Advisory Committee 1979: 1–2). After many months of arduous campaigning, the Census Advisory Committee on the Asian Pacific American Population for the 1980 Census was chartered in June 1976—almost two years after the creation of the Black Advisory Committee and the Hispanic Advisory Committee.

To ensure better coverage of the relevant populations, the Asian Pacific American Advisory Committee pushed for measures that would increase the 1980 count of its constituents or would make them more visible in census reports. For example, the committee demanded an estimate of the undercount of the Asian Pacific American population, suggested that the Census Bureau allocate money for advertising in minority media, and asked that the Bureau extend its affirmative action plan to the Asian Pacific community (Census Advisory Committee, 1979: 6–7).

The committee's most protracted struggle was over Asian Pacific American representation in the race item, which, in the preceding decades, had become the most controversial item on the census schedules. At the time of the 1960 census, the race question[8] had become discredited and would have been excluded in 1970 had it not been for the passage of the civil rights and equal opportunities laws, which made it necessary for the census to continue to compile racial statistics (Kaplan 1979: 4). In the 1970 census, the five Asian Pacific American groups identified in the "Color or Race" question were enumerated on a 100 percent basis. Asian Pacific groups not listed were relegated to the "Other" category and tallied from sample tabulations. Contending that a 100 percent enumeration would produce more accurate (i.e., larger) counts than a sample, the committee fought to increase the number of Asian Pacific categories in the race item so that fewer or no Asian Pacific groups would have to be enumerated as "Other" (Census Advisory Committee 1979: 9).

But more was at stake here than statistical reliability. Status perception was of equal concern. Asian Pacific American groups wanted the American public to regard them as significant populations; being listed alongside the major racial minorities (blacks and American Indians) helped their cause. The Hispanic Advisory Committee likewise asked the Census Bureau to move the "Spanish/Hispanic origin or descent" question from the sample portion of the 1970 census to the 100 percent portion in 1980, claiming that it was demeaning to them to be identified on merely a sample basis while other groups were enumerated on a 100 percent basis (Kaplan 1979: 4).

For the Asian Pacific American population, the category "Other" is also problematic because of inaccurate—and at times, racist—coding instructions for the write-in entries. For example, the Questionnaire Reference Manuals for the 1976 and 1977 census pretests include these inappropriate guidelines: "If a respondent's answer is 'American,' classify it as 'White'; if it is 'Nonwhite,' classify it as 'Black.'" The Census Bureau explained these guidelines on the logic of numerical majorities (i.e., most Americans are white, most nonwhites are black). Albert Yee, chairperson of the 1980 Asian Pacific Census Advisory Committee, denounced these racial designations:

> All Americans are not White and the history and laws of the land spell that fact out so vividly that it seems foreign or cynical to promulgate the notion that it does not matter for the 1980 census. Also, I need not stress the point that all Nonwhites are not Black. (Census Advisory Committee 1979: 17)

Besides the racist overtones, these instructions benefit the larger groups by adding more people to those categories. Given the official tendency to see only black and white and to define "American" as white, Asian American demands for precise census classification are part of a more general (and badly needed) project of education. In other words, Asian Americans are not only campaigning for immediate benefits but also expressing rage at past slights and attempting to head off future injustices.[9]

Other coding instructions reflect the Census Bureau's ignorance of, or indifference to, the complexities within the Asian American population. For example, "Cantonese," "Nipponese," and "Yellow" were reclassified as "Other" instead of as "Chinese," "Japanese," and "Other Asian," respectively (Census Advisory Committee 1979: 6).[10] To increase the total count of Asian Pacific American groups, the Advisory Committee recommended an "Other Asian" option for the following write-in responses: "Asian (Asian American), Asiatic, Bangladesh, Burmese, Cambodian, Ceylonese, Eurasian, Indonesian, Javanese, Laotian, Malayan, Mongolian, Okinawan, Oriental, Pakistani, Siamese, Thai, Yellow" (Census Advisory Committee 1979: 16). This catch-all category denotes the multiple levels of Asian American identifications: from regional (e.g., Okinawan) to national (e.g., Laotian) to panethnic (e.g., Asian American). It also claims the offspring of mixed parentage (e.g., Eurasian). Although the "Other Asian" category did not appear on the 1980 census questionnaire, it was shown in the tabulation of results.

In 1976, the Office of Management and Budget (OMB) issued a memorandum requiring all federal agencies to use the following racial categories in program administrative reporting and statistical activities: "American Indian or Alaskan Native, Asian or Pacific Islander, Black, and White."[11] An Asian or Pacific Islander is defined as "a person having origins in any of the original peoples of the Far East, Southeast Asia, the Indian subcontinent, or the Pacific Islands" (U.S. Equal Employment Opportunity Commission 1977). This classification scheme ignores subgroup boundaries, treating diverse populations as unitary groups. To satisfy the new federal guidelines on the collection of racial statistics, the Census Bureau proposed to collapse all Asian Pacific racial codes into one summary category (Asian or Pacific Islander). According to the Bureau, this single classification would provide a 100 percent count of the total Asian and Pacific Islander population, as required by the OMB (Plotkin 1977: 158; Census Advisory Committee 1979: 11).

The Bureau also opted for the blanket category "Asian or Pacific Islander" because it is the politically safest choice. With the listing approach, the Bureau is required to select the Asian Pacific groups to be identified separately on the census form. This practice is politically troublesome because the groups not selected will be sure to protest the Bureau's decisions. As the director of the Census Bureau testified before Congress, "From the representations made to us, even a listing of fifteen to twenty categories would not satisfy or meet the demands of the groups for which data are to be obtained" (Plotkin 1977: 158). But to include all of the Asian and Pacific Islander groups would require a great expansion of the race question—an expense the Census Bureau was unwilling to shoulder. With the proposed race question, the statistics on the individual Asian groups could emerge only from the respondents' write-in entries (Plotkin 1977: 162).

Asian American individuals, advocacy groups, and legislators united to fight the Census Bureau's attempt to lump all Asians together (Census Advisory Committee 1979: 11). At a congressional hearing on the 1980 census, the chair of the Asian Pacific American Census Advisory Committee cited the unfavorable pretest results in Oakland: "Many people were either confused by the category 'Asian or Pacific Islander' or they totally rejected the concept" (Azores 1977: 196). Contending that "identification along racial lines is primarily an American phenomenon, and is the creation of third and fourth generation immigrants," Azores argued that the concept "Asians" is particularly difficult for immigrants, and for limited- or non-English speakers who identify themselves only on the basis of their national origin. In contrast, another Asian American advocate espoused an Asian American perspective, testifying that Asians in the United States

> tend to view ourselves as a single minority group. This is the result of similarities in native cultures, cultural, and linguistic distance from Western society, and shared racial appearances. We also share a history of discrimination and ethnic stereotyping in the U.S. American culture nearly always views us as a single group and variously we have been called Asiatics, Orientals, and Asian and Pacific Americans. (Pian 1976: 32)

These contrasting testimonies reflect the range and complexity of ethnic identifications within the Asian American community, particularly along generational lines.

Mounting pressure from Asian American constituencies and unfavorable test results ultimately forced the Census Bureau to abandon the proposed summary category "Asian or Pacific Islander." Dealing yet another victory to the Asian Pacific American community, the Census Bureau also added Asian Indian, Vietnamese, Samoan, and Guamanian to the five groups originally listed in the 1970 Census (Census Advisory Committee 1979: 12) (see Figure 5.2). With sepa-

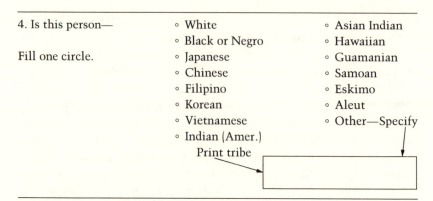

4. Is this person—

Fill one circle.

- White
- Black or Negro
- Japanese
- Chinese
- Filipino
- Korean
- Vietnamese
- Indian (Amer.)
  Print tribe

- Asian Indian
- Hawaiian
- Guamanian
- Samoan
- Eskimo
- Aleut
- Other—Specify

FIGURE 5.2
Census Bureau Question on Race, 1980

rate categories for nine Asian Pacific groups, the 1980 race question provided more than 95 percent of all Asians and Pacific Islanders with an easy method to indicate their cultural and racial background (Der 1988: 113).

Asian Indians and the 1980 Census

In implementing civil rights legislation, federal authorities specified four disadvantaged minority groups: American Indians or Alaskan Natives, Asian and Pacific Islanders, blacks, and Hispanics (Lowry 1982: 48–49). Substantial underrepresentation of any of the "Big Four" is grounds for civil rights compliance action. However, fair shares are usually not defined for the individual components of each of the four groups. In other words, among Hispanics Puerto Ricans are rarely distinguished from Cubans, and among Asians Japanese often are rarely distinguished from Vietnamese.[12]

The failure to draw finer ethnic distinctions allows some groups such as the Asian Indians to lobby for inclusion in one of the "Big Four." In the 1970 census, Asian Indians were relegated to the category "Other" and subsequently classified as whites as they had been since 1950.[13] In 1974, the Association of Indians in America (AIA) lobbied to have Asian Indians reclassified as Asian Americans. The major incentive for requesting the reclassification was possible economic gain: "Asians are officially recognized as minorities and therefore derive economic benefits in compensation for their past history of discrimination in this country" (Fisher 1980: 135).

Leaders of the AIA believed that government recognition of Asian Indians as a minority group would somehow confer affirmative action benefits on group members. They were particularly interested in the set-aside programs, which funnel government contracts to minority-owned businesses (Fisher 1980: ch. 8). Until 1980, these set-aside programs excluded Asian Americans. However, Japanese and Chinese Americans petitioned for designation as socially disadvantaged groups and gained this status in 1980. Asian Indians followed them in 1982. Under the current Small Business Administration 8(a) guidelines, the socially disadvantaged groups include blacks, Hispanics, Native Americans, and Asians and Pacific Islanders (U.S. Commission on Civil Rights 1988: 15–16).

Testifying at a congressional hearing on the 1980 Census, Manoranjan Dutta (1976: 35–36) called the exclusion of Asian Indians from the Asian American category "arbitrary." Dutta reminded the House Committee that the 1917 Immigration Act contained an Asiatic exclusion provision, which prohibited people in the region all the way from the Caucasus Mountains to Japan—a region that included India—from immigrating to the United States. The passage of this act prompted the State of Oregon to attempt to nullify the citizenship of Indian-born Bhagat Singh Thind. When the case reached the U.S. Supreme Court, the Court ruled in favor of the State of Oregon on the ground that Asian Indians were nonwhite. Citing this ruling, Dutta (1976: 36) recommended that Americans of Asian Indian heritage be reclassified as "Asians" rather than "Whites."

After a three-year campaign, the Association of Indians in America succeeded in obtaining the reclassification of Asian Indians as Asian Pacific Americans on the 1980 census. This shift means that Asian Indians are now eligible to seek minority status protection under affirmative action legislation and to participate in many federally funded programs (Fisher 1978: 280). For example, the Equal Employment Opportunity Commission deleted "Indian Subcontinent" from its "White" category and added it to the "Asian or Pacific Islander" category (U.S. Equal Employment Opportunity Commission 1977). In short, affirmative action protection generates incentive to identify oneself as a member of a minority group. As exemplified by the

Asian Indian case, the linkage between census ethnic classification and federal program benefits can result in a large number of "instant ethnics," as immigrant groups are designated as minorities.

The 1990 Census

In 1987, in yet another administrative turnabout, the Census Bureau announced that it would discontinue the check-off system and reintroduce the summary category "Asian or Pacific Islander" in the 1990 census. This format was the very same one that had been rejected by the 1980 Asian Pacific Islander Census Advisory Committee. A former member of the committee expressed his indignation this way: "We fought them tooth and nail [then]. They nonetheless proceeded to test it out during the 1978 Oakland pretest and they got a terrible return. It flopped. And because of that and our protests they went back to the detailed listing" (cited in S. Chen 1987).

The new format required respondents to check the "Asian or Pacific Islander" category and then write in their subgroup (see Figure 5.3). Further angering the Asian Pacific American community, the Census Bureau announced that it was not planning to tabulate the write-in responses from the short form, which goes to every American household. "In other words, Asian and Pacific Americans are being told to write in their subgroup even though the Bureau plans to ignore their answers" (R. Matsui 1988b: 62). Instead, the Census Bureau planned to count individual Asian Pacific groups only on the sample form, the longer questionnaire, which went to one in every six households. Arguing that detailed information is needed for policy decision-making and the delivery of services, U.S. Representative Robert Matsui drafted H.R. 3828, mandating that the Census Bureau tabulate the write-in entries on a 100 percent basis in the 1990 census. Two months later, the Census Bureau conceded, announcing that it would count Asian and Pacific Islanders on both the short and long forms (R. Matsui 1988b: 63).

Next, Asian American legislators and political organizations demanded a return to the 1980 check-off system, with separate categories for Asian American subgroups. Established advocacy groups —principally Chinese for Affirmative Action, the Organization of Chinese Americans, and the Japanese American Citizens League— initiated a lobbying campaign. Other organizations and individuals

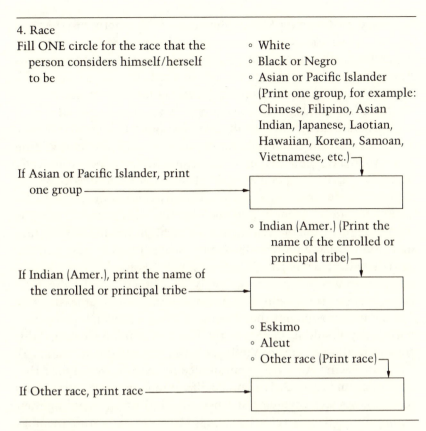

4. Race

Fill ONE circle for the race that the
  person considers himself/herself
  to be

○ White
○ Black or Negro
○ Asian or Pacific Islander
  (Print one group, for example:
  Chinese, Filipino, Asian
  Indian, Japanese, Laotian,
  Hawaiian, Korean, Samoan,
  Vietnamese, etc.)

If Asian or Pacific Islander, print
  one group

○ Indian (Amer.) (Print the
  name of the enrolled or
  principal tribe)

If Indian (Amer.), print the name of
  the enrolled or principal tribe

○ Eskimo
○ Aleut
○ Other race (Print race)

If Other race, print race

FIGURE 5.3
Census Bureau Recommended Question on Race, 1990

across the country followed suit, forming the National Coalition for an Accurate Count of Asian Pacific Americans[14] to push for detailed enumeration by subgroup. The 1990 Asian Pacific Census Advisory Committee similarly called for a return to the 1980 check-off format, pressing for a listing of at least the nine groups identified in the 1980 form (S. Chen 1988b). On the legislative side, U.S. Representative Matsui introduced H.R. 4432, mandating that the Census Bureau return to the 1980 check-off format and add at least two other Asian Pacific Islander groups to the list. The bill had over forty co-sponsors (R. Matsui 1988b: 65).

Dissatisfied with the Census Bureau's refusal to return to the 1980 format, Asian Pacific Americans took their fight to Congress. At a congressional hearing on the 1990 census, the director of the Census Bureau testified that, as in 1980, the proposed 1990 format was developed to satisfy governmental requirements for 100 percent data on the total Asian and Pacific Islander population (Keane 1988). In 1980, with separate categories for nine Asian Pacific groups, the Bureau provided 100 percent count only for the nine. Continuing immigration since 1980 has produced a more numerous and even more ethnically diverse Asian Pacific population. With so many Asian subgroups, the Census Bureau could not afford—politically or economically—to list them separately. According to the director, "There are simply too many. . . . Inclusion of even the nine specific groups in the 1980 race question provoked protests by some respondents and caused confusion that affected reporting" (Keane 1988: 62). Some Asian and Pacific Islander groups not listed separately had difficulty with the 1980 race question. For example, some non-Vietnamese Southeast Asian immigrants crossed out the "Vietnamese" category and wrote their nationality beside it, but since the form was tallied electronically, they were all registered as Vietnamese (Braun 1988; Keane 1988: 62).

Asian Pacific American community representatives argued that the collapsing of all Asian and Pacific groups into one tally would lead to gross stereotyping and other misinformation regarding their communities (Chow 1988; Der 1988; Mineta 1988). Citing the huge influx of recent immigrants from the Pacific Rim, U.S. Representative Robert Matsui (1988a: 46–47) testified that these newcomers have unique health, education, and welfare concerns that need to be separately identified. To emphasize his point, Matsui submitted for the record the hundreds of letters that he had received from community service groups and agencies claiming that incomplete data would hamper their delivery of services to individual Asian and Pacific Islander groups. Moreover, the write-in format is problematic because many recent immigrants do not know enough English to write in their subcategory. Because write-ins are hand tabulated, Matsui (1988a: 47) claimed that this format will further delay the publication of data on Asian and Pacific Islander subgroups: "What would happen if they are required to write these subcategories down with illegible signatures and all these problems? Would it be 1998 or the year 2000 before these groups were able to get accurate information?" Although the 1980 census data were electronically tabulated, the Census Bureau still took eight years to publish the tabulations for Asian and Pacific Islander subcategories.

In sum, the Asian Pacific American community wanted a speedy, 100 percent count for as many specified groups as possible. At stake in the battle was the potential loss of millions of dollars in public funding and services. Without a count of each group, Asian American activists feared that information needed for service delivery and identification of specific needs would not be available. According to the executive director of the Asian Pacific American Legal Center of Southern California, Asian immigrants were already severely undercounted. For instance, the 1980 census counted 28,000 Indochinese in the Los Angeles area, "when 50,000 of them were on the welfare alone" (Kwoh interview). Undercounting hurts in many areas other than affirmative action or federal aid. For example, when minority populations are underestimated as markets, their businesses have a harder time securing loans and investment, and their experiences and perspectives receive minimal representation in the media.

Reflecting the strength of Asian and Pacific American political lobbying, both the House and the Senate unanimously passed U.S. Representative Matsui's census bill, forcing the Census Bureau to agree to the nine-category check-off system and to tabulate Asians and Pacific Islanders on a 100 percent basis (Lyons 1988). However, it was a short-lived victory. A month later, on election night, President Ronald Reagan pocket vetoed the census bill, claiming that "the bill would unnecessarily restrict the form of the race question in the future" (S. Chen 1988c). In view of the veto, the Census Bureau wavered on its pledge to use a check-off system, stating that it was "reviewing its options." Two more months of uncertainty followed. With no word from the Census Bureau, Asian Pacific American groups intensified their political lobbying. On the legislative side, Representative Matsui reintroduced his census bill, which was expected to pass handily (W. Wong 1988b; Lyons 1989a).

Putting an end to the one-and-a-half-year-long struggle, the Census Bureau finally announced in January 1989 that it would use a check-off format to count Asian Pacific Americans in the 1990 census (Lyons 1989a). The Bureau also made two other concessions. In addition to the nine Asian Pacific subgroups listed in the 1980 census, two other Southeast Asian groups would be specially coded from

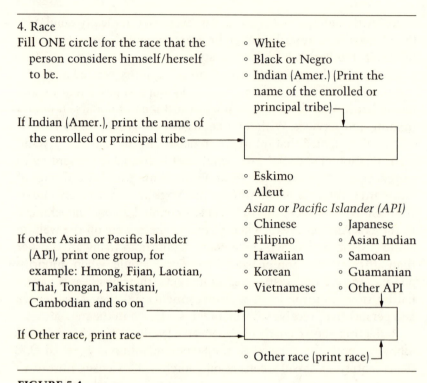

4. Race

Fill ONE circle for the race that the person considers himself/herself to be.

If Indian (Amer.), print the name of the enrolled or principal tribe ⟶

If other Asian or Pacific Islander (API), print one group, for example: Hmong, Fijan, Laotian, Thai, Tongan, Pakistani, Cambodian and so on ⟶

If Other race, print race ⟶

∘ White
∘ Black or Negro
∘ Indian (Amer.) (Print the name of the enrolled or principal tribe) ⟶

∘ Eskimo
∘ Aleut

Asian or Pacific Islander (API)
∘ Chinese   ∘ Japanese
∘ Filipino   ∘ Asian Indian
∘ Hawaiian   ∘ Samoan
∘ Korean   ∘ Guamanian
∘ Vietnamese   ∘ Other API ⟶

∘ Other race (print race) ⟶

FIGURE 5.4
Census Bureau Question on Race, 1990

the write-in portion and tabulated at the same time as the original nine (S. Chen 1989*a*).

More importantly, the Census Bureau agreed to include an "Other API" category in the 1990 census (see Figure 5.4). In previous years, Asian and Pacific Islander groups not identified separately shared the category "Other" with all other "races" not listed in the race item (see Figures 5.1 and 5.2). The inclusion of "Other API" allows for a quick total count of Asian Pacific Americans. This early count is important for electoral politics because the first set of census statistics to be released is used for the purpose of legislative redistricting.[15] In these statistics, Asian and Pacific Islanders are lumped together; subgroup data are not requested. In previous population reports to the states, Asian and Pacific Islander groups not listed separately showed up in the category "Other"; they were not included in the total count of Asian Pacific Islanders. With the "Other API" category, these groups would be counted with the rest, thus raising the total count of Asian Pacific Islander Americans. The crucial role of Asian American legislators in these census disputes underscores the importance of having ethnic representation in political struggles.

Census Classification and Asian American Ethnicity

As an agency of the federal government, the Census Bureau is susceptible to sociopolitical concerns and demands. It bows to ethnic pressure partly because it needs the assistance of the minority communities to improve its coverage of the population (Choldin 1986). The Bureau is also bound by other political and statistical constraints. Besides having to satisfy the more vocal ethnic lobbies, the Bureau has to group the population into recognizable categories that are mandated for civil rights enforcement; it also has to provide enough continuity with past census statistics to satisfy social scientists interested in longitudinal research. In other words, the Census Bureau cannot be an autocratic agency. Its job of counting the population is closely watched and contested by a broad-based coalition of local officials, ethnic activists, academics, and congresspersons (Anderson 1988).

Most important, these census disputes epitomize the multileveled organization of Asian American ethnicity. At first glance, Asian American demands to be counted separately in the 1980 and 1990 censuses suggest the absence of pan-Asian solidarity. However, this struggle for separate counts was waged by pan-Asian advocacy groups: the National Coalition for an Accurate Count of Asian Pacific Americans, the Asian Pacific American Census Advisory Committee, and the Pacific/Asian Coalition, with the combined efforts of single-ethnic advocacy groups such as the Japanese American Citizens League, the Chinese for Affirmative Action, and the Organization of Chinese Americans. Without the competitive advantage of these pan-Asian efforts, the Asian American struggle with the Census Bureau would probably not have been so successful. Thus, rather than demonstrating the lack of pan-Asian solidarity, the census struggles illustrate the organizational dialectic of Asian American ethnicity:

a demand for separate counts was waged by a pan-Asian coalition.[16] These disputes also call attention to the strategic and constructed nature of ethnicity as well as to the ways in which perceived discrimination from the American society at large can unite diverse groups.

It is noteworthy that Asian Americans who lobbied for individual group data also pushed for an accurate *total* count (Pian 1976: 32; Yung 1977: 201; R. Matsui 1988a: 46). Their desire was most evident in the community fight for the inclusion of the "Other API" category. The demand for the "Other API" category denotes an acceptance of the validity of an Asian Pacific American entity. In other words, the census protest was mostly against the *absence* of the subgroup categories, not against the *presence* of the umbrella category.

Aggregate data are necessary because of the federal tendency to lump all Asian Americans together. As one community advocate stated, "In this political system, we have to get thrown into one and we are being carried together as Asian American" (Woo 1979: 44). For example, some federal agencies such as the Equal Employment Opportunity Commission collect compliance data using the inclusive Asian Pacific Islander category. Similarly, the Votings Right Act and the redistricting process require data on the collective group, not on the individual subgroups (U.S. Bureau of the Census 1987). In fact, no federal legislation requires the Census Bureau to provide 100 percent data for the Asian Pacific subgroups, but only for the collective group (U.S. Bureau of the Census 1987). On the other hand, in the area of social and health services, aggregate data can be misleading, masking the bipolarity of the Asian Pacific groups and ignoring the needs of high-risk groups (Ponce interview). Thus, in the social service arena, the Asian Pacific American community must have accurate data on the specific needs of the individual groups.

Because they have to balance the needs of their own world with the demands of the outside world, Asian American ethnic organizations must of necessity be multitiered and situationally determined.

Conclusion

Politically dominant groups shape societal definitions of ethnic groups through the categories they use to count and classify them. These ethnic categories depend only partly on the population's perceptions of meaningful ethnic differentiations. More often, they reflect the view of the dominant group of what is expedient for the economic and political order (Petersen 1969: 868; Enloe 1981: 128). Once state officials designate particular categories to count, these terms enter "the language of administration and shape both private and government decisions" (Starr 1987: 53). Thus, ethnic groups often have to frame or reframe their common identity in response to these state-based ethnic categories.

However, although relatively autonomous, the state—in this case, the Census Bureau—must respond to the political demands of constituencies. Civil rights legislation since 1960 has stimulated vested interests in the census ethnic classification and enumeration. Because incomplete counts of minority groups can affect voting representation, geopolitical considerations, and federal allocation of funds in the areas of employment, education, and health services, underrepresented groups have fought for measures that would increase the counts of their constituents and make them more visible in census reports. Through political pressures, ethnic activists (and other interest groups) influence how the Census Bureau classifies and counts the population.

In 1980 and again in 1990, Asian American legislators, community leaders, and advocacy groups united to fight the Census Bureau's proposal to collapse all Asian codes into one umbrella category. When the Bureau refused to cooperate, Asian American advocates went to Congress and the media to press their case further. Partly due to the strength of the multigroup political lobbying, the Bureau finally conceded to the coalition's demand for a detailed enumeration of Asian Pacific Americans. This political victory suggests not only that ethnicity is constructed from above but also that aggrieved groups can engage in their own bottom-up construction of ethnicity within the limits of their situation. Asian Americans did not merely accept the pan-Asian concept imposed by outsiders but also used it to advance their political demands—including the demand that government bureaucracies treat them as separate groups within a larger category.

Chapter 6

Reactive Solidarity: Anti-Asian Violence

While political benefits certainly promote pan-Asian organization, it is anti-Asian violence that has drawn the largest pan-Asian support. Because the public does not usually distinguish among Asian subgroups, anti-Asian violence concerns the entire group—cross-cutting class, cultural, and generational divisions. Therefore, regardless of one's ethnic affiliation, anti-Asian violence requires counterorganization at the pan-Asian level.

Research on ethnicity has indicated that external threats intensify group cohesion as members band together in defensive solidarities. The threatened destruction creates a common interest where none may have existed before (Coser 1956; Portes 1984). Most often, a group is sanctioned for its actual or alleged wrongdoing. But a racially defined group can also suffer reprisals because of its externally imposed membership in a larger group. In the Asian American case, group members can suffer sanctions for no behavior of their own, but for the activities of others who resemble them (Light and Bonacich 1988: 324). Thus anti-Asian activities necessarily lead to protective pan-Asian ethnicity. True, as indicated by the discussion on ethnic "disidentification" in Chapter 2, external threat does not always consolidate groups, but can also disintegrate them. However, it is also true that these early attempts by Asian immigrant groups to "dis-identify" themselves from the targeted Asian group often failed.

The most notorious case of mistaken identity was the 1982 killing of Vincent Chin, a Chinese American who was beaten to death by two white men who allegedly mistook him for Japanese. The Chin case activated both Chinese and pan-Asian levels of solidarity. To understand the web of reactive solidarities better, this chapter analyzes Asian American organizational responses to anti-Asian activities, particularly their responses to the Chin case. The Chin case is substantively important because many Asian Americans now consider it to be the archetype of anti-Asian violence in this country. It is also theoretically instructive because it sheds light on the pluralism of reactive groups.

Anti-Asian Activities

Anti-Asian activities in the United States can be traced back to the middle of the nineteenth century. For the most part, Americans meted out sanctions against Asians via the political and legal systems (McKenzie 1928; Ichioka 1988). From the late nineteenth to the early twentieth century, more than six hundred pieces of anti-Asian legislation were enacted, either limiting or excluding persons of Asian ancestry from citizenship, intermarriage, land ownership, employment, and other forms of participation in American life (Japanese American Citizens League 1987: 65; Chan 1991: ch. 3). As indicated earlier, the gravest government mistreatment of Asians occurred when Japanese residents and citizens were placed in relocation camps at the beginning of World War II (Daniels 1971).

Anti-Asian hostility also took violent turns. In the mid-nineteenth century, whites "were stoning the Chinese in the streets, cutting off their queues, wrecking their shops and laundries" (Dulles 1946: 89). In some instances, such as the Rock Springs Massacre in Wyoming in 1885, these violent outbursts ended in brutal killings. For the most part, these atrocities were legally sanctioned. For example, in 1854, the California Supreme Court ruled that Chinese could not testify against whites. So long as no white person was available to witness on their behalf, any crime perpetrated against the Chinese went unpunished (Dulles 1946).

During World War II, the United States Congress began to chip away at the legislative barriers to Asian immigration and citizenship. By the early 1970s, Asian Americans were finally accorded the civil rights long guaranteed to other residents and citizens. But in the late 1970s, reports of rising anti-Asian activities also began to surface.[1] At a congressional hearing on the impact of the new Asian immigration, an Asian American attorney contended that "today we are witnessing a resurgence of anti-Asian sentiment manifest by growing problems of vandalism, physical attack, and on occasion murder" (K. Wong 1985: 173). In a statement submitted to the U.S. Commission on Civil Rights, U.S. Representative Robert Matsui (1984) warned of the danger of rising anti-Asianism. In a 1988 keynote speech, the founding president of the Asian/Pacific Bar of California similarly warned, "The danger I see in the next decade is the revitalization of anti-Asian hostility" (Asian Pacific American Coalition 1989a).

Because no systematic data on anti-Asian activities exist, it is difficult to substantiate the claim of rising anti-Asianism. As the U.S. Commission on Civil Rights (1986: 5) reported, "There is currently no way to determine accurately the level of activity against persons of Asian descent, or whether the number of incidents has increased, decreased, or stayed the same in recent years." On the other hand, rising anti-Asianism has become so alarming that it has entered the public discourse, as evidenced by an increase in the number of articles on anti-Asian violence published not only in the ethnic press but also in major newspapers such as the *New York Times*, *Wall Street Journal*, *Boston Globe*, *Washington Post*, *San Francisco Examiner*, and *Los Angeles Times* (Japanese American Citizens League 1987: 66–67).

Federal, state, and local civil rights bodies extended this public discourse by holding official hearings on anti-Asian crimes. At a Los Angeles County hearing, twenty-two persons testified that the "Asian community has been alarmed by an increase in anti-Asian vandalism and violence in Los Angeles County and in other parts of the country" (Los Angeles County Commission on Human Relations 1984). These racial incidents ranged from hostile bumper stickers to racial name-calling to physical assaults. In Washington, a state commission reported that Asians in the state had experienced harassment of "very serious proportions" at the hands of "native workers" (*Koreatown* 1983). In California, the attorney general's Asian and Pacific Islander Advisory Committee concluded that, "in recent years, there has been an intensification of anti-Asian hostility" (California, Attorney General's Asian and Pacific Islander Advisory Committee 1988: 23). At the national level, a multisite study by the U.S. Commission on Civil Rights (1986: 5) concluded that "anti-Asian activity exists in numerous and demographically different communities across the Nation." In the absence of longitudinal data, these studies cannot substantiate the claim of rising violence against Asians; however, they do confirm that anti-Asianism is, indeed, a serious problem.

Factors Contributing to Anti-Asian Activities

Social scientists continue to debate the etiology of intergroup conflicts. Most of the dialogue has been structured around a confrontation between class-based and race-based theorists. For class-based theorists, economic competition plays the central role in structuring social relations (Bonacich 1972; Cummings 1980). In contrast, race-based theorists insist that unfavorable attitudes toward a racial group cause intergroup conflicts (Allport 1958; Myrdal 1962). As in many cases of racial conflicts, factors that contribute to anti-Asian activities include class as well as ideational elements.

Economic Competition

Resource competition theory posits that self-interest explains public animosity toward immigrants. Especially during economic downturns, the native-born blame immigrants for the nation's problems and regard them as unwanted competitors (Bonacich 1972; Light 1983: ch. 13). Historically, Asians in the United States have borne most of the blame for economic woes (Saxton 1971; Kitano 1980; K. Wong 1985). Recent anti-Asian activities coincided with the deteriorating economic conditions that began after 1975. In a context of high unemployment, climbing inflation, and skyrocketing interest rates, competition between Asians and non-Asians often escalated into intergroup conflicts (California, Governor's Task Force on Civil Rights 1982; Los Angeles County Commission on Human Relations 1984; U.S. Commission on Civil Rights 1986). A 1980 poll conducted in nine cities indicated that 47 percent of the respondents believed that "Indochinese refugees take jobs away from others in my area"

(Starr and Roberts 1982). According to a 1989 *Los Angeles Times* poll, a quarter of the respondents believed that Asian Americans were gaining too much economic power; no other group was similarly described by more than 7 percent (Roderick 1989*a*). The mushrooming of Asian businesses across the country has also evoked anti-Asian sentiment, often expressed in efforts to ban Asian-language business signs (Fong 1987; Siao 1989*a*). The rapid influx of Asian immigrants to the United States since 1965 further exacerbated the tension between Asians and non-Asians (Desbarats 1985: 522–523). In particular, the growing presence of Korean businesses in black neighborhoods in Baltimore, Philadelphia, Washington, D.C., New York City, and Los Angeles has fueled black anger, at times leading to racial violence (I. Kim 1981; Light and Bonacich 1988: ch. 12; Cheng and Espiritu 1989).

In addition to actual or alleged domestic economic competition, Asian Americans are resented for the United States' international trade imbalances. A period of economic recession in the United States coincided with a rise of Pacific Rim economies, not only that of Japan but also those of Taiwan, South Korea, Hong Kong, and Singapore. Unable to keep pace with Asian competition, traditional industries such as steel and automobiles experienced severe downturns. American businesses and labor unions, as well as elected officials, blamed the ills of American industry on business competition with Asian countries (Smollar 1983; U.S. Commission on Civil Rights 1986: 36–37). A prime example is automobile manufacturing: many Americans attributed the unemployment among American automobile workers to the large Japanese share of automobiles sold in the United States (U.S. Commission on Civil Rights 1986: 36). A 1982 national poll indicated that 44 percent of the public blamed U.S. economic problems "almost completely" or "very much" on Japanese business competition (M. Woo 1983). Anti-Japanese sentiment appeared on bumper stickers that read "Toyota—Datsun—Honda—and Pearl Harbor" and "Unemployment Made in Japan" (U.S. Commission on Civil Rights 1986: 40). Unfortunately, anger against Asian nations is often transferred to Americans of Asian ancestry, who have suffered from a long history of anti-Asian attitudes and behaviors (Los Angeles County Commission on Human Relations 1984: 2; R. Matsui 1984: 63).

Anti-Asian Attitudes

Attitudinal surveys reveal that anti-Asian sentiments are still alive and well today. In a survey of 2,000 Americans, the Roper Organization (1982) asked respondents to indicate whether each of the fifteen ethnic groups listed has "on balance . . . been a good thing or a bad thing for this country." No European group received lower than a 53 percent positive rating; in contrast, no Asian group received higher than a 47 percent positive rating.

Survey results also indicate that many Americans do not welcome Asian immigrants and refugees. According to a 1975 Harris poll, more than 50 percent of the American people thought Southeast Asian refugees should not be allowed to enter the United States; only 26 percent favored their entry. Many seemed to share Congressman Burt Talcott's conclusion that, "Damn it, we have too many Orientals" (cited in Rose 1985: 205). Five years later, public opinion toward the refugees had not changed. A 1980 poll of American attitudes in nine cities revealed that nearly half of those surveyed believed that the Southeast Asian refugees should have settled in other Asian countries (Starr and Roberts 1981). This poll also found that over 77 percent of the respondents would disapprove of the marriage of a Southeast Asian refugee into their family and 65 percent would not be willing to have a refugee as a guest in their home (Roberts 1988: 81).

Anti-Asian sentiment seemed to be symptomatic of the general anti-immigrant mood beginning in the late 1970s. Poll results indicated that, between 1965 and 1981, the proportion of the U.S. public favoring a decrease in legal immigration rose sharply (California, Governor's Task Force on Civil Rights 1982: 52). However, opposition toward immigrants was not directed equally toward all groups. A survey of San Diego County found that 36 percent of the respondents believed Asian immigrants had a negative impact on the city, but only 17 percent thought Western European immigrants had a negative impact (Cornelius 1982: 16). Along the same lines, the media decry Japanese ownership of U.S. property but largely ignore European investment—even though Europeans own the most American real estate.[2] In 1985, the British held $44 billion and the Dutch $38 billion in U.S. real estate. In contrast, the Japanese owned $35 billion in U.S. real estate in 1988. The disproportionate political and media attention to Japanese ownership suggests "that the professed concern for overseas ownership is a smokescreen for racial animosity toward Asians" (California, Attorney General's Commission 1986: 27–28).

Asian Lumping

It is difficult to trace the etiology of any racial incident. Motives are often mixed, so economically motivated acts may also carry a racist message and vice versa (Light 1983: 354–355). For the purpose of this chapter, it is not necessary to choose between class-based and race-based explanations of anti-Asianism. What is important is to recognize that, whatever the cause, hostilities directed at any of the Asian subgroups tend to affect the others as well. All Asians are at risk because outsiders perceive them as a single group.

Because outsiders do not or cannot distinguish among Asian subgroups, they target all Asians for their "message of hate"[3] or punish one group for another's behavior. They also fail to distinguish recent immigrants and refugees from third- or fourth-generation citizens (Allen 1983: 62; U.S. Commission on Civil Rights 1986: 2–3; Harrison 1987: 16). Worse yet, non-Asians seldom distinguish Asian Americans from Asian nationals. In public discourse, victims of anti-Asian incidents are often referred to as foreign nationals when, in fact, they are American citizens (Japanese American Citizen League 1987: 69). In a testimony submitted to the U.S. Commission on Civil Rights, U.S. Representative Matsui (1984: 64) contended that "the difference between Asian nations and Americans of Asian ancestry becomes so blurred that Asian Americans are the scapegoats to foreign industries." This misconception is reflected in the recurrent blaming of Japanese Americans for the bombing of Pearl Harbor and for the trade imbalance with Japan. Along the same lines, those who resent Asian entrepreneurs often confuse small-scale Asian American businesses with high-profile investment projects funded largely with overseas Asian capital (Fong 1987). More than any other incident, the beating death of Vincent Chin epitomizes the racism of Asian lumping: blamed for Japan's economic advantage, a Chinese American, mistaken for Japanese, was murdered.

The Vincent Chin Case

On the night of 19 June 1982, Vincent Chin, a twenty-seven-year-old Chinese American draftsman, stopped in a Detroit bar with three friends to celebrate Chin's upcoming wedding. While in the bar, Chin became involved in a fist fight with Ronald Ebens, a white Chrysler factory foreman. The dispute continued into the parking lot, where Ebens pulled a baseball bat from his car. Chin and his friends fled. For the next half-hour, Ebens and his stepson, Michael Nitz, allegedly stalked Chin, eventually locating him in front of a fast food restaurant. There, while Nitz grabbed Chin from behind, Ebens struck at least four blows to Chin's head. The Highland Park police arrested Ebens and Nitz at the scene. Chin died four days later from severe head injuries. Instead of celebrating Chin's wedding, his guests attended his funeral (American Citizens for Justice 1983a; Beer 1983; Weingarten 1983).

In filing charges, the Wayne County prosecutor opted for second-degree murder—homicide with no premeditation. In a later plea bargain, Ebens pleaded guilty to manslaughter (a lesser charge); Nitz did not contest his charge (Zia 1984a). Although a manslaughter conviction in Michigan carries a maximum sentence of fifteen years in prison, Wayne County Judge Charles Kaufman imposed no prison time on Ebens and Nitz. Instead, he sentenced both to three years' probation and fined each a mere $3,000 (American Citizens for Justice 1983a; Kaufman 1983).[4] In explaining his lenient sentence, Judge Kaufman cited the defendants' stable working backgrounds and lack of criminal records: "You don't make the punishment fit the crime; you make the punishment fit the criminal" (cited in American Citizens for Justice 1983a).

Although shocked by Chin's brutal death, Detroit's Asian American community did not immediately respond to the killing. They fully expected the court to punish the killers. When the court did not, the outraged and disbelieving community quickly formed American Citizens for Justice (ACJ) to seek prosecution of Chin's killers. Kaufman's lenient sentence also outraged Asian Americans across the country, who read in it an official condonation of anti-Asian violence. Letters of protest streamed into Kaufman's office from as far away as New York and San Francisco (Beer 1983). Kaufman's decision also received extensive and bitter media coverage.[5] "The headlines can only be described as scathing. One large cartoon . . . even showed the trial judge putting a baseball bat in one ear, as if it were a pencil, and sharpening it with a pencil sharpener in the opposite ear" (U.S. Court of Appeals, Sixth Circuit 1986: 1426). In June 1983, a year after Chin's death, Kaufman announced that he would not reverse his sentence (Weingarten 1983).

Initially, ACJ did not call the killing a racial attack. Its focus of protest was Kaufman's lenient sentence. But as ACJ's members reconstructed the events of that evening, they became convinced that the slaying had been racially motivated. Three eyewitnesses stated that Ebens directed racial slurs at Chin. One witness recalled hearing, "Because of you . . . we're out of work" (U.S. Court of Appeals, Sixth Circuit 1986).[6] It was this testimony that gripped the nation. It implied that Chin's killers mistook him for Japanese and blamed him for the layoffs in the automobile industry (Zia 1984a: 18).

In 1980, Detroit City had one of the highest unemployment rates in the country, 18.5 percent compared to the national average of 5.8 percent (U.S. Bureau of the Census 1983a: table 120 and 1983b: table 124). In this Motor City, where one in three auto workers had lost his or her job in the five preceding years, Japanese imports—almost a quarter of the market—took the blame (Weingarten 1983: 12; Nanto 1985). A recent film documentary on the Chin case showed Detroit in deep recession with long unemployment lines and closed car plants (Tajima and Choy 1988). At the United Auto Workers headquarters, a red and white sign summed up anti-Japanese sentiments: "300,000 laid-off UAW members don't like your import. Please park it in Tokyo" (Weingarten 1983). Numerous videocasts showed auto workers and others in Detroit attacking Japanese-made automobiles with sledgehammers (U.S. Court of Appeals, Sixth Circuit 1986: 1439). Calling for a new U.S. industrial policy that would limit imports, a Michigan congressman labeled Japanese trade practices "an economic Pearl Harbor" and another referred to Japanese workers as "little yellow people" (Smollar 1983).

The linkage between Chin's death and anti-Japanese sentiment became the hallmark of the case.[7] Because of the racial overtones, ACJ petitioned the U.S. Justice Department to bring civil rights charges against Chin's killers.[8] Responding to heavy public pressure, the Justice Department ordered an FBI investigation of Chin's death for possible civil rights violations (American Citizens for Justice

1983*b*). Applying additional pressure, California Congressman Norman Mineta wrote the U.S. attorney general urging him to act on the Chin case (*Rafu Shimpo* 1983). In November 1983, a federal grand jury indicted Ebens and Nitz on two counts of civil rights violations (U.S. Court of Appeals, Sixth Circuit 1986: 1427).[9]

Seven months later, a federal jury convicted Ebens of violating Chin's civil rights but acquitted him of conspiracy; Nitz was acquitted on both charges. Ebens was sentenced to twenty-five years in prison but was freed after posting a $20,000 bond (U.S. Court of Appeals, Sixth Circuit 1986: 1425). In 1986, the Chin case hit another legal snag when a federal appeals court overturned the civil rights conviction on a technicality.[10] Deluged with letters demanding a retrial, the Department of Justice agreed to retry Ebens. Citing the extensive publicity surrounding the case in Detroit, the department moved the trial to Cincinnati.[11] In May 1987, five years after Chin's death, the Cincinnati jury acquitted Ebens of federal civil rights charges. Much to the outrage of Asian Americans across the country, neither Ebens nor Nitz ever spent any time in prison for the killing (Mar 1987). Though the case did not turn out to the satisfaction of Asian Americans, it did leave an important organizational legacy.

Reactive Solidarity: Pan-Asian Organization

American Citizens for Justice

In 1980, the Asian American population in Detroit was 7,614, accounting for less than 1 percent (0.6) of the city's population (U.S. Bureau of the Census 1983*a*). Neither the Chinese nor the Japanese, the focus of attention in the Chin case, were the largest subgroups (see Table 6.1). For the most part, Detroit's Asian American communities did not coalesce. In 1972, representatives from different Asian American groups came together for the first time in the city-sponsored ethnic festival (Shimoura interview). Since then, this small group of Asian Americans has attempted several times to establish a pan-Asian group. Two years after the festival, these same individuals formed the Asian American Council to address common concerns. However, there was no burning issue to sustain the group; it eventually dissolved into competing factions and died (Covert 1983). In 1981, a Japanese American attorney brought together a group of close

TABLE 6.1
Asian Population in Detroit, 1980

Ethnic Group	Population	Percentage of Total Population
Asian Indian	1,965	25.8
Chinese	1,213	15.9
Filipino	2,089	27.4
Guamanian	71	0.9
Hawaiian	244	3.2
Japanese	637	8.4
Korean	571	7.5
Samoan	27	0.4
Vietnamese	270	3.6
Other Asian	527	6.9
Total	7,614	100.0

Source: U.S. Bureau of the Census (1983a: table 58).

to twenty community leaders, attorneys, and professionals to discuss the possibility of starting a pan-Asian organization because "a larger coalition means greater strength, more political power" (Shimoura interview). However, after the initial enthusiasm, the group began to look for issues: "There just wasn't any burning cause, no agenda to focus on" (Shimoura interview; also Fukuzawa 1989a: 1–2). It took the tragedy of Chin's death to transform Detroit's fragmented Asian American groups into a united community.

Initially, the Chin case was handled by the Chinese American community. Distressed by Kaufman's ruling, Chin's mother turned to the local Chinese organizations, the On Leong Association and the Chinese Welfare Council, for assistance (D. Wong 1983b). Five days after Judge Kaufman's decision, the On Leong Association held a meeting of about thirty people at a local Chinese restaurant. The group vowed to fight Kaufman's sentence, maintaining that the ruling "essentially declared 'open season' against Chinese, provided that the attackers were white and held steady jobs" (Chinese On Leong Association 1983: 3; Zia 1984a: 4). Except for Japanese American attorney Jim Shimoura, the meeting was an all-Chinese gathering. Shimoura was invited because he was the only Asian American attorney in town (Shimoura interview).

Although the Chin case started out as a Chinese American issue, it quickly became an Asian American cause. One week after the initial gathering, more than eighty people attended a second meeting at the Chinese Welfare Council Hall. Unlike the first meeting, this one drew Japanese, Korean, and Filipino American community representatives, many of whom had worked together in the city's ethnic festivals (Shimoura interview; Zia interview). A former ACJ president described the meeting:

> In the drafty hall of the Detroit Chinese Welfare Council, there was a joining of liberals and conservatives, youths and seniors, scientists, businessmen, Chinese, Japanese, Filipinos, and Koreans, Christians, and Buddhists, Cantonese- and Mandarin-speakers, American-born and immigrants—all of us put aside the differences that kept us apart and agreed that night to form a new organization to protect our rights as Americans of Asian ancestry. (Zia 1984a: 20–21)

The diversity of the group suggests that anti-Asian violence unites Asian Americans across class, ethnic, generational, and political lines.

At issue was the appropriate level of organization: Chinese American or Asian American? In other words, should Chin's supporters organize at the ethnic-specific or panethnic level? The names suggested for the organization reflected this debate: "Chinese Americans for Justice" or "Asian Americans for Justice"? Although predominantly Chinese, the group opted for a pan-Asian strategy. Race was a decisive factor: the group concluded that Chin was killed because of his racial membership; therefore, his death affected all Asian Americans. As a key organizer of the case explained, "People understood that it involved more than Chinese, more than one nationality. Anybody who looked Asian could be attacked. It just happened that Chin was Chinese. He could have been Korean or any other Asian nationality" (Zia interview). Another key organizer concurred:

> People felt that the group ought to reflect the Asian American community because the Chin case touched all Asian groups. Individuals realized that they could have been Chin. Because of the car import question, Asians who lived in Detroit understood that

Asians were targets as scapegoats. They had seen the anti-Asian bumper stickers. (Shimoura interview)

The predominantly Chinese American group also chose the pan-Asian framework for strategic reasons: to enlarge its own political effectiveness. "Being in Detroit, in the Midwest, we don't have a huge Chinese population. We knew we had to work with other Asian groups. We needed every source of support. The broader, the better" (Zia interview). In the end, the group named itself American Citizens for Justice (ACJ) because "it would be less offensive, less intimidating to people" than Asian Americans for Justice (Shimoura interview).

Mutual needs brought the traditional Chinese associations and ACJ members together. Unversed in the American legal system, the older Chinese community understood that, to win the case, they had to coalesce with Asian American professionals: "The On Leong Association lacked the verbal skills. Many of them did not speak English well. They knew that they needed help" (Shimoura interview). On the other hand, the Chinese networks "could raise money and reach many people" and thus were instrumental in the formation of ACJ (Zia interview).

However, the alliance between the traditional Chinese associations and the ACJ was often strained. Contention was brewing over money: who should handle fund-raising efforts for the Chin case? In the community newspapers, ACJ and the Detroit Chinese Welfare Council aired their differences. One newspaper article asserted that ACJ was subordinate to the Detroit Chinese Welfare Council, and that the Council was handling all fund-raising efforts. To separate itself from Chinese-only organizations, ACJ organizers stressed the pan-Asian and independent nature of the group: "We will proceed as independently as possible because our group is more than just Chinese. It also has Japanese, Koreans and Filipinos" (cited in D. Wong 1983b). The group also asserted that it was the only organization recognized and authorized to handle the Chin case legally and administratively. In a statement to the Chinese community, the group stated:

> ACJ is the only group which has hired attorneys to work on the criminal and civil rights avenues for legal redress. [It] is the only group which has won recognition in Wayne County, Michigan, and federal courts as a party in this case, at considerable expense, pre-

TABLE 6.2
Composition of American Citizens for Justice Board, 1983–89

Ethnic Group	1983	1984	1985	1986	1987	1988	1989	Total
Asian Indian	0	0	0	0	0	0	3	3
Chinese	6	5	5	5	5	4	2	32
Filipinos	0	0	1	1	2	2	2	8
Japanese	1	2	2	3	2	2	2	14
Koreans	0	0	1	3	4	4	2	14
Vietnamese	0	0	0	1	0	0	0	1
Other	0	0	0	0	0	1	2	3
Total	7	7	9	13	13	13	13	75

Source: Records on file at the Asian American Center for Justice of the American Citizens for Justice, Southfield, Mich.

senting a 150 page report to the FBI and the Department of Justice. [And it] is the only group that is paying the legal bills. (Cited in D. Wong 1983*b*)

Therefore, any money collected on behalf of the case should be forwarded to ACJ. The ACJ president claimed that the Chinese Welfare Council was holding onto the donations because they wanted to control how the money was going to be spent (D. Wong 1983*b*).

Although ACJ purported to be a pan-Asian American organization, its organizers were primarily Chinese Americans. Its first president, Kin Yee, was concurrently president of the On Leong Association and past president of the local Chinese Welfare Council. In its first year, six of the seven executive board members of ACJ were Chinese Americans; in its second year, five of the seven were Chinese Americans (see Table 6.2). Moreover, in its first two years, 80 percent of the financial contributors to ACJ in support of the Chin case were Chinese Americans (Zia 1984*b*).

These statistics suggest that at least initially the Vincent Chin case touched primarily Chinese Americans. However, as the case evolved, other Asian American groups joined the fight—often at the urging of ACJ organizers. For example, in May 1983, ACJ staged a mass rally in downtown Detroit to protest Kaufman's lenient sentences. To

TABLE 6.3
***Private Contributors to American Citizens for Justice
by Ethnic Group, 1988***

Ethnic Group	Number of Contributors	Percentage of Contributors*	Total ($)	Percentage $ Contributions*
Chinese	78	37.1	3,215	45.1
Japanese	60	28.6	1,740	24.4
Asian Indian	24	11.4	645	9.0
Filipino	14	6.7	400	5.6
Korean	14	6.7	445	6.2
African American	7	3.3	325	4.6
Jewish	5	2.4	155	2.2
Euro-American	4	1.9	115	1.6
Hmong	3	1.4	35	0.5
Malaysian	1	0.5	50	0.7

Source: Records on file at the Asian American Center for Justice of the American Citizens for Justice, Southfield, Mich.

* Percentages refer only to the contributors who identified their ethnic background. In 1988, 66.7 percent of contributors identified their backgrounds. This 66.7 percent represented 64 percent of the 1988 private contributors.

display widespread Asian American support for the case, ACJ organizers invited leaders from the Japanese, Korean, and Filipino American communities to speak at the rally (American Citizens for Justice 1983*a*; Shimoura interview). Between five hundred and a thousand persons attended the demonstration, making it the largest rally in support of an Asian American cause in Detroit (*Asian Week* 1983*a*; D. Wong 1983*a*). As the case built momentum, the ACJ's board composition also became more pan-Asian. As indicated in Table 6.2, the ACJ board expanded to include Filipinos, Koreans, Vietnamese, and Asian Indians. Contributors to ACJ also became more pan-Asian in later years (see Tables 6.3 and 6.4). These changes suggest that in building itself, ACJ also built pan-Asian consciousness. Although ACJ's membership was not initially pan-Asian, its self-conscious Asian panethnicity drew other Asian groups. In other words, ethnic organizations

TABLE 6.4

Private Contributors to American Citizens for Justice
by Ethnic Group, January–September 1989

Ethnic Group	Number of Contributors	Percentage of Contributors*	Total ($)	Percentage $ Contributions*
Chinese	37	33.9	1,660	37.0
Japanese	26	23.8	765	17.0
Asian Indian	19	17.4	570	12.7
Korean	8	7.3	590	13.1
Filipino	7	6.4	405	9.0
African American	4	3.7	125	2.8
Euro-American	3	2.7	240	5.3
Chaldean	2	1.8	60	1.3
Hmong	1	0.9	15	0.3
Jewish	1	0.9	50	1.1
Vietnamese	1	0.9	10	0.2

Source: Records on file at the Asian American Center for Justice of the American Citizens for Justice, Southfield, Mich.

* Percentages refer only to the contributors who identified their ethnic background. In 1989, 76.8 percent of contributors identified their backgrounds. This 76.8 percent represented 77 percent of the 1989 private contributors.

do not merely reflect existing ethnic consciousness; they can also create it.

The ACJ also generated pan-Asian consciousness by getting involved in multi-Asian issues. Because ACJ's raison d'être was to prosecute Chin's killers, membership and meeting attendance dropped after Ebens' acquittal in 1987 (Fukuzawa 1989a; Su 1989). To survive, ACJ had to broaden its scope. In 1988, ACJ members set up permanent representation for themselves by establishing the Asian American Center for Justice. With a paid full-time director, ACJ's Center began to monitor anti-Asian incidents. Since 1987, Asian Indians in Detroit have experienced increasing racial violence (American Citizens for Justice 1989a). This surge in "Dotbuster"[12] incidents may explain the recent increase in Asian Indian participation in ACJ (see Tables

6.2, 6.3, and 6.4). It also has broadened its scope to include health and mental health services, primarily targeting the Southeast Asian population. For example, ACJ received funding to conduct a health survey of the Detroit-area Hmong population (Su 1989). For the most part, the Southeast Asian community has not participated in ACJ, but ACJ's involvement in the community indicates that its definition of Asian American extends beyond its current membership.

The organization and the Chin case also received critical support from non-Asians, especially from the black and Jewish American communities (see Tables 6.3 and 6.4). According to a former ACJ executive director, "Experienced hands from the NAACP, the Anti-Defamation League of B'nai B'rith and the Detroit Association of Black Organizations provided invaluable contacts and information" (Fukuzawa 1989a: 2). Even though non-Asians were involved, the Chin case remained an Asian American cause, because "it had its most immediate impact on Asians. We are the victims" (Zia interview). Moreover, non-Asians approached the case from the legal —rather than the racial—angle. For example, the NAACP protested Judge Kaufman's lenient sentence because "Black people know that when punishment is meted out to fit the perpetrator, rather than the crime itself, we as victims become the ultimate, unrequited losers" (National Association for the Advancement of Colored People 1983). Similarly, in a letter of support for the Chin case, the Jewish Federation Council wrote, "The Vincent Chin case brought to greater light an especially troubling miscarriage of justice" (Glenn and Habush 1983). For the Asian American community, the Vincent Chin case meant more than a failure of the criminal system. Because they share a racial commonality with Chin, his death meant that "all Asian Americans are in jeopardy" (Zia 1984a: 18). Takaki (1983) expressed this fear and rage when he wrote, "[Asian Americans] know Vincent Chin was killed because of his racial membership; they realize it could happen to anyone of them—to anyone with black hair and slanted eyes." It was precisely because of this recognition that the Vincent Chin case managed to touch off an outcry beyond Detroit.

National Response
Across the country, Asian Americans came together to demand the prosecution of Chin's killers. Demonstrations and support

activities took place in San Francisco, Oakland, Los Angeles, Denver, Chicago, Toronto, and New York (Zia 1984a). In addition to the long-established Japanese American Citizens League, Organization of Chinese Americans, and National Chinese Welfare Association, Asian Americans also formed new pan-Asian organizations to seek justice for Chin's death (Zia 1984a). In San Francisco, concerned individuals from the Chinese, Japanese, Korean, Filipino, and Vietnamese communities founded Asian Americans for Justice to raise funds and publicize the case (*Asian Week* 1983b). In Los Angeles, more than fifty organizations representing various Asian American communities formed the Southern California Justice for Vincent Chin Committee. According to the committee's spokesperson, "In my lifetime in Los Angeles, this is the first time that I think such a broad coalition has come together. There's Chinese Americans, Japanese Americans, Korean Americans, Filipino Americans, Thai, Vietnamese" (cited in Feldman 1983). As a result of the mass support for the case in Los Angeles, the Los Angeles city council joined other governmental bodies in petitioning the Justice Department to commence an investigation into Chin's murder.

For the most part, Asian American organizations across the country adhered to the agenda set by Detroit's American Citizens for Justice (ACJ). As a Los Angeles organizer contended, "Los Angeles early on worked with ACJ. If they had not existed, we wouldn't have been able to organize" (Louie interview). To subsidize ACJ's legal expenses, many organizations and businesses around the nation collected money on behalf of the case and forwarded the sum to ACJ (see Table 6.5). During the period from March 1983 to December 1984, ACJ received close to $83,000 from supporters across the country. The largest sums came from the Asian Americans for Justice in San Francisco ($22,000), the Southern California Justice for Vincent Chin Committee in Los Angeles ($13,000), and the National On Leong Associations ($12,070) (Zia 1984b: 15). Supporters of the Chin case also participated in ACJ's nationwide letter-writing campaign to government officials and the press. The Justice Department reportedly received more than fifteen thousand letters; "They got more mail from the Chin case than from any other case in the department's recent history" (Shimoura interview). The indictment of Chin's killers came only as a result of this massive campaign.

To build pressure on Justice Department officials and to raise

TABLE 6.5

Organizations and Businesses Contributing to the American Citizens for Justice by State, 31 March 1983–31 December 1984

State	Number of Contributors	Percentage of Total
California	28	27.2
Michigan	23	22.3
New York	11	10.7
Illinois	6	5.8
Ohio	5	4.8
Canada	4	3.9
Missouri	3	2.9
Georgia	3	2.9
New Jersey	3	2.9
Washington D.C.	3	2.9
Indiana	2	1.9
Florida	2	1.9
Wisconsin	2	1.9
Pennsylvania	2	1.9
Colorado	2	1.9
Nevada	1	1.0
Massachusetts	1	1.0
Louisiana	1	1.0
Minnesota	1	1.0

Source: Compiled from "ACJ Contributors List, 3/31/83 to 12/31/84" (Zia 1984*b*).

funds, community organizations also sponsored speaking tours for Chin's mother and ACJ representatives. In July of 1983, Chin's mother and ACJ members toured the West Coast, addressing thousands of people in Los Angeles, San Diego, San Francisco, Oakland, San Jose, and Sacramento about the Chin case and "its implication for Asian Americans." Later that year, the group attended similar fund-raisers in Denver and Chicago and addressed the founding meeting of the Democratic Party's Asian Pacific American Caucus (American Citizens for Justice 1983*c*; Zia 1984*a*). Members also reached a national audience by appearing on all three national television networks, by way of the Donahue Show, NBC's First Camera, and local television documentaries in Sacramento and Detroit (Zia 1984*a*; 1984*b*).

Through all its efforts, ACJ organizers emphasized the pan-Asian nature of the case and the importance of pan-Asian coalition. As a former ACJ president wrote:

> To the extent that what happened to Vincent Chin could happen to any one of us, all Asian Americans are in jeopardy. This case has proven that Americans from China, Japan, Korea, the Philippines, Southeast Asia, India, and other Asian heritages can make a powerful impact by working together for our mutual interests. (Zia 1984*a*: 18)

Legacy of the Chin Case

Considered the archetype of anti-Asian violence, the Chin killing has "taken on mythic proportions" in the Asian American community (W. Wong 1989*a*). As a result of the Chin case, Asian Americans today are much more willing to speak out on the issue of anti-Asianism; they are also much better organized than they were at the time of Chin's death. Across the country, Asian Americans have formed new organizations to monitor, report, and protest anti-Asian incidents. Some of the newly formed organizations include the Bay Area's Break the Silence Coalition and Asian Network for Equality and Justice, Boston's Asians for Justice Coalition, Cincinnati's Americans for Asian Concerns, Davis, California's Asians for Racial Equality, New York's Coalition against Anti-Asian Violence, and Sacramento's Coalition of Asians for Equal Rights (Mar 1987). In 1988, the Asian Foundation for Community Development in northern California established the Vincent Chin Memorial Grant to fund projects that aim to reduce anti-Asian violence and to improve intergroup relations (*Rafu Shimpo* 1989).

Besides combating anti-Asian violence, these pan-Asian organizations provide a social setting for building pan-Asian unity. As Asian Americans came together to fight anti-Asian bigotry, "a new understanding about each other has developed, increasing the potential for stronger united efforts" (Song 1987: 22). For example, the establishment of the Asian American Resource Workshop in Boston has spawned similar pan-Asian organizations, including the Asian American Lawyers Association, the Massachusetts Asian American Forum, the National Association of Young Asian Professionals, Asian Sisters in Action, and many campus-based Asian American student organizations (Song 1987: 28).

Because no systematic data exist on anti-Asian violence, Asian Americans have pushed for the collection and reporting of statistics on anti-Asian crimes at the local, state, and national levels (Ochi 1985: 177). Chin's death and the subsequent Asian American activism have forced government officials to respond to these demands. In California, following the Chin killing and other racially motivated incidents, Attorney General John Van de Kamp formed the Commission on Racial, Ethnic, Religious and Minority Violence and the Asian Pacific Islander Advisory Committee to determine the nature and extent of hate crimes in California (California, Attorney General's Asian and Pacific Islander Advisory Committee 1988). Similarly, at the urging of American Citizens for Justice (ACJ), Michigan's governor established the Advisory Commission on Asian American Affairs (Fukuzawa 1989a: 2). At the federal level, Asian Americans (and other aggrieved groups) actively lobbied for the passage of the Hate Crime Statistics Act (Lyons 1990a), which requires the U.S. attorney general to collect and publish statistics on crimes motivated by prejudice against race, religion, sexual orientation, or ethnicity. In sum, the Chin case has forced Asian Americans as well as government officials to be more responsive to anti-Asian violence.

The legacy of the Chin case is most evident in the responses to two subsequent anti-Asian killings. In 1989, in two separate racially motivated incidents, six Asian Americans were killed. In the first incident, five Southeast Asian elementary school students were shot to death in Stockton, California; in the second, a Chinese American, Jim Loo, was killed in Raleigh, North Carolina, because he was allegedly mistaken for Vietnamese. Unlike the Chin case, these two events did not seem to ignite the Asian American community: there was no noisy demonstration, no national news media exposure, no national call for donations. At first glance, this apparent lack of response suggests that the organization around the Chin case was a one-time phenomenon and that anti-Asian violence does not necessarily generate a pan-Asian response. However, closer analysis indicates that, in these two cases, a nationwide protest was not necessary because Asian Americans acted immediately to prevent any breakdown in the justice system. For the most part, government officials were also more responsive to the racial motive of these crimes.

Such a quick response can be traced to the lessons learned from the Chin case. "The Chin case provided a blueprint for what to do. People are now in a better position to address the issue" (Shimoura interview). In the Chin case, Asian Americans did not act until after the local courts had issued the lenient sentences—eight months after Chin's murder. By that time, media-grabbing demonstrations were necessary to protest the court decision. But in the Southeast Asian children and the Jim Loo cases, they mobilized immediately to monitor the government responses to the killings.

Southeast Asian Children Killings

On 17 January 1989, Patrick Purdy, dressed in combat fatigues, sprayed 105 rounds from his semiautomatic AK-47 assault weapon into a crowd of children at the Cleveland Elementary School in Stockton, California, killing five and wounding thirty more before killing himself. While the shootings horrified everyone, they especially touched Asian Americans because all those killed and most of those wounded were Southeast Asians (Kempsky 1989: 1–6; Lyons 1989b). Two weeks later, over one hundred Asian Americans convened at the West Berkeley Senior Center to discuss a community response to the killing (East/West 1989a; Jue 1989). Because Cleveland Elementary School's student population was predominantly Southeast Asian (70 percent), Asian Americans instantaneously labeled the slayings racially motivated (Asian Pacific American Coalition U.S.A. 1989b; Jue 1989; W. Wong 1989b). On the other hand, Stockton police and local officials quickly dismissed the racial aspect of the case, claiming that the shooting was the singular act of a paranoid psychotic (Jue 1989).

Public attention then turned almost completely to the issue of gun control. In a letter to *Asian Week*, Governor George Deukmejian (1989) detailed new legislative measures banning the sale and possession of semiautomatic weapons in California. In contrast, Asian American leaders emphasized the racial aspect of the slayings. In an editorial to the *Los Angeles Times*, Stewart Kwoh, executive director of the Asian Pacific American Legal Center of Southern California, argued:

> While [gun-control proposals] may be useful, our state would be negligent or worse if we do not at least have parallel initiatives to reduce hate crimes and group hatred. . . . Too many assault rifles are on the street, but we cannot forget that Vincent Chin, whose racially motivated killing seven years ago sparked national outrage, was beaten to death with a baseball bat. (Kwoh 1989)

In a letter to Attorney General Van de Kamp, community leader David Fukuzawa (1989b) similarly emphasized the importance of race: "We hope that in the din of all the voices calling for a ban on semiautomatic weapons, the racial element of this massacre is not overlooked."

Unlike the Chin case, there was no one to prosecute in the Stockton killings. Purdy was dead. But Asian Americans wanted to establish that the slayings were racially motivated. Within two weeks after the shooting, Asian American leaders from Stockton and the San Francisco Bay Area appealed to the attorney general's office to investigate the possibility that the shooting might have been "triggered by racism, ethnic hostilities, or fears of being edged out of employment opportunities by hard-working immigrants" (Kempsky 1989: 10). Responding to the charges that the Stockton police dismissed the racial aspect of the case too hastily, Attorney General Van de Kamp launched an inquiry into Purdy's background for any possible racial biases. Nine months after the shootings, the attorney general's office released an extensive report on Purdy's life, habits, and psychological makeup. Confirming the suspicion of the Asian American community, the report concluded:

> It appears highly probable that Purdy deliberately chose Cleveland Elementary School as the location for his murderous assault in substantial part because it was heavily populated by Southeast Asian children. His frequent resentful comments about Southeast Asians indicate a particular animosity toward them. (Kempsky 1989: 12)

According to the report, Purdy resented Southeast Asians because they "got benefits and didn't have to work for it." Purdy was quoted as saying that "the government was giving jobs to the Vietnamese and they also got money to live on before they got their jobs" (Kempsky 1989: 11).

As in the Chin case, Asian American leaders contended that the Stockton killings affected all Asians (Asian Pacific American Coalition U.S.A. 1989b; Fukuzawa 1989b; Kwoh 1989). In a letter to *Asian Week*, an angry Asian American wrote, "The Stockton massacre was not just a refugee situation. This could happen anywhere with Asian Americans. The rest of the Americans cannot tell us apart" (Gate 1989). Asian American community leaders asked Van de Kamp to investigate the case because "they saw it as a piece of a disturbing rise of anti-Asian sentiments" (W. Wong 1989b). However, unlike the Chin case, the racial aspect of the Stockton case received prompt attention from Asian American leaders as well as government officials. The investigation into Purdy's possible racial motives took place within two weeks after the children were killed.

Jim (Ming Hai) Loo Case

In late July 1989, in another tragic case of mistaken racial identification, two white men, Robert and Lloyd Piche, pistol-whipped a Chinese American man in a North Carolina pool hall after allegedly mistaking him for Vietnamese. Jim Loo died two days later from severe head injuries. According to eyewitnesses, the Piche brothers directed racial slurs at Vietnamese while attacking Loo and his Asian American friends. The two men were quoted as saying that they did not like Vietnamese because they had lost a brother in the Vietnam war. Of the five Asian Americans present that night, only one was in fact Vietnamese (Glascock 1989; Siao 1989b).

Fearing a repeat of the Chin case, Asian Americans responded immediately to the Loo killing. Less than a month after Loo's death, Asian Americans in Raleigh formed the Jim Loo American Justice Coalition to ensure the prosecution of Loo's killers. The coalition's chairman explained the group's strategy: "We know that in the Chin case, there was no Asian representation in the early stage. No one paid attention until the judge announced the sentence. In this case, we tried to get involved early in the game" (Chan interview). Although the core organizers of the coalition were Chinese Americans, they solicited and received support from other local Asian groups. As Chan explained, "Like the Chin case, the Loo case is an Asian case. In both

157

instances, the victim was mistaken for another Asian nationality. The perpetrators cannot tell the difference between Asians. That's why it is an Asian problem" (Chan interview).

Early on, Asian American organizations across the country contacted the Jim Loo Coalition and later the Jim Loo Memorial Fund Committee to offer their assistance. For example, a representative from the Oakland-based Asian Law Caucus visited the coalition in Raleigh to lend his legal advice and counsel (Chan interview). The national president of the Organization of Chinese Americans vowed to fight at both the state and federal levels to ensure the prosecution of Loo's killers (Organization of Chinese Americans 1989). The San Francisco–based Asian Pacific American Coalition wrote to the state attorney general in North Carolina demanding justice for Loo's murder (Asian Pacific American Coalition U.S.A. 1989c). Detroit's American Citizens for Justice also offered its support and monitored the case to ensure that no travesty of justice occurred (American Citizens for Justice 1989b; W. Wong 1989a; Chan interview).

In addition to the local criminal charges, the New York–based Asian American Legal Defense and Education Fund called for a letter-writing campaign to request an immediate civil rights investigation into the killing (East/West 1989b). In an open letter to Asian Americans, the president of the Organization of Chinese Americans in San Francisco urged Asian Americans to unite behind the Loo case: "What we can do is to mobilize a letter-writing campaign to let the governmental authorities and agencies know that we have learned our lessons from the Vincent Chin case and will not stand by and suffer another incidence of mock justice and ridicule" (Cheng 1989).

Although poised to wage a nationwide protest on behalf of Loo, Asian Americans in this instance did not have to do so because, for the most part, the legal system was responsive and responsible. The Raleigh police described the killing as racially motivated. A grand jury indicted Robert Piche on second-degree murder. In addition, four members of the U.S. Commission on Civil Rights visited Raleigh to investigate the case (American Citizens for Justice 1989b). At the urging of these civil rights officials and Asian American representatives across the country, the Justice Department ordered an FBI investigation for possible civil rights violations. An active participant in both the Chin and the Loo cases contrasted the responses to the two incidents: "So far the Loo case has not been a Vincent Chin case. The community was unable to react quickly in the Vincent Chin case, and the district attorney didn't do a good job" (cited in Siao 1989c).

On the day that Robert Piche was to be sentenced, the Jim Loo Coalition readied for a protest march (Chan interview). Said a coalition leader, "If the system lets Robert Piche off lightly, then expect some loud protests" (cited in W. Wong 1989a). However, surprising his own attorney and the coalition, Robert Piche decided at the last minute to plead not guilty. The case then went to trial. In March 1990, the Wake County jury found Robert Piche guilty of second-degree murder and sentenced him to thirty-seven years in prison.

In July 1991, Lloyd Piche, who received only a six-month sentence for disorderly conduct and assault, was tried and convicted by a federal jury for violating the civil rights of Loo and his six Asian American friends. Piche's conviction was the first successful federal prosecution of a civil rights violation case in which the victim was an Asian American. Attending the proceedings were representatives from Asian American organizations across the country: the Jim Loo Memorial Fund Committee, the Asian Law Caucus, National Network Against Anti-Asian Violence, and the Organization of Chinese Americans (Zia 1991).

The lesson learned in the Chin case was not lost on the organizers of the Loo case; in the Loo case, Asian Americans (in Raleigh as well as across the country) mobilized *before* any verdict had been reached. This early mobilization was instrumental in forcing the legal system to be more responsive to anti-Asian crimes.

Conclusion

For Asian American groups in the United States, Asian American identity is not always an identity of choice. Largely on the basis of race, all Asian Americans have been lumped together and treated as if they were the same. When manifested in anti-Asian violence, racial lumping necessarily leads to protective pan-Asian ethnicity. Because the public does not usually distinguish among Asian subgroups, all Asians face the same real and dangerous threat of anti-Asianism.

As this chapter shows, the tragedy of Chin's death united Asian American groups across generational, ethnic, class, and political lines. Their belief that all Asian Americans are potential victims propelled them to work in concert to monitor, report, and protest anti-Asian violence. As evident in the dispute over money between ACJ and the Chinese Welfare Council, pan-Asian alliances can be tenuous. However, pan-Asian organizations can breed pan-Asian consciousness. For example, in the process of building itself, American Citizens for Justice in Detroit built pan-Asian consciousness. Although ACJ's membership was not initially pan-Asian, its very existence and concerns drew in other Asian groups. The history of ACJ suggests that ethnic organizations do not merely reflect existing ethnic consciousness; they can also generate it. At the same time, pan-Asian consciousness, such as that which emerged in the Chin case, can survive and, in some cases, materialize into pan-Asian organizations. Because of this national network, Asian Americans were able to respond quickly and effectively to the massacre of the Southeast Asian children and the Loo killing.

Pan-Asian
American Ethnicity:
Retrospect and Prospect

*Ethnicity is forged and changed in encounters among groups. Be-*cause groups possess unequal power, they face unequal choices in these encounters. For the less powerful groups, ethnicity is not always voluntary, but may be imposed by a more powerful group. This imposed ethnicity may or may not match the subordinate group's established cultural and organizational practices. When there is a mismatch, members of the subordinate group often have to change their world to adapt to the demands of the outside world.

For Asian Americans, changing their world has meant expanding their social frame of reference and assuming a pan-Asian identity. But this process of change has not been simply unilateral. Within the limits of their situations, Asian Americans have transformed not only themselves but also the conditions under which they act. Adopting the dominant group's categorization of them, Asian Americans have institutionalized pan-Asianism as their primary political entity—thereby enlarging their own capacities to make claims on the resources of the dominant group. Nor has this process of change been unilinear. Within the broad pan-Asian boundaries, subgroup identifications remain important, leaving room for shifting levels of solidarity, backsliding, or dropping out of the pan-Asian framework altogether.

Dominant Group Categorization and
Subordinate Group Response

To a large degree, the process of pan-Asianization began with non-Asians. Unable or unwilling to make correct ethnic distinctions, outsiders often lump all Asian Americans together and treat them as if they were the same. While regional and national chauvinism organizes life within ethnic enclaves, movement into the mainstream necessitates a broadened scope of ethnic identity. Once outside these enclaves, Asian Americans find themselves in political and social situations that demand that they act on a pan-Asian basis. Unable to alter this demand, they eventually form an identity based in part upon it.

Although the pan-Asian concept may have originated in the minds of non-Asians, it is today more than a reflection of this misperception. Asian Americans did not just adopt the concept but also transformed it to conform to their ideological and political needs. As discussed in Chapter 2, young Asian American activists rejected the stereotyped term "Oriental" and coined their own term, "Asian American." Although both terms denote the consolidation of group boundaries, Asian American activists insisted on their term because they wanted to define their own image—one that would connote political activism rather than passivity. The term "Asian American" subsequently replaced "Oriental" in public, academic, and government discourse—so much so that to use "Oriental" today is to commit a faux pas in many social circles.

Not only did Asian Americans consolidate, but they also politicized, using the very pan-Asian concept imposed from the outside as their political instrument. In particular, possible affirmative action benefits provide compelling material reason for Asian American subgroups to consolidate their efforts. Because the welfare state bureaucracy often treats all Asian Americans as a single administrative unit in distributing economic and political resources, it imposes a pan-Asian structure on persons and communities dependent on government support. In yielding to this pressure, a minority group is rewarded by being heard—and possibly by having its demands granted.

As dealings with government bureaucracies increased, political organization along a pan-Asian line became advantageous—not only because numbers confer power but also because the pan-Asian category is the institutionally relevant category in the political and legal system. Administratively treated as a homogeneous group, Asian Americans found it necessary to respond as a group. The pan-Asian strategy has led to some political victories. As detailed in Chapter 5, Asian American legislators, community leaders, and organizations united to fight the Census Bureau's proposal to collapse all Asian racial codes into one summary category for the 1980 and 1990 censuses; partly due to the strength of their political lobbying, the Census Bureau finally conceded to the coalition's demand for a detailed enumeration of Asian subgroups. Indeed, the emergence of the pan-Asian entity may be the most significant political development in Asian American affairs.

When pan-Asian ethnicity is a political option, individuals and groups can choose to join—or to ignore—the coalition according to their changing political and economic needs. However, when pan-Asian lumping means anti-Asian activities, then the enrollment of Asian American subgroups in the pan-Asian movement is no longer an option, but a necessity. Because non-Asians do not distinguish among Asian American subgroups, group members can suffer sanctions for no behavior of their own, but for the alleged or actual misconduct of others who resemble them. Therefore, regardless of one's ethnic background, anti-Asian violence requires counter organization at the pan-Asian level.

As detailed in Chapter 6, Asian Americans across the nation were drawn together by the "mistaken identity" murder of Chinese American Vincent Chin. For some Asian Americans, the Chin case marked their first participation in a pan-Asian effort. Their belief that all Asian Americans are potential victims propelled them to join together in self-defense and to monitor, report, and protest anti-Asian violence. In particular, Asian Americans pushed for the collection and reporting of statistics on anti-Asian crimes at the local, state, and federal levels. This pan-Asian activism has forced government officials, the media, and the public to be more attentive and responsive to anti-Asian crimes. Indeed, in the 1990 California election, to woo Asian American votes and money, all three gubernatorial candidates pledged to toughen existing laws in order to combat anti-Asian violence. The Chin case makes it clear that, while political benefits certainly promote pan-Asian organization, it is anti-Asian violence that has drawn the largest pan-Asian support because it cross-cuts class, cultural, and generational divisions and necessarily leads to protective panethnicity. Thus, we can expect that, if racial hostilities against Asians escalate, pan-Asian organization will correspondingly increase.

Constructing and Sustaining Asian Panethnicity

The primordialist–instrumentalist debate in the ethnicity literature is primarily a debate over the relative importance of internal, cultural factors as opposed to external, structural factors in explaining the development and maintenance of ethnic groups. The present study indicates that, at least in its origin, pan-Asian ethnicity was the product of material, political, and social processes rather than cultural bonds. Asian Americans came together because they recognized that pan-Asian alliance was important, even essential, for the protection and advancement of their interests. But this is not to say that pan-Asian ethnicity is devoid of culture and sentiment. On the contrary, while panethnic groups may be circumstantially created, they are not circumstantially sustained (see Cornell 1988b). Once established, the panethnic group—through its institutions, leaders, and networks—produces and transforms panethnic culture and consciousness. In the process, the panethnic idea becomes autonomous, capable of replenishing itself. Over time, it may even outlive the circumstances and interests that produced it, creating conditions that sustain and revivify it.

Pan-Asian Institutions

Pan-Asian institutions are important because they provide a setting for persons of diverse Asian backgrounds to establish social ties and to discuss their common problems and experiences. As Asian Americans come together to coordinate, plan, and participate in the activities of these organizations, they become tied together in a cohesive interpersonal network (Breton 1964). As Melford Weiss (1974: 242) reported, a strong esprit de corps was established among the more active members at a local pan-Asian center. Many secondary relationships among these activists eventually developed into primary ones.

While it is true that panethnic consciousness sustains panethnic institutions, it is also true that this consciousness does not necessarily precede organizational consolidation. As indicated in previous chapters, pan-Asian organizations, publications, and Asian American Studies programs are important producers and carriers of pan-Asian consciousness. By participating in these pan-Asian institutions, Asian Americans begin to develop common views of themselves and of one another, and similar interpretations of their experiences and of the larger society. According to Cornell (1988b: 19), "Culture is forever created by persons consciously sharing social experiences." Furthermore, some pan-Asian organizations have become the institutional symbol of Asian American unity and the political voice of Asian American interests. As the de facto representatives of Asian American concerns, these organizations influence a much wider Asian American audience than their membership rosters suggest.

Pan-Asian institutions are also important because their very existence can spawn similar organizations. Once institutionalized in the late 1960s, the pan-Asian structure reinforced the cohesiveness of already existing networks and expanded these networks. However, this structure has taken different forms—at times quite different from its original form. Although originated by young Asian American activists, the pan-Asian concept was subsequently institutionalized by middle-class professionals and special interest groups. The radical and confrontational politics of the activists eventually gave way to the conventional and electoral politics of the professionals, lobbyists, and politicians—as Asian Americans continued to use the pan-Asian framework to enlarge their political capacities.

Once formed, pan-Asian institutions can become independent of the conditions that created them and defy, for a time at least, changes in these originating conditions. As indicated in Chapter 6, many of the pan-Asian organizations established in the wake of Vincent Chin's death endured even after the Chin case had ended. Some organizations have continued to monitor, report, and protest anti-Asian activities; others have had to introduce new activities and services to retain current participants and attract new members.

"Panethnic Entrepreneurs"

The case studies presented in this book show that the construction of panethnic consciousness is not merely the gradual, unconscious work of persons sharing social experiences. It can also be the deliberate work of "panethnic entrepreneurs,"[1] individuals who have a vested interest in pan-Asian activities (see Cornell 1988b). Leaders of pan-Asian organizations have the most obvious motive for strengthening pan-Asian consciousness: to maintain as large a clientele as possible. In the interest of survival, the leaders of some single-ethnic organizations have also adopted a pan-Asian stance. For example, faced with dwindling numbers and a lack of urgent political issues within their own community, the leaders of the Japanese American Citizens League have become active defenders of pan-Asian causes (Morimoto 1989a).

Although all leaders have some interest in the survival of their organizations, those who have an economic or occupational stake in these organizations have been the most active promoters of pan-Asianism. As indicated in Chapter 4, the livelihood of most Asian American social workers is directly tied to their ability to procure funding for their social service agencies. Because funding sources prefer pan-Asian projects, these agency directors actively coordinate multigroup programs and promote pan-Asian unity. At times, they have joined together to create new pan-Asian organizations solely for the purpose of keeping alive their own programs or centers. For example, to compete for the shrinking pools of public monies, Asian American social service groups in Los Angeles County established the Asian Pacific Planning Council (APPCON) to lobby on their behalf.

Asian American political officials have also actively promoted pan-Asian consciousness. Because individual Asian American groups lack the numbers to mount a strong political voice by themselves, politically minded Asian Americans find it necessary to aggregate Asian American subgroups when seeking political recognition. Chapter 3 indicates that, to win elections, Asian American candidates need coalition support. For many Asian American politicians, coalition building naturally and necessarily begins with other Asian American communities. Notwithstanding their small electorate, their support —especially financial contributions—continues to be important for Asian American candidacies. Even when Asian American compatriots are a numerical minority, they can provide the foundation for building a victorious campaign.

But political expediency is only one reason that Asian American politicians assume a pan-Asian posture. Public expectation is another. Regardless of the ethnic composition of their electoral districts, Asian American elected and appointed officials are expected (by Asians as well as non-Asians) to understand and respond to the needs of all Asian Americans. In other words, whatever their specific ethnic backgrounds, Asian American political officials become the de facto representatives of the wider Asian American community and the carriers of its political agenda. Consequently, they are often the ones to spearhead policies and programs that affect the Asian American community.

Because the political structure requires that a minority community deal with the external bodies through only one or two delegates, it provides incentives for ambitious individuals seeking leadership positions to promote the pan-Asian line. Responding to these incentives, these community representatives corroborate the misperception that there is a generalized Asian American constituency with a generalized interest. Moreover, as dealings with government bureaucracies increase, the ability to deal successfully with non-Asians as well becomes an ever more desirable qualification for leadership. This development favors more acculturated persons.

Individual Panethnicity

To be sure, pan-Asian ethnicity affects different individuals to varying degrees. For some Asian Americans, pan-Asian ethnicity is their sole identity; for many others, it is only one of their many levels of ethnic identity. As discussed above, those who have a vested interest in pan-Asian activities will be most vocal in promoting and strengthening pan-Asian consciousness. Also, as indicated in Chapter 2, native-born, American-educated Asians are much more receptive to pan-Asian ethnicity than their immigrant parents are. These second- and third-generation Asian Americans often consider themselves to have more in common culturally with other American-born Asians than they do with foreign-born compatriots.

This book focuses primarily on the institutionalization of pan-

Asian consciousness. An important next step would be to quantify this consciousness by studying interpersonal pan-Asian ethnicity—most important, its marriage patterns. Most often used to study rates of overall assimilation, intermarriage between ethnic subgroups is an equally good measure of panethnicity at the individual level. Just as intermarriage between major ethnic groups can obliterate boundaries, so intermarriage within these categories can fuse subgroups into one panethnic group (Lopez and Espiritu 1990: 219).

Although Asian-white marriages continue to be the most common type of intermarriage for Asian Americans, there is evidence that a "relatively high proportion of [Asian] outmarriages were to other Asian groups" (Kitano et al. 1984: 181). When controlling for the size of the population, Larry Shinagawa and Gin Yong Pang (1988: 101) found that "an Asian American is more likely to marry a member of another Asian ethnic group than to marry a white American." In Hawaii, where there is a large Asian population, inter-Asian marriages appear to be much more common than Asian-white marriages (M. Wong 1989: 92). Moreover, these studies indicate that Japanese and Chinese Americans, when they marry interethnically, are most likely to marry each other, suggesting that pan-Asian ethnicity is most developed between these two most established Asian American groups (Shinagawa and Pang 1988; M. Wong 1989).

Cooperation and Conflict

The consolidation of group boundaries has produced not only new links among Asian Americans but also new cleavages. Because the process of organizational consolidation reduces the power of some individuals and groups and elevates the influence of others, it inevitably results in struggles for control and competition for resources. In many instances, Asian American subgroups have competed directly with the pan-Asian group for power, members, and monies—often from the same sources. Because the pan-Asian category is the institutionally prescribed and socially relevant ethnic category in American society, the needs of the subgroups have often been subordinated to the interests of the larger entity, resulting in a loss of autonomy for these communities and declining power for their leaders. Under these conditions, inter-Asian conflicts ramify. Within the broad pan-Asian boundary, constituent communities have also competed for their shares in the benefits of membership: the jobs, money, and services won by their collective efforts. As these resources become scarce, the determination of who gets served—or, more aptly, who gets the jobs and the promotions—at times polarizes the pan-Asian coalitions.

In other words, the gradual consolidation of group boundaries is often met by a countertendency toward intergroup divisions. While prevalent, these divisions are barriers not to the development of panethnicity, but to its effectiveness as a political instrument (see Cornell 1988a: chs. 8–9). Because of the political need to present a united front to the public, many Asian American subgroups have continued to pursue their interests and to fight for their autonomy *within* the pan-Asian framework. A few groups, however, have attempted to pursue their goals outside this framework—with varying degrees of success.

Web of Associations

Given the benefits and limitations of the pan-Asian framework, the organization of ethnicity among Asian Americans has existed on multiple levels—not only on consolidation or fragmentation. When external threats appear minimal, intergroup divisions tend to weaken pan-Asian coalitions. Yet, whenever there is a need to combine their resources, Asian Americans act as a cohesive unit, presenting a united front against the dominant society. This united front does not mean that Asian Americans dismiss internal differences and divisions, but only that they look beyond them.

In part, this multitiered pattern of organization exists because ethnic and panethnic groups need each other to survive. Because numbers count in American politics, the political effectiveness of the subgroups depends on panethnic solidarity—the ability of Asian Americans to speak with one voice, and, in so doing, to confront the dominant society on their own terms. The less powerful the subgroup, the more dependent it will be on the panethnic group. In such a system, ethnic solidarity is linked to panethnic solidarity while ethnic politics becomes panethnic politics. The 1980 and 1990 census disputes illustrate this organizational dialectic: a demand for separate counts of Asian American subgroups was waged by a pan-

Asian coalition. Without this multigroup effort, the Asian American struggle with the Census Bureau would probably not have been so successful.

On the other hand, the longevity and effectiveness of the pan-Asian group hinges on the cooperation and support of the subgroups. A pan-Asian organization is most attractive when it succeeds in providing thorough and equal representation for all Asian American subgroups. When this is not the case, members may threaten to secede and would-be members can refuse to join—thereby reducing the federation's legitimacy, and thus its effectiveness. Thus, in the interest of survival, a pan-Asian organization has to continue to expand its base of support by retaining existing members and attracting new ones. As discussed in Chapter 4, responding to charges of ethnic chauvinism and inadequate representation, the Asian Pacific Planning Council (APPCON) in Los Angeles introduced an outreach program to attract new Asian American groups. Altruism was not the only reason for APPCON's reaching out to these new communities. The council also instituted these outreach measures for a practical reason: if it did not recruit new members, its credibility, and thus its effectiveness, would be reduced. Also, to make themselves accessible to the broadest constituency, panethnic organizations often lobby simultaneously for both panethnic and ethnic-specific causes—thereby emphasizing both a commonality of interest and the preservation of the rights and existence of subgroups. In other words, panethnic associations thrive when they are willing to include and share power with the ethnic subgroups.

Finally, this multitiered framework prevails because of the strategic utility of a flexible organizational framework. The strongest social support is derived from a web of affiliations, linking Asian Americans simultaneously to many levels of solidarity; stripping any level renders them more insecure (Light and Bonacich 1988: 327). This flexible framework allows Asian Americans to coalesce and to fragment, and to shift identity and reference groups to meet situational needs. A single organizational structure—either ethnic or panethnic—would leave Asian Americans only two choices: to join or to withdraw. Today's Asian American population is diverse, ranging from affluent, fourth-generation Japanese Americans to impoverished, newly arrived Southeast Asians. To accommodate this high level of diversity, the Asian American community needs an organizational structure allowing multiple choices.

"Dropping Out": Class and Class-Based Ethnic Divisions

Class and class-based ethnic divisions halt the development of panethnic solidarity. In the Asian American instance, class polarization is, ironically, most evident within the very organizations that claim to promote pan-Asian unity. As we have seen, pan-Asian organizations and activities are dominated by middle-class professionals. This class bias precludes a broad-based membership, thus undercutting the legitimacy of these organizations and the use of panethnicity as their organizing principle. Worse yet, as evident in the case of Filipino Americans and other nondominant Asian American groups, class differences often correlate with ethnicity, generating internal conflicts over power and control that assume an ethnic appearance (Espiritu and Ong 1991). As outlined in Chapters 3 and 4, the fights over scarce resources were often waged in ethnic terms: some Asian American subgroups accused the more established Chinese and Japanese Americans of monopolizing the funding and jobs meant for all Asian Americans; the dissidents complained that newer and more impoverished groups were simply used as window display. Under these conditions, historical intergroup enmities were often made worse by intergroup competition.

When communities feel inadequately represented by the panethnic coalition, they may go outside this framework to pursue their goals. But dropping out is not an option for all subgroups. Less established groups that lack numbers, political experience, and material resources often have little choice but to stay within the panethnic coalition. Being a member of the coalition brings them instant political visibility—if not always benefits. As discussed in Chapter 4, to receive social service funding, less established Asian American groups often have to depend on the technical assistance and political clout of the more established and experienced pan-Asian groups.

Post-1965 Asian immigration has made it more feasible for some Asian American groups to secede. The new immigrants revive cultural traditions, reinforce national differences, and remind co-ethnics of how little they have in common with other Asian groups. More important, immigration has added to the numerical strength of previously smaller Asian American groups. With their newly found numerical dominance, these groups have begun to challenge the established power structure of the Asian American community, charging that their needs have not been met. As these new constituencies have become more numerous and more active, they have vastly complicated pan-Asian organization.

With the new immigration, Filipino Americans became the largest Asian American group in the United States in 1980 and the second largest in 1990 (next to Chinese Americans). Their numbers have given them political clout. Consequently, some Filipino Americans contend that they no longer need to coalesce with other Asian American groups. However, recognizing the competitive advantage of a web of associations, not all Filipino Americans wish to leave the pan-Asian framework. Thus, at present, dissenting Filipino Americans, although very vocal, are in the minority.

The pan-Asian coalition is not the only panethnic option available to Filipino Americans. The Hispanic coalition is another. As a result of the Spanish colonization of the Philippines, Filipinos share many cultural characteristics with Hispanic American groups—including Catholicism. Filipino and Hispanic Americans also face many of the same social and economic difficulties, such as low educational participation rates (Azores 1986–87). As a "borderline"—and large—group, Filipino Americans have been courted by both the Asian American and the Hispanic American communities. There remain many obstacles to the Filipino-Hispanic alliance, including government bureaucracies that continue to treat Filipino Americans as Asian Americans. Although the option of joining the Hispanic coalition remains a remote possibility, it could nevertheless give Filipino Americans more political clout within the pan-Asian grouping: to keep Filipino Americans within their fold, pan-Asian leaders would need to open up leadership positions and champion Filipino American causes.

Looking Ahead

Since the pan-Asian concept was forged in the late 1960s, the Asian American population has become much more variegated.

The removal of racial barriers in the economic sector and the preference for highly educated labor in immigration legislation have increased the rank of the educated professionals, thus fragmenting Asian Americans more clearly than in the past along class lines. The post-1965 immigration has also brought new ethnic constituencies into the pan-Asian fold, many of which are unfamiliar with or indifferent to the pan-Asian concept. Coming from different worlds, the post-1965 Asian immigrants and the American-born (or American-raised) Asians do not share a common history, sensibility, or political outlook. Without shared worldviews, collective modes of interpretation, and common class interests, the prospects of a viable pan-Asian ethnicity appear bleak. Evolving efforts to construct a meaningful pan-Asian ethnicity often lag behind the rate of change.

Racial politics has also changed in the last two decades. In the 1960s, race (as a social, legal, and administrative concept) was a legitimate basis for making claims on the resources of the state. Today, race-oriented social programs are largely discredited. With the restructuring of the global order and the recurring economic crises in this country, the "federal government has reversed itself and switched sides on racial policy" (Omi and Winant 1986: 135). The 1980s was a decade of right-wing politics, in which Republican administrations in general attempted to reverse the political gains of the racial minority movements of the 1960s. The public and legal attack on affirmative action (viewed as "reverse discrimination" and "preferential treatment") has been nationwide.

As this book documents, affirmative action programs have provided a material incentive for Asian Americans to organize along pan-Asian lines. Thus, the dismantling of race-oriented programs should spell the end of racially based mobilization. On the other hand, notwithstanding recent calls for a "colorblind" society, America remains a race-conscious society, though race may be "rearticulated" in other terms (Omi and Winant 1986: ch. 7). Whether overtly or covertly, racial issues continue to color American politics, from campaign tactics that exploit racial fears[2] to the confirmation of a black conservative who opposes affirmative action programs to the U.S. Supreme Court. Indeed, the very call for a "colorblind" society is itself an implicit attack on the racial groups that affirmative action programs purport to protect.

Hate crimes and racial incidents are also on the rise. Survey data reveal that anti-Asian bigotry continues to plague Asian Americans. In a 1984 survey of minority groups in California, 45 percent of the Asian Americans polled indicated that they had personally experienced serious discrimination; 57 percent thought that some or most Americans were prejudiced against Asian Americans (Cain 1988). In short, although the content of racial politics may have changed, race—or more accurately, the exploitation of race—remains central to American politics.

In this "new" racial order, Asian Americans continue to be defined as a distinct race. Although the Asian American population has changed, outsiders have not changed in how they view Asian Americans. State policy and the majority of the American public persist in identifying Asian Americans along racial lines (i.e., as "Asians")—discounting class, ethnic, and generational cleavages.[3] This classification system is so entrenched that, when new Asian immigrants and refugees arrive, they are automatically assigned to the Asian American collectivity. As a consequence, Asian American lives are *still* strongly influenced by their racial status—regardless of whether or not they choose to identify themselves in racial terms (Waters 1990: 157).

Racial lumping is also an effective unifying force among other racial minority groups in the United States. Like Asian Americans, Native Americans face a conceptual scheme that emphasizes their racial boundary, not their tribal identity (Cornell 1988a: chs. 7–8). Even the racially variable Latino American population is, from an outsider's point of view, something of a race apart (Lopez and Espiritu 1990: 220). As a result of internal diversity and the persistent sense of tribe among Native Americans and homeland among Latino Americans, panethnicization has been a slow and uneven process for these two groups. But if there is even a hint of such panethnic group evolution, it is due in no small part to the prevailing categorization scheme that treats them as united populations (Enloe 1981: 134).

Racial lumping and stigmatizing have been most widespread against African Americans, the earliest and most developed panethnic group in the United States. The tendency to see African Americans in racial terms often obscures the fact that these Americans originally came to this country not as "blacks" or "Africans," but as members of distinct and various ethnic populations. A comprehensive racial consciousness was constructed only after extended interaction with Euro-American society (Cornell 1990). In the United States, the black–white distinction has been so rigidly defined and enforced—more so than the distinction between whites and other nonwhites—that, even as recently as 1980, blacks were nearly twice as segregated residentially as were Hispanic Americans or Asian Americans. Whites apparently view blacks as "qualitatively different and, by implication, less desirable as neighbors, than members of other racial or ethnic groups" (Massey and Denton 1987: 823). Marriages between whites and blacks have also been less prevalent than marriages between whites and other nonwhites (Fuchs 1987–88). Recent opinion polls indicate that many whites continue to cling to negative stereotypes of blacks. For example, in a 1991 poll by the University of Chicago's National Opinion Research Center, 56 percent of whites said blacks were likely to be less intelligent than whites (Richter 1991). This rigid black–white distinction helps to explain why African Americans have been more cohesive, and thus more successful politically, than Asian Americans and other racial minority groups. Granted, relative homogeneity along class and generational lines contributes to this cohesiveness. But given the harsh and uncompromising black–white model in American society, African American racial solidarity is due in large part to the unity that has been imposed upon them.

The continuing importance of race and the persistence of racial lumping in American society suggest that, at present and in the immediate future, Asian Americans cannot—and perhaps should not—do away with the notion of pan-Asian ethnicity. Pan-Asian unity is necessary if Asian Americans are to contest systems of racism and inequality in American society—systems that seek to exclude, marginalize, and homogenize them. Given the external pressures and the benefits it promises, panethnicity, in contrast to ethnic particularism or assimilation, may well define the future of ethnicity for other racial minority groups in the United States as well.

That said, there remains the problem of internal diversity: how to bridge the class, ethnic, and generational chasms dividing Asians in the United States. This task of "bridging" belongs to Asian Americans: outsiders may have drawn the pan-Asian boundary, but it will be Asian Americans who design the content within that boundary. This content can be exclusive, ignoring diverse viewpoints and subsuming nondominant groups, or it can be inclusive, incorporating conflicting perspectives and empowering less established communities. Class, ethnic, and generational divisions can be obscured and perpetuated or they can be recognized and addressed. If Asian Americans are to build a self-consciously pan-Asian solidarity, they need to take seriously the heterogeneities among their ranks and overcome the narrow dominance of one class or that of the two oldest Asian American groups. This task of "bridging" reminds us that ethnicization—the process of boundary construction—is not only reactive, a response to pressures from the external environment, but also creative, a product of internally generated dynamics.

Notes

Chapter 1

1. In this book, the term *ethnicity* refers to differentiation on the basis of race (socially defined) and cultural characteristics such as language and religion.

2. The phrases "communities of culture" and "communities of interests" were coined by Stephen Cornell (1988b: 20).

3. I thank Steve Cornell for sharing his thoughts with me on the role of culture.

4. In general, most ethnic protests are inspired and led by higher-status persons (Yinger 1985: 173). For example, the racial issues that were defined and articulated by black activists in the early 1960s reflected the orientations and specific needs of the growing black middle class (Wilson 1980).

Chapter 2

1. On the other hand, due to the relative strength of Japan in the world order, Japanese immigrants at times received more favorable treatment than other Asian immigrants. For example, in 1905, wary of offending Japan, national politicians blocked an attempt by the San Francisco Board of Education to transfer Japanese students from the public schools reserved for white children to the "Oriental" school serving the Chinese (Chan 1991: 59).

2. Although many Korean laborers were sympathetic to the 1920 strike, because of their hatred for the Japanese, they did not participate. As the Korean National Association announced, "We do not wish to be looked upon as strikebreakers, but we shall continue to work in the plantation and we are opposed to the Japanese in everything" (cited in Melendy 1977: 164).

3. The same is true with other racial groups. For example, American-born Haitians are more like their African American peers than like their Haitian parents (Woldemikael 1989: 166).

4. Ideally, residential patterns should be analyzed at the census tract

level. However, this analysis cannot be done because Asians were not tabulated by census tracts until the 1980 census.

5. The units of analysis used by Lam (1986) were 822 suburbs with a population in 1960 of 10,000 or more located within the 212 SMSA that could be identified in 1970 as well as in 1980.

6. The Index of Dissimilarity (ID) is the leading measure of residential segregation. The index of dissimilarity ranges from 0 to 1 (some researchers prefer 0 to 100) and reflects the percentage of a group that would have to move to obtain equivalent proportional distributions. In general, values of dissimilarity above .600 are considered high, while those under .300 are low; values from .300 to .600 indicate a moderate level of residential segregation (Denton and Massey 1988: 804).

7. The 1980 census provided a first-time opportunity to examine the census tract separation of Asian subgroups. Analyses of the 1980 data show a relatively high level of residential segregation among Asian subgroups. In selected areas in Southern California, the level of segregation between Asian subgroups is (in some cases) as high as that between each group and non-Asians (Hodge, Arsdol, Ko, and Gorwaney 1986: table 2; White 1986: table 1). In the absence of longitudinal data, these findings do not necessarily invalidate the claim made in this section that residential segregation among Asian subgroups has declined over time. Moreover, this section is concerned primarily with the immediate postwar period, when the majority of the Asian population was native born. In 1980, the Asian population was, once again, an immigrant population (73 percent foreign born). Rapid growth through immigration promotes the formation of new ethnic-specific enclaves, thereby reducing contact with other Asian groups as well as with non-Asians (Massey and Denton 1987: 821).

8. During the late 1960s, in radical circles, the term *third world* referred to the nation's racially oppressed people.

9. According to Yuji Ichioka, potential members were drawn from the Peace and Freedom Party roster: "We went down the list and picked out identifiable Asian names. AAPA participants were younger people in their twenties and thirties. They were more Americanized. All American-born. We felt we had to do something because we were part of American society. We were not new immigrants" (Ichioka interview).

10. I thank Jesse Hiraoka for sharing his thoughts with me on this subject.

11. A 1978 survey identified the following longstanding Asian American Studies programs in the United States: California State Universities at San Francisco, Fresno, Sacramento, and Long Beach; Universities of California at Berkeley, Santa Barbara, Davis, and Los Angeles; University of Southern California; University of Washington; University of Colorado; City College of New York; and the University of Hawaii. Harvard, Yale, Columbia, and

Princeton offered courses once but never established programs (Nakanishi and Leong 1978).

12. As stated in the 1991 program of the Association for Asian American Studies Conference, one of the purposes of the association is to promote "better understanding and closer ties among the various groups within the Asian American community."

13. In 1990, some of the former *Gidra* staff reunited to publish a twentieth-anniversary issue of the paper. Reflecting the ethnic diversity of the Asian Pacific American population in the 1990s, the 128-page publication included many articles on and by the post-1965 Asian immigrants and refugees.

14. The publication of *Rice* magazine was suspended in 1989.

15. For example, the Red Guards accepted an invitation to guard a meeting of the Chinese Contractors' Association against a threatened assault by the Teamsters who sought to organize Chinatown's heavily exploited seamstresses (Lyman 1973: 29).

16. IWK later merged with the August Twenty-Ninth Movement (ATM) and changed its name to the League for Revolutionary Struggle.

17. For example, the staff of the movement publication *Gidra* were predominantly Japanese Americans.

18. For a discussion of the role of "cultural entrepreneurs," see Cornell (1988*b*).

Chapter 3

1. For example, in South Pasadena, a suburb of Los Angeles, Asian Americans had a higher median family income, a higher percentage of college-educated persons, and a higher percentage of professionals and managers than did the city's overall population, but their voter registration rate of 35 percent was only slightly more than one-half the total population's rate of almost 68 percent (Nakanishi 1986: 13).

2. Simulating comparable levels of English-language competence, Carole J. Uhlaner, Bruce Cain, and D. Roderick Kiewiet (1987) found that Asian Americans would have voted at approximately the same levels as whites in the 1984 election.

3. At the time of the November 1988 election, one-third of Hispanic Americans aged eighteen and over were ineligible to vote because they were not U.S. citizens (U.S. Bureau of the Census 1989*a*:: 1).

4. See the following newspaper stories: "Group Seeks to Reverse Voter Apathy by Asians," *Los Angeles Times*, 3 March 1986; "Voters Group Reaches Out to ¼ Million Asians in Texas," *Asian Week*, 8 July 1988; "Korean-American Group Seeks to Register Voters," *Orange County Register*, 16 April

1988; "Low Voter Registration Retards New York Asians' Political Clout," *Asian Week*, 7 September 1990; "AAC Launches Voter Registration Drives," *Asian Week*, 1 February 1991.

5. Naturalized Latino immigrants also display weak party ties. According to a 1989 study by the National Association of Latino Elected and Appointed Officials (NALEO), 25 percent of naturalized Latino immigrants have not aligned themselves with either the Democratic or the Republican Party, and 62 percent of legal immigrants who are eligible for citizenship have no party preference (Davis 1989).

6. Cain and Kiewiet also reported that Japanese (of whom 29 percent were foreign born in 1980) had issue preferences most like those of the whites in the sample. In contrast, Koreans (of whom 83 percent were foreign born in 1980) were the most like Latinos on issues of bilingualism and immigration reform.

7. According to these right-wing groups, support for renewed diplomatic relations with Vietnam is the same as support for communism in Vietnam.

8. In the 1986 Los Angeles gubernatorial campaign, about 10 percent of Mayor Tom Bradley's statewide financial support came from Asian Americans, who made up less than 6 percent of the state's population (Tachibana 1986a).

9. In 1985, stung by criticism that the party is controlled by special interest groups, the Democratic Party's executive committee voted to abolish many of its caucuses, including the Asian Pacific Caucus. The National Democratic Council of Asian and Pacific Americans was formed to fill that political vacuum for Asian Americans (Zane 1985; Iwata 1987).

10. Asian American candidates' fund-raising prowess has at times drawn criticism from non-Asian candidates. For example, in the 1990 city council election in Cerritos, a suburb of Los Angeles, candidate Charles Kim raised $96,000—almost double the amount raised by all twelve of his competitors combined. According to Cerritos city officials, the most successful fund raising in previous council elections generated only about $36,000. Kim's campaign funding reports indicated that the overwhelming majority of his contributors were fellow Koreans who did not live in Cerritos. The size of Kim's campaign treasury "has raised the hackles of most of the candidates and generated charges that he is a carpetbagger" (Feutsch 1990).

11. Both Furutani and Woo were the first Asian Americans to be elected to their respective offices.

12. These campaign disclosure statements do not give a complete list of all the donors; they contain the names only of those contributors who have donated a hundred dollars or more. Asian contributors were identified through sight recognition of their surnames. This method has several well-

known limitations (see Nakanishi 1985–86: 8–10). One involves the identification of Asian women who married non-Asian men and adopted their husbands' surnames. Although these women cannot be identified systematically, it was possible to include those who have distinctly Asian given names. The second limitation involves Asian surnames (particularly Filipino names) that are identical to those of non-Asians. Names that are not readily identifiable were relegated to the "Unknown" category. This limitation probably leads to an undercount of Filipino contributors, and thus of Asian contributors. Finally, some Asian surnames are common for more than one Asian group, as in Lee, Young, and Chang for Chinese and Koreans. In Michael Woo's case, these names were counted as Chinese given the likelihood that more Chinese than Koreans would contribute to a Chinese candidate. When the surnames common for both Chinese and Koreans were treated as Chinese, 364 contributors with Chinese surnames were counted. When these surnames were treated as Koreans, 348 contributors with Chinese surnames were counted—a difference of 16 contributors. However, this limitation does not affect the Furutani analysis because only Japanese contributors were separated from the Asian sample.

13. According to the coordinator of the fund-raiser, who declined to be named, the main concern was Asian representation: "Dolores was the first Asian Pacific person in the nation to run for mayor of a major metropolitan area. We wanted to support her. Besides, Dolores does not consider herself only as a Filipina, but as an Asian representative." To rally the broadest Asian support, different strategies were used in different Asian communities: "For the Filipino community, we presented her as a Filipino candidate. But for the other Asian Pacific communities, we presented her as an Asian Pacific candidate."

14. In its original form, the bill proposed to eliminate the family visa preferences often used by Asians and Latinos; it also favored English-speaking immigrants. Asian American and Latino lobbying efforts led to a revised bill, which restored the family preference category and eliminated the points preference given to English-speaking immigrants.

15. For a good discussion of organizational networks, see Cornell (1988a: 173–176).

16. In 1956, Dalip Singh Saund from the Imperial Valley, California, a native of India, became the first American of Asian ancestry to win a seat in the U.S. House of Representatives.

17. Even as late as the 1980s, Asian American elected officials continued to hold the dubious distinction of being the first of their group to win a particular office. Some examples include Michael Woo's 1985 election to the Los Angeles city council, Warren Furutani's 1987 election to the Los Ange-

les board of education, Al Sugiyaman's 1988 election to the Seattle board of education, and Sylvia Sun Minnick's 1990 election to the Stockton city council.

18. See the following stories from *Asian Week*: "2 Asians Running for Houston City Council," July 1991 (Southern California issue); "Teng Running for New York Council," and "Ambalada Joins Race for Seattle Council," 15 July 1991.

19. For example, in 1975, Norman Mineta was elected to the U.S. House of Representatives in a district that was only 2.5 percent Asian American. Similarly, in 1985, Michael Woo became the first and only Asian American ever elected to the Los Angeles city council in a district that was only 5 percent Asian American.

20. In the 1988 calendar year, Chu received close to $16,000 from contributions of a hundred dollars or more. An analysis of Chu's campaign disclosure statements indicated that 77 percent of the contributors were Chinese. Even though Chu was running for a local election, 76 percent of her funders lived outside Monterey Park, suggesting ethnic support by the wider Chinese community.

21. As U.S. Representative Robert Matsui related, "When I became a congressman, I wanted to get on a monopoly subcommittee. . . . But, that great liberal, Peter Rodino [D–N. J.], said, 'I thought someone like you would want to work on the immigration subcommittee.' He thought my one interest is immigration since I am an Asian American. I told him he was stereotyping me" (cited in Lau 1989).

22. Then president of the college, Hayakawa proposed to deliver ultimatums, restrict due process, suspend students, and fire disobeying faculty. On 2 December 1968, at a mass campus rally, Hayakawa himself jumped onto the sound truck and ripped off the speaker cords. Defending the use of police repression, Hayakawa described the student strikers as a "gang of goons, gangsters, con-men, neo-Nazis, and common thieves" (Umemoto 1989: 31–33).

23. For example, in 1974, Los Angeles County Supervisor Kenneth Hahn invited Gardena City Councilman Mas Fukai to join his staff as liaison with the county's rapidly growing Asian American community. A Japanese American, Fukai became Hahn's representative "at anything to do with the Asian community" (Vollmer 1987).

24. In 1976, 39 percent of the voters in Hawaii were of Japanese ancestry (Haas 1987: 659).

1. Following the example of the Black Panthers, the San Francisco Red Guards instituted a free breakfast program for indigent Chinatown children. It also initiated a successful petition drive to prevent the closing of the tuberculosis treatment center and forced the federal government to hire more Chinese-speaking staff (Lyman 1970: 106; A. Hing 1989: 138). In New York City, the I Wor Kuen (IWK) provided numerous social service programs to the largely Chinese American community. In Los Angeles, East Wind worked for the rights of young, poor, elderly, and non-English-speaking Asians (East Wind 1979: 110).

2. By the late 1960s, drugs had become an epidemic in the Asian American community. In 1972, at least thirty Asian American youths in the Los Angeles area died of drug overdose (Ling 1989: 57).

3. For example, in 1969, ex-drug users and community volunteers in Los Angeles formed the Asian American Hard Core to help other young Asians. In San Francisco, Leway (Legitimate Ways) was founded by juvenile delinquents to "help street people keep out of trouble" (Gotanda 1970).

4. Los Angeles County provides an example. Between 1969 and 1972, fifty to sixty Asian health and human service community-based agencies were established in the county (Spector-Leech 1988). In the 1970s, the county provided seed money for the incorporation of the Asian, Samoan, and Indochinese service centers, the Asian American Drug Abuse Program, the Asian Pacific Treatment and Counseling Center, and the Asian Pacific Resource Center. In 1971, the Greater Los Angeles Community Action Agency financed the Service for Asian American Youth. In 1975, Los Angeles City money funded the Asian Pacific Coalition on Aging. City and county community block grants continue to finance many Asian American social service projects in the 1980s (Coalition for Asian Mental Health 1976: 22; Kokubun 1987; Asian American Drug Abuse Program 1988).

5. In the early 1970s, "Asian Pacific Islander" became the broader racial category used by many funding agencies and social service providers. Before this time, Pacific Islanders were subsumed under the rubric "Asian American." For example, the Office of Asian American Affairs and the Department of Health, Education, and Welfare initially listed Samoans with the other four Asian groups, Chinese, Japanese, Koreans, and Filipinos (Department of Health, Education, and Welfare 1974: 1).

6. For example, although the needs of Laotian refugees are numerous, Lao Vathana, a Los Angeles agency serving these refugees, faced a multitude of barriers when applying for social service funding. Responding to Lao Vathana's complaint of inadequate funding, the program manager of the Refugee Training Program stressed that funding is "based on an agency's ability

to provide facts about their needs. That includes a thorough investigation of the organization based on a performance basis. Bring us the facts. We're quite willing to hear the case." But Lao Vathana lacks the technical expertise to prepare such a professional proposal. According to the agency's chairman, "What is needed is for someone to volunteer to write a grant proposal to be presented at the federal level" (cited in Yablonka 1989).

7. In Los Angeles, Special Services for Groups (SSG), a predominantly Japanese American agency, acts as a fiscal agent for many new Asian American projects. Founded in the 1940s, SSG has accumulated a good record on fiscal and program management. Expounding on the agency's qualifications, the director of SSG stated, "When you apply for federal money, you have to be knowledgeable. They have substantial requirements. We know the game of how to do it. And we have the staff to provide technical assistance" (Hatanaka interview).

8. For example, the Asian Health Services in Oakland, the International District Community Health Center in Seattle, the North East Medical Services in San Francisco, the South Cove Community Center in Boston, and the Kokua Kalihi Valley Health Center in Honolulu all provide health care for multiple Asian groups.

9. The Asian American population includes the Japanese, Chinese, Filipino, Korean, and Hawaiian populations.

10. For example, a 1989 Los Angeles County request for a proposal for AIDS funding stipulated that prospective bidders must serve at least six Asian groups. This stipulation effectively ruled out applications from agencies serving single Asian groups.

11. Reflecting the ethnic diversity of the county's Asian Pacific American population in 1990, the project proposed to serve the following Asian groups: Chinese, Japanese, Korean, Thai, Vietnamese, Chinese Vietnamese, Lao, and Filipino.

12. In 1960, Chinese Americans constituted 76 percent of all Asian Americans in New York City; in 1970, 73 percent; and in 1980, 52 percent (U.S. Bureau of the Census 1963: table 21; 1973b: table 23; 1983d: table 58).

13. HR 4922 is a component of the Disadvantaged Minority Health Improvement Act (HR 5702), which was signed into law (PL 101-527) by President George Bush on 6 November 1990.

14. To be sure, Filipino Americans are not homogeneous economically, particularly since the post-1965 arrival of highly educated and professional Filipino immigrants. However, my concern here is not with the class variation within any given Asian American population, but rather with the systematic variations in the class distributions among Asian American subgroups (see Espiritu and Ong 1991).

15. For example, citing the high unemployment rate of Samoan Ameri-

cans in California, a study conducted by the National Office of Samoan Affairs recommended that government agencies create a separate category of "Samoan Americans" for employment purposes (Gladstone 1981). Similarly, at a 1990 public hearing on Asian American education at the California State University at Fullerton, Southeast Asian community representatives argued that, as the poorest group among the Asian American minority, Southeast Asians should be placed in a separate category and be given special assistance in the higher education system.

16. For example, the fund organizers received little support from the county, which is the largest employer of Asian Pacific Americans. According to the group's president: "The county people give United Way half an hour to speak to the employees about their program, but they only give us two seconds" (Woo interview).

Chapter 5

1. According to the instructions to enumerators: "A person of mixed White and Negro blood was to be returned as Negro, no matter how small the percentage of Negro blood. . . . A person of mixed White and Indian blood was to be returned as Indian" (U.S. Bureau of the Census 1979: 52).

2. The 1890 census schedule epitomizes the problem of misclassification. This census instructs census takers to "be particularly careful to distinguish between blacks, mulattoes, quadroons, and octoroons. The word 'black' should be used to describe those persons who have three-fourths or more black blood; 'mulatto,' those persons who have from three-eighths to five-eighths black blood; 'quadroon,' those persons who have one-fourth black blood; and 'octoroon,' those persons who have one-eighth or any trace of black blood" (U.S. Bureau of the Census 1979: 28). It is doubtful that these distinctions can be made by observation.

3. A combination of laws and executive orders prohibited discrimination based on race in voter registration, education, public facilities, the sale or rental of housing, mortgage lending, property insurance, and the selection of beneficiaries for federal grants. The principal laws were the Civil Rights Act of 1964 (PL 88-352), the Voting Rights Act of 1965 (PL 89-110), the Civil Rights Act of 1968 (PL 90-284), the Equal Employment Opportunity Act of 1972 (PL 92-261), and the Voting Rights Act of 1975 (PL 94-73). The principal executive orders were 11603 (Equal Opportunity in Housing), 1962; 11246 (Equal Employment Opportunity), 1965; 11478 (Equal Employment Opportunity in the Federal Government), 1969; and 11764 (Nondiscrimination in Federal Assisted Programs), 1974 (Lowry 1982: 58).

4. Other federal agencies that use census data for affirmative action

purposes include the Equal Employment Opportunity Commission, Department of Health, Education, and Welfare, Department of the Treasury, Law Enforcement Assistance Administration, Small Business Administration, and Commission on Civil Rights.

5. Representatives of organizations of white ethnic groups such as Irish Americans and Slavic Americans also demanded better statistics on their groups, pressuring the Census Bureau to add a question on ethnic ancestry that would allow them to identify their potential members—the third and later generations (Waters 1990: 9).

6. The Korean government ended emigration in 1905 and the number of Koreans did not rise much until the 1960s.

7. For example, the National Institute of Mental Health uses the census data to create mental health demographic profile information tapes. These tapes are then disseminated to the states and the local counties so that they can plan mental health and other kinds of services. If Asian Pacific Americans are not properly counted, there is little chance that they will be able to receive adequate services (Nguyen 1979).

8. The count of a racial group can be derived from one of the following three items on the census schedules: racial membership, ancestry, or place of birth. Each of these variables provides slightly different and occasionally conflicting counts of the population. The controversy discussed in this chapter is over the racial membership question.

9. I thank George Lipsitz for pointing this out to me.

10. At the request of the Advisory Committee, these misclassifications were corrected for the 1980 census tabulations (U.S. Bureau of the Census 1983b: B-3).

11. The OMB is charged with setting statistical standards for federal data collection. Prior to the 1976 directive, racial designations included only three categories: "Negro, White, and Other Races." Although federal data collection was not restricted to these three categories, no classification was prescribed for any other racial or ethnic group. Ethnic enumeration had become such a political issue that OMB had to impose a uniform system of counting on all federal agencies, including the Bureau of the Census (U.S. Commission on Civil Rights 1973: 34).

12. To establish a uniform federal position in the area of employment discrimination, the Equal Employment Opportunity Commission, the Civil Service Commission, the Department of Labor, and the Department of Justice jointly issued the "Uniform Guidelines on Employee Selection Procedures." According to section 4 of these 1978 guidelines, records are to be maintained by the following racial and ethnic groups: Blacks, American Indians, Asians, Hispanics, and Whites. The guidelines do not ask for data on the

individual components of these general groupings (U.S. Equal Employment Opportunity Commission 1979: II-45).

13. The 1946 Luce–Celler bill permitted India to have a small immigration quota and made it possible for Asian Indians in the United States to become naturalized citizens.

14. Organizations endorsing the coalition include: Association of Health Organizations, National Japanese American Citizens League, East Bay Asian Local Development Corporation, Center for Southeast Asian Refugee Resettlement, Korean Community Center of the East Bay, Asian American Health Forum, Asian American Communities for Education, Equal Rights Advocates, Asian Health Services, Chinese for Affirmative Action, and the Asian Foundation for Community Development.

15. In 1975, Congress passed Public Law 94-171 giving the Census Bureau a legal role in providing census counts for redistricting state legislatures. Under this law, the Census Bureau must provide population counts to the legislature and governor of each state one year after census day.

16. To be sure, the census fights did not originate at the grass-roots level. Rather, they were led by established Asian Americans, well versed in the political system.

Chapter 6

1. See the following newspaper stories: "Asians Harassed in Washington," *Koreatown*, 4 January 1983; "Increasing Attacks on Minorities Cited," *Korea Times English Section*, 15 February 1983; "Assaults on Asian Immigrants Increase in Boston," *New York Times*, 11 August 1983; "Hostilities Build between Vietnamese, White Fishermen," *East/West*, 14 September 1983; "Korean Merchants, Black Customers—Tensions Grow," *Los Angeles Times*, 15 April 1985.

2. In a segment of the *60 Minutes* television show, Andy Rooney (1989) lamented Japanese ownership of Washington, D.C.: "I know they [Japanese] own most of Hawaii, a lot of Los Angeles and big parts of New York. I thought our nation's capital would be different. Well, I got the shock of my life. Through half a dozen different sources, we found out what the Japanese do own in Washington." Rooney went on to list the hotels, companies, and office buildings owned by the Japanese. He ended with, "This is the Washington Monument. This is the Jefferson Memorial. And this is the Capitol, of course. The Japanese don't own any of those. Yet."

3. For example, the White American Resistance (WAR) group accused all Asians of trading in illegal drugs and urged whites to resist this "Yellow Peril" (Harrison 1987).

4. In Michigan that year, 28 percent of all defendants convicted of manslaughter received probation.

5. Within two months after Kaufman's decision, the Chin case was covered by the following local and national news media: Channel 7 (ABC Detroit); Channel 4 (NBC Detroit); Channel 2 (CBS Detroit); Channel 7 Action News Commentary by Bill Bonds; Cable News Network by Robert Vitto; Channel 56 (PBS Detroit); CBS Evening News with Dan Rather; David Newman Show on WXYZ Radio; WJR Radio; Mort Crim's Free 4 All on Channel 4; Associated Press; United Press International; Channel 50 (Independent Detroit); WCHB Radio; *Windsor Star* (Windsor, Ontario, Canada); *USA Today*; Chung Wah Commercial Broadcasting Co.; *New York Times*; *Detroit News*; and numerous Asian-language and English-language ethnic newspapers (American Citizens for Justice 1983*a*).

6. At the time of Chin's death, Ebens was a foreman at an automobile plant, and Nitz had been laid off. Ebens lost his job soon after.

7. The linkage between Chin's death and anti-Japanese sentiments even reached Japan. Television crews from Japan flew to Detroit to investigate, and Japanese businessmen "felt that you cannot come to this country and conduct business because you can be subject to indiscriminate violence" (Ochi 1985).

8. This tactic was widely used in the South in the 1960s, when all-white state juries routinely acquitted whites who murdered blacks; justice then had to be sought in federal courts under statutes that made it a crime to deny a person's civil rights because of his or her race.

9. The first count charged them with "conspiracy to deprive Chin of his civil rights," the second with "interfering with Chin's civil rights by willfully injuring, intimidating, and interfering with Chin on account of his race or national origin and because the latter has been employing the privileges and accommodations of . . . a place of entertainment open to the public" (U.S. Court of Appeals, Sixth Circuit 1986: 1427).

10. During the first trial, Ebens and Nitz had sought to introduce as evidence a taped conversation between an ACJ attorney and the witnesses to demonstrate that the witnesses were improperly coached. Their petition was denied. The Court of Appeals ruled that the tapes should have been admitted and that "failure to admit tapes mandated reversal" (U.S. Court of Appeals, Sixth Circuit 1986: 1422–1431).

11. According to the U.S. Court of Appeals (1986: 1425), "The joint appendix filed in the appellate record contains sixty-eight pages of articles from Detroit newspapers about the Chin matter. . . . The publicity was not only extensive but was all adverse."

12. "Dotbuster" refers to the dots worn by Asian Indian women on their foreheads.

1. For a discussion of "cultural entrepreneurs," see Cornell (1988*b*).

2. For example, in his 1988 campaign against a black Democrat, Harvey Gantt, Senator Jesse Helms (R–N.C.) commissioned a television ad that showed the hand of a white job applicant crumpling a rejection slip he received supposedly because of an employer's affirmative action hiring plan. George Bush also used racial ads in his 1988 presidential campaign, featuring Willie Horton, the black Massachusetts convict who had been furloughed on weekends by then Governor Michael Dukakis, the Democratic nominee (Richter 1991).

3. For a comparative analysis of panethnic groups in the United States, see Lopez and Espiritu (1990).

References

Allen, Irving Lewis. 1983. *The Language of Ethnic Conflict*. New York: Columbia University Press.

Allport, Gordon W. 1958. *The Nature of Prejudice*. Boston: Beacon.

American Citizens for Justice. 1983a. "The Case for Vincent Chin: A Tragedy in American Justice (the Official Position of American Citizens for Justice)." Press release, 4 May.

———. 1983b. "Legal Status Update on Vincent Chin Case." *Justice Update*, September.

———. 1983c. "Mrs. Chin and ACJ Reps Sweep through California." *Justice Update*, September.

———. 1989a. "The Center Is One Year Old!: A Status Report from the Executive Director." *Justice Update*, Winter.

———. 1989b. Press release, 11 August.

Andersen, Patrick. 1990a. "Wilson Brings Governor's Race to S.F. Chinatown." *Asian Week*, 16 February.

———. 1990b. "Demos Hire Nguyen to Lure Asians." 9 March.

———. 1990c. "7,000 L.A. Korean Voters Registered in Six Weeks." *Asian Week*, 30 March.

Anderson, Margo. 1988. *The American Census: A Social History*. New Haven, Conn.: Yale University Press.

Asamura, Gary. 1989. "The Unsung Heroes of the Yellow Brotherhood." *Amerasia Journal* 15 (1): 156–158.

Asian American Drug Abuse Program. 1988. *People Need People*. Los Angeles: Asian American Drug Abuse Program.

Asian American Mental Health Research Center. 1977. *Asian/Pacific American Mental Health Directory*. Chicago: Asian American Mental Health Research Center.

Asian Pacific American Coalition U.S.A. 1989a. "AACI Celebrates 15th Anniversary." *APAC Alert*, February.

———. 1989b. "Stockton: Brutal Reminder of Racism." *APAC Alert*, February.

———. 1989c. "North Carolina Asian Murdered Stirs Memory of Vincent Chin Killing." *APAC Alert*, September.

Asian/Pacific American Municipal Officials. 1990. *Directory of Asian/Pacific Elected and Appointed Officials*. Washington, D.C.: Asian/Pacific American Municipal Officials.

Asian Week. 1983a. "1,000 Detroit Asians Protest Sentences," 12 May.

———. 1983b. "National Day of Mourning Slated for Vincent Chin," 2 June.

———. 1989a. "CAA Celebrates 20th Anniversary," 19 May.

———. 1989b. "GOP Taps 2 Chinese for Asian Outreach," 14 July.

———. 1990. "S.F. Asians Besieged with Candidates' Pleas for Money," 2 March.

Asians in America: A Selected Annotated Bibliography. 1983. Davis: University of California, Davis Asian American Studies Center.

Azores, Tania. 1977. "Statement of Tania Azores." Pp. 195–198 in U.S. House, Committee on Post Office and Civil Service, Subcommittee on Census and Population Hearings, *1980 Census Hearing*, 95th Congress, 1st session, 24 June.

———. 1986–87. "Educational Attainment and Upward Mobility: Prospects for Filipino Americans." *Amerasia Journal* 13 (1): 39–52.

Azores, Tania, and Yen Espiritu. 1990. "Least Studied: California Filipinos and Southeast Asians." Pp. 22–25 in *California's Asian Population: Looking Toward the Year 2000*, presented by Lucie Cheng and Paul Ong. Los Angeles: UCLA Center for Pacific Rim Studies.

Azores, Tania, and Paul Ong. 1991. *Reapportionment and Redistricting in a Nutshell*. Los Angeles: UCLA Asian American Studies Center.

Bagasao, Brad. 1989. "Asian-American No More." *LA Weekly* 1 (12): 43.

Banton, Michael. 1983. *Racial and Ethnic Competition*. Cambridge: Cambridge University Press.

Barth, Frederick. 1969. *Ethnic Groups and Boundaries*. Boston: Little, Brown.

Bates, Jim. 1988. Letter to Assemblyman Peter Chacon, 79th district, Calif., 5 April.

Beer, Matt. 1983. "Does 'Buy American' Buy Trouble?" *Los Angeles Times*, 2 June.

Bell, Daniel. 1975. "Ethnicity and Social Change." Pp. 141–166 in *Ethnicity: Theory and Experience*, edited by Nathan Glazer and Daniel P. Moynihan. Cambridge, Mass.: Harvard University Press.

Bello, Madge, and Vince Reyes. 1986–87. "Filipino Americans and the Marcos Overthrow: The Transformation of Political Consciousness." *Amerasia Journal* 13 (1): 73–83.

Bhachu, Parminder. 1985. *Twice Migrants: East African Sikh Settlers in Britain*. London: Tavistock.

Blauner, Robert. 1972. *Racial Oppression in America*. New York: Harper & Row.

Bonacich, Edna. 1972. "A Theory of Ethnic Antagonism: The Split Labor Market." *American Sociological Review* 37: 547–559.

———. 1973. "A Theory of Middleman Minorities." *American Sociological Review* 38: 583–594.

Bonacich, Edna, and John Modell. 1980. *The Economic Basis of Ethnic Solidarity: A Study of Japanese Americans*. Berkeley: University of California Press.

Braun, Stephen. 1988. "Simpler 1990 Census Form Upsets Asian Americans." *Los Angeles Times*, 12 April.

Breton, Raymond. 1964. "Institutional Completeness of Ethnic Communities and the Personal Relations of Immigrants." *American Journal of Sociology* 70: 193–205.

Bridge. 1973. "Editorial: What Price 'Peace with Honor.' " 2 (4): 3.

Browne, Blaine T. 1985. "A Common Thread: American Images of the Chinese and Japanese, 1930–1960." Ph.D. dissertation, University of Oklahoma.

Burstein, Paul. 1985. *Discrimination, Jobs, and Politics: The Struggle for Equal Employment Opportunity in the United States since the New Deal*. Chicago: University of Chicago Press.

Cabezas, Amado, Larry Shinagawa, and Gary Kawaguchi. 1986–87. "New Inquiries into the Labor Force: Pilipino Americans in California." *Amerasia Journal* 13 (1): 1–21.

Cain, Bruce E. 1988. "Asian-American Electoral Power: Imminent or Illusory?" *Election Politics* 9 (2): 27–30.

Cain, Bruce E., and D. Roderick Kiewiet. 1986. *Minorities in California*. Proceedings from a public symposium, 5 March, Pasadena, Calif.

California, Attorney General's Asian and Pacific Islander Advisory Committee. 1988. *Final Report*. Sacramento: California Department of Justice.

California, Attorney General's Commission on Racial, Ethnic, Religious and Minority Violence. 1986. *Final Report*. Sacramento: California Department of Justice.

California, Department of Economic Opportunity. 1989. *California's Unfinished Battle: The War on Poverty*. Sacramento: Department of Economic Opportunity.

California, Governor's Task Force on Civil Rights. 1982. *Report on Racial, Ethnic, and Religious Violence in California*. Sacramento: Department of Fair Employment and Housing.

Census Advisory Committee on the Asian and Pacific American Population. 1979. "Summary Report by the Census Advisory Committee on the

Asian and Pacific American Population for the 1980 Census." Mimeograph. Los Angeles: UCLA Asian American Studies Center.

Chan, Sucheng. 1991. *Asian Americans: An Interpretive History*. Boston: Twayne.

Chen, May Ying. 1976. "Teaching a Course on Asian American Women." Pp. 234–239 in *Counterpoint: Perspectives on Asian America*, edited by Emma Gee. Los Angeles: UCLA Asian American Studies Center.

Chen, Serena. 1987. "Matsui Charges 1990 Census Shortchanges Asians." *East/West*, 1 October.

———. 1988a. "National Coalition Urges Support for an Accurate Census Count." *East/West*, 17 March.

———. 1988b. "Census Officials Take Hard Line with Own Advisory Committee." *East/West*, 28 April.

———. 1988c. "Reagan Vetoes Asian Census Bill." *East/West*, 10 November.

———. 1989a. "Census Seeks Asian/Pacific Workers." *East/West*, 9 March.

———. 1989b. "Asians Assail Cap on Immigration Reform Bill." *East/West*, 15 June.

Cheng, Claudine. 1989. "Let Your Voices Be Heard." *Asian Week*, 8 September.

Cheng, Lucie, and Yen Le Espiritu. 1989. "Korean Businesses in Black and Hispanic Neighborhoods: A Study of Intergroup Relations." *Sociological Perspectives* 32: 521–534.

Chin, Rocky. 1971a. "Getting beyond Vol. 1, No. 1: Asian American Periodicals." *Bridge* 1 (2): 29–32.

———. 1971b. "NY Chinatown Today: Community in Crisis." Pp. 282–295 in *Roots: An Asian American Reader*, edited by Amy Tachiki, Eddie Wong, and Franklin Odo. Los Angeles: UCLA Asian American Studies Center.

Chin, Rocky, and May Ying Chen. 1990. "Inside the Historic Dinkins Campaign and the Future of Asian American Political Organizing." *Gidra* (20th anniversary issue), pp. 57–58.

Chinese On Leong Association. 1983. Press release, 23 March.

Choi, Portia, Keith Kawaoka, Barbara Kitashima, and Bob Matsushima. 1975. *Asian Americans and Health Care in Los Angeles County*. Los Angeles: UCLA Asian Health Team.

Choldin, Harvey M. 1986. "Statistics and Politics: The 'Hispanic Issue' in the 1980 Census." *Demography* 23 (3): 403–418.

Chow, Franklin Fung. 1988. "Statement of Franklin Fung Chow, Asian Pacific American Coalition." Pp. 115–117 in U.S. House Committee on Post Office and Civil Service, *Review of 1990 Decennial Census Questionnaire Hearing*, 100th Congress, 2nd session, 14 April.

Chun-Hoon, Lowell. 1975. "Teaching the Asian-American Experience: Alternative to the Neglect and Racism in Textbooks." *Amerasia Journal* 3 (1): 40–59.

Chun-Hoon, Lowell, Lucie Hirata, and Alan Moriyama. 1973. "Curriculum Development in Asian American Studies: A Working Paper." Pp. 83–90 in *Proceedings of the National Asian American Studies Conference II: A Tool of Change or a Tool of Control?*, edited by George Kagiwada, Joyce Sakai, and Gus Lee. Davis: University of California, Davis Asian American Studies Center.

Clifford, Frank. 1989. "Census Mired in Dispute over Counting the Hidden." *Los Angeles Times*, 15 March.

———. 1991. "Asian, Latino Numbers Soar in U.S. Census." *Los Angeles Times*, 11 March.

Coalition for Asian Mental Health. 1976. "Serving the Needs of the Asian Communities: Current Issues and Alternative Approaches." Proceedings from the symposium, November 20–21, California State University, Los Angeles.

Cohen, Abner. 1969. *Customs and Politics in Urban Africa*. Berkeley and Los Angeles: University of California Press.

———. 1981. "Variables in Ethnicity." Pp. 307–331 in *Ethnic Change*, edited by Charles F. Keyes. Seattle: University of Washington Press.

Conk, Margo. 1984. "The Census, Political Power, and Social Change." *Social Science History* 8: 81–106.

Conlan, Timothy. 1988. *New Federalism: Intergovernmental Reform from Nixon to Reagan*. Washington, D.C.: Brookings Institution.

Connor, W. 1978. "A Nation Is a Nation, Is a State, Is an Ethnic Group, Is a . . . ." *Ethnic and Racial Studies* 1: 377–400.

Contemporary Asian Studies Division, University of California, Berkeley. 1973. "Curriculum Philosophy for Asian American Studies." *Amerasia Journal* 2 (1): 35–46.

Cornelius, Wayne A. 1982. "America in the Era of Limits: Nativist Reactions to the 'New' Immigration." Pp. 1–31 in *Working Papers in US–Mexican Studies*, vol. 3. San Diego: University of California, San Diego.

Cornell, Stephen. 1988a. *The Return of the Native: American Indian Political Resurgence*. New York: Oxford University Press.

———. 1988b. "Structure, Content, and Logic in Ethnic Group Formation." Working Paper series, Center for Research on Politics and Social Organization, Department of Sociology, Harvard University.

———. 1990. "Land, Labour, and Group Formation: Blacks and Indians in the United States." *Ethnic and Racial Studies* 13 (3): 368–388.

Coser, Lewis A. 1956. *The Functions of Social Conflict*. Glencoe, Ill.: Free Press.

Covert, Colin. 1983. "Japanese-Americans in Detroit." *Detroit Free Press*, 10 July.

Cummings, Scott. 1980. "White Ethnics, Racial Prejudice, and Labor Market Segmentation." *American Journal of Sociology* 85: 938–950.

Daniels, Roger. 1971. *Concentration Camps USA: Japanese Americans and World War II.* Hinsdale, Ill.: Dryden Press.

————. 1988. *Asian America: Chinese and Japanese in the United States since 1850.* Seattle: University of Washington Press.

Davis, Kevin. 1989. "81% Naturalized Latinos Sign Up to Vote, Study Says." *Los Angeles Times*, 8 September.

Denton, Nancy A., and Douglas S. Massey. 1988. "Residential Segregation by Socioeconomic Status and Generation." *Social Science Quarterly* 69 (4): 797–817.

Department of Health, Education, and Welfare. 1974. *A Summary of Asian American Health, Education, and Welfare.* Washington, D.C.: U.S. Government Printing Office.

Der, Henry. 1988. "Statement of Henry Der, Executive Director, Chinese for Affirmative Action, on Behalf of National Coalition for an Accurate Count of Asian/Pacific Americans." Pp. 112–115 in U.S. House, Committee on Post Office and Civil Service, *Review of 1990 Decennial Census Questionnaire Hearing*, 100th Congress, 2nd session, 14 April.

Desbarats, Jacqueline. 1985. "Indochinese Settlement in the United States." *Annals of the Association of American Geographers* 75: 522–538.

————. 1986. "Ethnic Differences in Adaptation: Sino-Vietnamese Refugees in the United States." *International Migration Review* 20: 405–427.

Deukmejian, George, Governor of California. 1989. Letter: "Legislative Measures and Semi-Automatic Weapons." *Asian Week*, 26 May.

Din, Grant. 1984. "An Analysis of Asian/Pacific American Registration and Voting Patterns in San Francisco." M.A. thesis, Claremont Graduate School, California.

Dulles, Foster Rhea. 1946. *China and America.* Princeton, N.J.: Princeton University Press.

Dutta, Manoranjan. 1976. "Statement of Manoranjan Dutta, on Behalf of the Association of Indians in America, Inc." Pp. 33–37 in U.S. House, Committee on Post Office and Civil Service, *1980 Census Hearing*, 94th Congress, 2nd session, 1–2 June.

East/West. 1988a. "New Executive Director," 19 May.

————. 1988b. "Editorial: Asian Community Activists and JFK," 24 November.

————. 1989a. "Community Forum on Stockton Tragedy," 16 February.

————. 1989b. "Raleigh Killing Draws National Support," 24 August.

Editorial Board. 1971. "An Interview with L. Ling-Chi Wang." Pp. 275–281 in

Roots: An Asian American Reader, edited by Amy Tachiki, Eddie Wong, and Franklin Odo. Los Angeles: UCLA Asian American Studies Center.

Efron, Sonni. 1990. "Politics Are Changing for Asian-Americans." *Los Angeles Times*, 16 August.

Enloe, Cynthia H. 1980. *Police, Military and Ethnicity: Foundations of State Power*. New Brunswick, N.J.: Transaction Books.

———. 1981. "The Growth of the State and Ethnic Mobilization: The American Experience." *Ethnic and Racial Studies* 42 (2): 123–136.

Espiritu, Yen Le, and Paul Ong. 1991. "Class Constraints on Racial Solidarity among Asian/Pacific Americans." Working Paper, Department of Ethnic Studies, University of California, San Diego.

Feldman, Paul. 1983. "Asian Groups Stage Protest on Slaying." *Los Angeles Times*, 19 June.

Feraru, Arthur N. 1950. "Public Opinions Polls on Japan." *Far Eastern Survey* 19 (10): 101–103.

Field Institute. 1990. "A Digest on California's Political Demography." *California Opinion Index*, August.

Fisher, Maxine P. 1978. "Creating Ethnic Identity: Asian Indians in the New York City Area." *Urban Anthropology* 7: 271–285.

———. 1980. *The Indians of New York City*. Columbia, Mo.: South Asia Books.

Fong, Tim. 1987. "Asian Small Business Growth Becomes Lightning Rod for Anti-Asian Sentiment." *East/West*, 9 July.

Fuchs, Lawrence H. 1987–88. "Assimilation in the U.S.: Identities and Boundaries." *La Revue Tocqueville* 9: 181–199.

Fuetsch, Michele. 1990. "Big Spender in Cerritos Campaign Draws Criticism." *Los Angeles Times*, 18 March.

Fugita, Stephen S., and David J. O'Brien. 1991. *Japanese American Ethnicity: The Persistence of Community*. Seattle: University of Washington Press.

Fukuzawa, David. 1989a. "The Vincent Chin Case and the Detroit Asian American Community." *EWGAPA (Ecumenical Working Group of Asian and Pacific Americans) News*, Winter 1989.

———. 1989b. Letter to California Attorney General John Van de Kamp, 2 February.

Fulwood III, Sam. 1991. "U.S. Refuses to Alter Contested Census Figures." *Los Angeles Times*, 16 July.

Gardner, Robert W., Bryant Robey, and Peter Smith. 1985. "Asian Americans: Growth, Change, and Diversity." *Population Bulletin* 40: 4. Washington, D.C.: Population Reference Bureau.

Gate, Jamieson. 1989. "Letter to the Editor." *Asian Week*, 24 March.

Getting Together. 1972. 3–17 March, p. 1.

Gil, Dinora. 1968. "Yellow Prostitution." *Gidra*, April, p. 2.

Gladstone, Mark. 1981. "Migrants from South Pacific Seek Better Life, Jobs in L.A.'s Din, Clamor." *Los Angeles Times*, 1 October.

Glascock, Ned. 1989. "Chinese Slain in Raleigh Pool Hall Attack." *News and Observer*, 1 August.

Glazer, Nathan, and Daniel Patrick Moynihan. 1963. *Beyond the Melting Pot: The Negroes, Puerto Ricans, Jews, Italians, and Irish of New York City*. Cambridge, Mass.: M.I.T. Press.

Glenn, Martin, and Ferry Freedman Habush. 1983. Letter from the Jewish Federation Council of Greater Los Angeles to the *Los Angeles Times*, 13 June.

Gordon, Milton. 1964. *Assimilation in American Life: The Role of Race, Religion, and National Origins*. New York: Oxford University Press.

Gotanda, Neil. 1970. "Interview with Alex Hing, Minister of Information of the Red Guard Party." *Aion* 1 (1): 32–42.

Greenberg, Stanley. 1980. *Race and State in Capitalist Development*. New Haven, Conn.: Yale University Press.

Haas, Michael. 1987. "Comparing Paradigms of Ethnic Politics in the United States: The Case of Hawaii." *Western Political Quarterly* 40 (4): 647–672.

Hannan, Michael T. 1979. "The Dynamics of Ethnic Boundaries in Modern States." Pp. 253–275 in *National Development and the World System*, edited by John Meyer and Michael Hannan. Chicago: University of Chicago Press.

Harris, Marvin. 1964. *Patterns of Race in the Americas*. New York: W. W. Norton.

Harrison, Laird. 1987. "White Supremacist Group Targets Asians." *Asian Week*, 4 December.

Hayano, David M. 1981. "Ethnic Identification and Disidentification: Japanese-American Views of Chinese-Americans." *Ethnic Groups* 3 (2): 157–171.

Hechter, Michael. 1975. *Internal Colonialism: The Celtic Fringe in British Natural Development*. Berkeley: University of California Press.

———. 1978. "Group Formation and the Division of Labor." *American Journal of Sociology* 84: 293–318.

Hein, Jeremy. 1989. "States and Political Migrants: The Incorporation of Indochinese Refugees in France and the United States." Ph.D. dissertation, Northwestern University.

Hill, Herbert. 1973. "Anti-Oriental Agitation and the Rise of Working-Class Racism." *Society* 10 (2): 43–54.

Hing, Alex. 1970. "The Need for a United Asian American Front." *Aion* I (1): 9–11.

———. 1989. "The Main Focus . . . Was to Change Substandard Conditions in Chinatown." *Amerasia Journal* 15 (1): 138–139.

Hing, Bill Ong. 1986. "Current Factors in the Re-Emergence of Anti-Asian Violence." Pp. 11–15 in *Break the Silence: A Conference on Anti-Asian Violence May 10, 1986 Proceedings.* San Francisco: Break the Silence Coalition.

Hiraoka, Jesse. 1986. "Asian American Literature." Pp. 93–97 in *Dictionary of Asian American History,* edited by Hyung-Chan Kim. New York: Greenwood Press.

Hodge, Robert W., Maurice D. Van Arsdol, Jr., Chyong-Fang Ko, and Naintara Gorwaney. 1986. "New Patterns of Ethnic Residential Segregation in Los Angeles." Paper presented at the International Sociological Association, XI World Congress of Sociology, New Delhi, India, 18–23 August.

Horowitz, Donald L. 1985. *Ethnic Groups in Conflict.* Berkeley: University of California Press.

Horton, John. 1988. "Ethnicity and the Politics of Growth." Paper presented at the Conference on Comparative Ethnicity, 1–3 June, UCLA.

Hoyt, Edwin P. 1974. *Asians in the West.* New York: Thomas Nelson.

Ichioka, Yuji. 1977. "Japanese Associations and the Japanese Government: A Special Relationship, 1909–1926." *Pacific Historical Review* 46: 409–437.

———. 1988. *The Issei: The World of the First Generation Japanese Americans, 1885–1924.* New York: Free Press.

Ignacio, Lemuel F. 1976. *Asian Americans and Pacific Islanders (Is There Such an Ethnic Group?)* San Jose: Pilipino Development Associates.

Isaacs, Harold. 1975. *Idols of the Tribe.* New York: Harper & Row.

Ito-Adler, James. 1980. *The Portuguese in Cambridge and Somerville,* pt. 2, 1977 supp. Cambridge, Mass.: Department of Planning and Development.

Iwata, Edward. 1987. "Asian Americans Host Democratic Hopefuls." *San Francisco Chronicle,* 20 October.

I Wor Kuen. 1974. "The National Question & Asian Americans." *IWK Journal* 1 (August).

Jacaban, Melecio H. 1988a. "SB 1813 Gives Filipinos Full Benefits of Affirmative Action Law." *Philippine News,* 24 February.

———. 1988b. Memo to the Committee on Senate Bill 1813. San Fernando Valley: Office of Senator Alan Robbins.

Japanese American Citizens League. 1987. "Testimony of the Japanese American Citizens League." Pp. 63–82 in U.S. House, Committee on the Judiciary, *Anti-Asian Violence,* 100th Congress, 1st session, 10 November.

Jenkins, Richard. 1986. "Social Anthropological Models of Inter-Ethnic Relations." Pp. 170–186 in *Theories of Race and Ethnic Relations,* edited by John Rex and David Mason. Cambridge, Eng.: Cambridge University Press.

Jensen, Richard J., and Cara J. Abeyta. 1987. "The Minority in the Middle: Asian-American Dissent in the 1960s and 1970s." *Western Journal of Speech Communications* 51: 402–416.

Johanessen, Edward L. H. 1950. *The Labor Movement in the Territory of Hawaii*. M.A. thesis, University of California, Berkeley.

Jue, Linda. 1989. "Anti-Asian Violence: Confronting an Old Demon." *East/West*, 18 May.

Kaplan, David L. 1979. "Politics and the Census." *Asian and Pacific Census Forum* 6 (2): 1+.

Kaufman, Charles. 1983. "Response to Concerns Raised Regarding Probation Sentences in the Killing of Vincent Chin." Press release, 4 May.

Keane, John. 1985. "Increasing Reliance on the Decennial Census." *Government Information Quarterly* 2 (4): 341–353.

———. 1988. "Statement of Dr. John G. Keane, Director, U.S. Bureau of the Census, Accompanied by Paula Schneider, Chief, Population Division, Census Bureau." Pp. 60–63 in U.S. House, Committee on Post Office and Civil Service, *Review of 1990 Decennial Census Questionnaire Hearing*, 100th Congress, 2nd session, 14 April.

Kempsky, Nelson. 1989. *A Report to Attorney General John K. Van de Kamp on Patrick Edward Purdy and the Cleveland School Killings*. Sacramento: California Department of Justice.

Keyes, Charles F. 1981. "The Dialectics of Ethnic Change." Pp. 4–30 in *Ethnic Change*, edited by Charles F. Keyes. Seattle: University of Washington Press.

Kim, Elaine H. 1982. *Asian American Literature: An Introduction to the Writings and Their Social Context*. Philadelphia: Temple University Press.

Kim, Illsoo. 1981. *New Urban Immigrants: the Korean Community in New York*. Princeton, N.J.: Princeton University Press.

Kimura, Naomi. 1990. "A Study of Charitable Giving and Financial Support to Asian Pacific Human Service Organizations in Los Angeles." Los Angeles: Special Services for Groups.

Kirschten, Dick. 1989. "Looking for Everybody." *National Journal*, 1 April, p. 782.

Kitano, Harry. 1976. *Japanese Americans: The Evolution of a Subculture*. Englewood Cliffs, N.J.: Prentice-Hall. First published 1969.

———. 1980. *Race Relations*. Englewood Cliffs, N.J.: Prentice-Hall.

Kitano, Harry H. L., and Roger Daniels. 1988. *Asian Americans: Emerging Minorities*. Englewood Cliffs, N.J.: Prentice-Hall.

Kitano, Harry H. L., Wai-Tsang Yeung, Lynn Chai, and Herbert Hatanaka. 1984. "Asian-American Interracial Marriage." *Journal of Marriage and the Family* 46 (1): 179–190.

Koreatown. 1983. "Asians Harassed in Washington," 7 January.

Kokubun, Kei. 1987. "The Roots of the Asian Pacific Human Resources Development." Speech presented at the "Looking to 2010: The Asian Pacific Community, Survival or Growth" conference, Los Angeles, 25 February.

Kuo, Wen H. 1979. "On the Study of Asian-Americans: Its Current State and Agenda." *Sociological Quarterly* 20 (Spring): 279–290.

Kuramoto, Ford H. 1976. "Lessons Learned in the Federal Funding Game." *Social Casework* 57 (3): 208–218.

Kuramoto, Ron. 1987. "Asian Pacific Americans and United Way in the 'Era of the Pacific.'" Statement presented at the Alternative Funds National Strategy Meeting, 25–28 April, Washington, D.C.

Kushida, Arlene Hori, Marilyn Montenegro, Paul Chikahisha, and Royal F. Morales. 1976. "A Training Program for Asian and Pacific Islanders." *Social Casework* 57 (3): 185–194.

Kwoh, Stewart. 1989. "Bitter Lesson from Stockton Schoolyard." *Los Angeles Times*, 2 February.

Kwong, Peter. 1987. *The New Chinatown*. New York: Hill & Wang.

Lai, Him Mark. 1987. "Historical Development of the Chinese Consolidated Benevolent Association/*Huiguan* System." *Chinese America: History and Perspectives, 1987*. San Francisco: Chinese Historical Society of America, pp. 13–52.

Lal, Barbara B. 1990. *The Romance of Culture in an Urban Civilisation: Robert E. Park on Race and Ethnic Relations in Cities*. London: Routledge.

Lam, Frankie. 1986. "Suburban Residential Segregation of Chinese and Japanese Americans, 1960, 1970, and 1980." *Sociology and Social Research* 70 (4): 263–265.

Lau, Don. 1989. "CAA Celebrates 20 Years with Anniversary Banquet." *Asian Week*, 9 June.

Lew, Julie. 1987. "Asian Americans More Willingly Stuff Campaign Warchests than Ballot Boxes." *East/West*, 27 August.

Library of Congress, Congressional Research Service. 1975. *Federal Formula Grant-in-Aid Programs That Use Population as a Factor in Allocating Funds*. Washington, D.C.: U.S. Government Printing Office.

Lieberson, Stanley. 1980. *A Piece of the Pie: Blacks and White Immigrants since 1880*. Berkeley: University of California Press.

Light, Ivan. 1972. *Ethnic Enterprise in America: Business and Welfare among Chinese, Japanese, and Blacks*. Berkeley: University of California Press.

―――. 1981. "Ethnic Succession." Pp. 54–86 in *Ethnic Change*, edited by Charles F. Keyes. Seattle: University of Washington Press.

―――. 1983. *Cities in World Perspective*. New York: Macmillan.

Light, Ivan, and Edna Bonacich. 1988. *Immigrant Entrepreneurs: Koreans in Los Angeles, 1965–1982*. Berkeley: University of California Press.

Ling, Susie Hsiuhan. 1984. "The Mountain Movers: Asian American Women's Movement in Los Angeles." M.A. thesis, University of California, Los Angeles.

―――. 1989. "The Mountain Movers: Asian American Women's Movement in Los Angeles." *Amerasia Journal* 15 (1): 51–67.

Lipset, Seymour Martin, and Stein Rokkan. 1967. *Party System and Voter Alignments*. New York: Free Press.

Lipsitz, George. 1988. *A Life in the Struggle: Ivory Perry and the Culture of Opposition*. Philadelphia: Temple University Press.

Liu, John. 1988. "The Relationship of Migration Research to Asian American Studies: Unity and Diversity within the Curriculum." Pp. 117–125 in *Reflections on Shattered Windows*, edited by Gary Okihiro, Shirley Hune, Arthur Hansen, and John Liu. Pullman: Washington State University Press.

Liu, John M., and Lucie Cheng. 1986. "A Dialogue on Race and Class: Asian American Studies and Marxism." Pp. 139–163 in *Left Academy: Marxist Scholarship on American Campuses*, edited by Bertell Ollman and Edward Vernoff. New York: Praeger.

Liu, William. 1976. "Asian American Research: Views of a Sociologist." *Asian Studies Occasional Report*, no. 2.

Lopez, David. 1988. "The Organization of Ethnicity: Asian Indian Associations in the United States." Research proposal submitted to the Social Science Research Council, Los Angeles.

Lopez, David, and Yen Espiritu. 1990. "Panethnicity in the United States: A Theoretical Framework." *Ethnic and Racial Studies* 13 (2): 198–224.

Los Angeles County Commission on Human Relations. 1984. *New Asian Peril*. Los Angeles: Los Angeles County Commission on Human Relations.

Los Angeles Times. 1979. "Asians Win Relisting as Minorities," 24 May.

Los Angeles Times Magazine. 1989. "89 for 1989," 1 January.

Lott, Juanita Tamayo. 1976. "The Asian American Concept: In Quest of Identity." *Bridge*, November, pp. 30–34.

Lowe, Lisa. 1991. "Heterogeneity, Hybridity, Multiplicity: Marking Asian American Differences." *Diaspora* 1: 24–44.

Lowry, Ira S. 1982. "The Science and Politics of Ethnic Enumeration." Pp. 42–61 in *Ethnicity and Public Policy*, vol. 1, edited by Winston A. Van Horne. Madison: University of Wisconsin System.

Lyman, Stanford M. 1970. *The Asian in the West*. Reno and Las Vegas: Desert Research Institute, University of Nevada.

———. 1973. "Red Guard on Grant Avenue: The Rise of Youthful Rebellion in Chinatown." Pp. 20–44 in *Asian Americans: Psychological Perspectives*, edited by Stanley Sue and Nathaniel Wagner. Palo Alto, Calif.: Science and Behavior Books.

Lyons, Judith A. 1988. "Census Bill Passes Senate." *Asian Week*, 21 October.

———. 1989a. "Census Bureau Bows to Asians." *Asian Week*, 20 January.

———. 1989b. "Killer Opens Fire on Asian Children." *Asian Week*, 20 January.

———. 1990a. "Senate Passes Hate Crimes Statistics Act." *Asian Week*, 16 February.

———. 1990b. "Brown, Running for Treasurer, Vows More State Contracts for Asians." *Asian Week*, 23 February.

Mar, Eric. 1987. "Vincent Chin's Killers Go Free." *People's Monitor/Third World Forum*, 28 May.

Masada, Saburo. 1970. "Stockton's Yellow Seed." *Pacific Citizen*, 9 October.

Massey, Douglas S., and Nancy A. Denton. 1987. "Trends in the Residential Segregation of Blacks, Hispanics, and Asians, 1970–1980." *American Sociological Review* 52 (December): 802–825.

Matsui, Jeffrey. 1968. "Asian Americans." *Pacific Citizen*, 6 September.

Matsui, Robert T. 1984. Testimony submitted to the U.S. Commission on Civil Rights, 31 October.

———. 1988a. "Statement of Hon. Robert T. Matsui, a Representative in Congress from CA." Pp. 45–47 in U.S. House, Committee on Post Office and Civil Service, *Review of 1990 Decennial Census Questionnaire Hearing*, 100th Congress, 2nd session, 14 April.

———. 1988b. "Statement of Hon. Robert T. Matsui, a Representative in Congress from the State of CA, Read by Mr. Fujioka, President Elect, Japanese American Bar Association." Pp. 62–65 in U.S. House, Committee on Post Office and Civil Service, *Role of Minority Communities in Decennial Censuses Hearing*, 100th Congress, 2nd session, 20 May.

Maurice, Arthur J., and Richard P. Nathan. 1982. "The Census Undercount Effects on Federal Aid to Cities." *Urban Affairs Quarterly* 17 (3): 251–284.

McKay, James. 1982. "An Exploratory Synthesis of Primordial and Mobilizationist Approaches to Ethnic Phenomena." *Ethnic and Racial Studies* 5 (4): 395–420.

McKenzie, R. D. 1928. *Oriental Exclusion*. Chicago: University of Chicago Press.

McWilliams, Carey. 1964. *Brothers under the Skin*. Boston: Little, Brown.

Mears, Eliot Grinnell. 1928. *Resident Orientals on the American Pacific Coast*. New York: Arno Press.

Melendy, H. Brett. 1977. *Asians in America: Filipinos, Koreans, and East Indians*. Boston: Twayne.

Melnick, Daniel. 1981. "The 1980 Census: Recalculating the Federal Equation." *Publius: The Journal of Federalism* 11 (3–4): 39–65.

Millard, Max. 1987. "Mandy Au Challenges UC Berkeley for Rejecting Valedictorian Son." *East/West*, 4 June.

Miller, Alan C. 1988. "Political Newcomer's Bid for Congress Sparks Korean Community Involvement." *Los Angeles Times*, 16 February.

Min, Pyong Gap. 1986–87. "Filipino and Korean Immigrants in Small Business: A Comparative Analysis." *Amerasia Journal* 13 (1): 53–71.

Mineta, Norman Y. 1988. "Statement of Hon. Norman Y. Mineta, a Rep. in Congress from CA." Pp. 58–60 in U.S. House, Committee on Post Office and Civil Service, *Review of 1990 Decennial Census Questionnaire Hearing*, 100th Congress, 2nd session, 14 April.

Montero, Darrell. 1979. *Vietnamese Americans: Patterns of Resettlement and Socioeconomic Adaptations in the United States*. Boulder, Colo.: Westview Press.

Moore, Joan, and Harry Pachon. 1985. *Hispanics in the United States*. Englewood Cliffs, N.J.: Prentice-Hall.

Mori, Floyd. 1980. "Political Cooperation and the Asian Americans." Pp. 21–29 in *Political Participation of Asian Americans: Problems and Strategies*, edited by Yung-Hwan Jo. N.p.: Pacific/Asian Mental Health Research Center.

Morimoto, Joy. 1989a. "Japanese Americans Chart Future Course." *Asian Week*, 14 April.

———. 1989b. "Japanese Americans and Others Ponder the JACL's Future Role." *Asian Week*, 21 April.

Murase, Mike. 1976a. "Ethnic Studies and Higher Education for Asian Americans." Pp. 205–223 in *Counterpoint: Perspectives on Asian America*, edited by Emma Gee. Los Angeles: UCLA Asian American Studies Center.

———. 1976b. "Toward Barefoot Journalism." Pp. 307–319 in *Counterpoint: Perspectives on Asian America*, edited by Emma Gee. Los Angeles: UCLA Asian American Studies Center.

Myrdal, Gunnar. 1962. *An American Dilemma: The Negro Problem and Modern Democracy*. New York: Harper & Row. First published 1944.

Nagel, Joane. 1982. "The Political Mobilization of Native Americans." *Social Science Journal* 19: 37–45.

———. 1986. "The Political Construction of Ethnicity." Pp. 93–112 in *Com-*

petitive Ethnic Relations, edited by Susan Olzak and Joane Nagel. San Diego: Academic Press.

———. 1989. "American Indian Repertoires of Contention." Paper presented at the 84th Annual Meeting of the American Sociological Association, San Francisco, 9–13 August.

Nakamura, Norman. 1971. "The Nature of G.I. Racism." Pp. 24–26 in *Roots: An Asian American Reader*, edited by Amy Tachiki, Eddie Wong, and Franklin Odo. Los Angeles: UCLA Asian American Studies Center.

Nakanishi, Don T. 1980. "The National Asian-American Roster: 1978." Pp. 197–210 in *Political Participation of Asian Americans: Problems and Strategies*, edited by Yung-Hwan Jo. N.p.: Pacific/Asian American Mental Health Research Center.

———. 1985–86. "Asian American Politics: An Agenda for Research." *Amerasia Journal* 12 (2): 1–27.

———. 1986. "The UCLA Asian Pacific American Voter Registration Study." Unpublished report, UCLA Asian American Studies Center.

Nakanishi, Don T., and Bernie C. LaForteza. 1984. *The National Asian Pacific American Roster, 1984*. Los Angeles: UCLA Asian American Studies Center.

Nakanishi, Don T., and Russell Leong. 1978. "Toward the Second Decade: A National Survey of Asian American Studies Programs in 1978." *Amerasia Journal* 5 (1): 1–19.

Nakano, Roy. 1984. "Marxist Leninist Organization in the Asian American Community: Los Angeles, 1969–79." Unpublished student paper, UCLA Asian American Studies Center.

Nanto, Dick K. 1985. "Automobiles Imported from Japan." Washington, D.C.: Congressional Research Service, 4 September.

National Association for the Advancement of Colored People (Detroit Branch). 1983. Letter from the Detroit NAACP branch to participants of the NAACP Region III Leadership and Development Conference, 26 March.

Nee, Victor, and Jimy Sanders. 1985. "The Road to Parity: Determinants of the Socioeconomic Achievements of Asian Americans." *Ethnic and Racial Studies* 8 (1): 75–93.

Ng, Franklin C. 1980. "Asian-American Politics in Hawaii." Pp. 90–97 in *Political Participation of Asian Americans*, edited by Yung-Hwan Jo. N.p.: Pacific/Asian American Mental Health Research Center.

Ng, Johnny. 1989. "Asian Foundation Gives $38,000 to 12 Groups." *Asian Week*, 8 September.

———. 1991a. "Asian Pacifics 62% of Hawaii's Population." *Asian Week*, 1 March.

———. 1991b. "Houston Eyes Asian District." *Asian Week*, 5 April.

Nguyen, Tuan. 1979. "Statement of Tuan Nguyen, Ph.D., Department of Psychiatry, University of San Francisco." Pp. 53–54 in U.S. House, Committee on Post Office and Civil Service, *Oversight Hearings on the 1980 Census*, pt. 3: *S.F., CA*, 96th Congress, 1st session, 17 April.

Nielsen, Francois. 1985. "Toward a Theory of Ethnic Solidarity in Modern Societies." *American Sociological Review* 50: 133–149.

Nishida, Mo. 1989. "Shitamachi." *Amerasia Journal* 15 (1): 126–134.

Nishio, Alan. 1982. "Personal Reflections on the Asian National Movements." *East Wind*, Spring/Summer, pp. 36–38.

Ochi, Rose. 1985. "Statement of Rose Ochi of the Office of the Mayor of the City of Los Angeles." Pp. 175–178 in U.S. House, Committee on Post Office and Civil Service, *Demographic Impact of Immigration on the U.S. Hearings*, 99th Congress, 1st session, 19 July.

Office of the Secretary. 1978. "Transfer of Responsibility for Certain Statistical Standards From OMB to Commerce." *Federal Register* 43 (87): 19260–19270.

O'Hare, William P., and Judy C. Felt. 1991. *Asian Americans: America's Fastest Growing Minority Group*. Washington, D.C.: Population Reference Bureau.

Ohnuma, Keiko. 1991. "Asian Plurality District in Lower Manhattan." *Asian Week*, 7 June.

Olzak, Susan. 1985. "Ethnicity and Ethnic Collective Behavior." Pp. 65–85 in *Research in Social Movements, Conflict, and Change*, edited by Louis Kriesberg. Greenwich, Conn.: JAI Press.

Omi, Michael, and Howard Winant. 1986. *Racial Formation in the United States: From the 1960s to the 1980s*. New York: Routledge and Kegan Paul.

Ong, Paul. 1989. "California's Asian Population: Past Trends and Projections for the Year 2000." Los Angeles: Graduate School of Architecture and Urban Planning.

Ong, Paul, Yen Espiritu, and Tania Azores. 1991. "Redistricting and Political Empowerment of Asian Pacific Americans in Los Angeles: A Position Paper." Los Angeles: UCLA Asian American Studies Center.

Ono, Shin'ya. 1973. "Dancing to a Sour Tune." *Gidra*, 19 May.

Organization of Chinese Americans (Washington, D.C.). 1989. Press release, 11 August.

Pacific Citizen. 1985. "Asian Students Retain Minority Status," December.

Padgan, Art. 1989. Letter to Honorable David Roberti, 28 February. Pomona, Calif.: Filipino-American Public Affairs Council.

Padilla, Felix M. 1985. *Latino Ethnic Consciousness: The Case of Mexican Americans and Puerto Ricans in Chicago*. Notre Dame, Ind.: Notre Dame University Press.

————. 1986. "Latino Ethnicity in the City of Chicago." Pp. 153–171 in *Competitive Ethnic Relations*, edited by Susan Olzak and Joane Nagel. New York: Academic Press.

Park, Robert. 1950. *Race and Culture*. Glencoe, Ill.: Free Press.

Parsons, Talcott. 1975. "Some Theoretical Considerations on the Nature and Trends of Change of Ethnicity." Pp. 53–83 in *Ethnicity: Theory and Experience*, edited by Nathan Glazer and Daniel P. Moynihan. Cambridge, Mass.: Harvard University Press.

Patterson, Orlando. 1975. "Context and Choice in Ethnic Allegiance." Pp. 305–349 in *Ethnicity: Theory and Experience*, edited by Nathan Glazer and Daniel P. Moynihan. Cambridge, Mass.: Harvard University Press.

Petersen, William. 1969. "The Classification of Subnations in Hawaii: An Essay in the Sociology of Knowledge." *American Sociological Review* 53: 863–877.

————. 1987. "Politics and the Measurement of Ethnicity." Pp. 187–233 in *The Politics of Numbers*, edited by William Alonso and Paul Starr. New York: Russell Sage Foundation.

Pian, Canta. 1976. "Statement of Ms. Canta Pian, Pacific-Asian Coalition." Pp. 32–33 in U.S. House, Committee on Post Office and Civil Service, *1980 Census Hearing*, 94th Congress, 2nd session, 1–2 June.

Plotkin, Manuel D. 1977. "Statement of Manuel D. Plotkin, U.S. Census Bureau, Accompanied by Leobardo F. Estrada, Special Assistant to Division Chief, Population Division; Nampeo D. R. McKenney, Chief Ethnic and Racial Statistics Staff, Population Division; and Daniel B. Levine, Associate Director for Demographic Fields." Pp. 156–173 in U.S. House, Committee on Post Office and Civil Service, *1980 Census Hearing*, 95th Congress, 1st session, 9–10, 24 June.

Polenberg, Richard. 1980. *One Nation Divisible: Class, Race, and Ethnicity in the United States since 1938*. New York: Viking Press.

Portes, Alejandro. 1984. "The Rise of Ethnicity: Determinants of Ethnic Perceptions among Cuban Exiles in Miami." *American Sociological Review* 49: 383–397.

Portes, Alejandro, and Robert L. Bach. 1985. *Latin Journey: Cuban and Mexican Immigrants in the United States*. Berkeley: University of California Press.

Portes, Alejandro, and Rubén G. Rumbaut. 1990. *Immigrant America: A Portrait*. Berkeley: University of California Press.

Quinsaat, Jesse. 1976. "Asians in the Media: The Shadows in the Spotlight." Pp. 264–268 in *Counterpoint: Perspectives on Asian America*, edited by Emma Gee. Los Angeles: UCLA Asian American Studies Center.

Rabaya, Violet. 1971. "I Am Curious (Yellow?)." Pp. 110–111 in *Roots: An*

Asian American Reader, edited by Amy Tachiki, Eddie Wong, and Franklin Odo. Los Angeles: UCLA Asian American Studies Center.

Rafu Shimpo. 1983. "Mineta Pushes Feds for Action on Chin Case," 12 July, p. 1.

———. 1989. "Vincent Chin Memorial Grant Recipients Named," 6 January.

Reitz, Jeffrey G. 1980. *The Survival of Ethnic Groups.* Toronto: McGraw-Hill.

Rice Paper. 1975. 1 (2): (whole issue).

Richter, Paul. 1991. "Beneath the Bitterness of Race." *Los Angeles Times,* 13 August.

Ridley-Thomas, Mark, Manuel Pastor, and Stewart Kwoh. 1989. "The 'New Majority' Wants Its Share." *Los Angeles Times,* 12 October.

Roberts, Alden E. 1988. "Racism Sent and Received: Americans and Vietnamese View One Another." *Research in Race and Ethnic Relations* 5: 75–97.

Robey, Bryant. 1989. "Two Hundred Years and Counting: The 1990 Census." *Population Bulletin* 44 (1). Washington, D.C.: Population Reference Bureau.

Rodan. 1971. "Asian Women as Leaders." 1 (9).

Roderick, Kevin. 1989a. "Speaking Out." *Los Angeles Times,* 13 February.

———. 1989b. "Deciding What Counts in the '90s." *Los Angeles Times,* 14 March.

Rooney, Andy. 1989. Transcript of "A Few Minutes with Andy Rooney." *60 Minutes,* 10 February.

Roosens, Eugeen E. 1989. *Creating Ethnicity: The Process of Ethnogenesis.* Newbury Park, Calif.: Sage.

Roper Organization. 1982. *Roper Reports,* vols. 82–84. Storrs, Conn.

Rose, Peter I. 1985. "Asian Americans: From Pariahs to Paragons." Pp. 181–212 in *Clamor at the Gates: The New Immigration,* edited by Nathan Glazer. San Francisco: Institute of Contemporary Studies.

Ross, Jeffrey A. 1982. "Urban Development and the Politics of Ethnicity: A Conceptual Approach." *Ethnic and Racial Studies* 5 (4): 440–456.

Saito, John. 1968. "Council of Oriental Organizations (COO)." Mimeograph. Los Angeles: Asian Community Service Center.

Sano, Roy. 1970. "Asiantown in Oakland." *Pacific Citizen,* 4 August.

Saxton, Alexander. 1971. *The Indispensable Enemy: Labor and the Anti-Chinese Movement in California.* Berkeley: University of California Press.

Shibutani, Tamotsu, and Kian M. Kwan. 1965. *Ethnic Stratification.* New York: Macmillan.

Shinagawa, Larry Hajime, and Gin Yong Pang. 1988. "Intraethnic, Interethnic, and Interracial Marriages among Asian Americans in California,

1980." *Berkeley Journal of Sociology* 13: 95–114.

Siao, Grace Wai-Tse. 1988. "CACA's Irvin Makes Civil Rights Almost a Full-Time Job." *Asian Week*, 21 October.

———. 1989a. "Monterey Park Council Votes for English on All Signs." *Asian Week*, 27 January.

———. 1989b. "Chinese Man Beaten to Death in North Carolina." *Asian Week*, 11 August.

———. 1989c. "Judge Clears Way for Murder Charge in N.C." *Asian Week*, 25 August.

———. 1990. "Feinstein Meets with 40 LA Asian Leaders." *Asian Week*, 6 April.

Skinner, Kenneth, and Glen Hendricks. 1979. "The Shaping of Self-Identity among Indochinese Refugees." *Journal of Ethnic Studies* 7: 25–41.

Smollar, David. 1983. "U.S. Asians Feel Trade Backlash." *Los Angeles Times*, 14 September.

Snyder, Louis L. 1984. *Macro-Nationalisms: A History of the Pan-Movements.* Westport: Greenwood Press.

Song, Elaine. 1987. "To Live in Peace . . . Responding to Anti-Asian Violence in Boston." A report of the Civil Rights Capacity-Building Project of the Asian American Resource Workshop, Boston.

Sowell, Thomas. 1981. *Ethnic America: A History.* New York: Basic Books.

Spector-Leech, Garrett. 1988. "Ethnic Community Mobilization within an Urban Environment: An Analysis of Asian/Pacific Community and Advocacy Organizations in Los Angeles County." M.A. thesis, University of Southern California.

Starr, Paul. 1987. "The Sociology of Official Statistics." Pp. 5–57 in *Politics and Numbers*, edited by William Alonso and Paul Starr. New York: Russell Sage Foundation.

Starr, Paul D., and Alden Roberts. 1981. "Attitudes toward Indochinese Refugees: An Empirical Study." *Journal of Refugee Resettlement* 1 (4): 51–61.

———. 1982. "Attitudes toward New Americans: Perceptions of Indo-Chinese in Nine Cities." *Research in Race and Ethnic Relations* 3: 165–186.

Stewart, Jill. 1989. "State Could Lose $683 Million in Census Undercount." *Los Angeles Times*, 15 August.

Su, Joanna. 1989. Personal correspondence, 8 September.

Sumi, Pat. 1971. "An Interview with Pat Sumi." Pp. 253–264 in *Roots: An Asian American Reader*, edited by Amy Tachiki, Eddie Wong, and Franklin Odo. Los Angeles: UCLA Asian American Studies Center.

Sung, Betty Lee. 1967. *Mountain of Gold: The Story of the Chinese in America.* New York: Macmillan.

Tachibana, Judy. 1986*a*. "California's Asians: Power from a Growing Population." *California Journal*, November, pp. 535–543.

———. 1986*b*. "Michael Woo—Los Angeles City Councilman." *California Journal*, November, pp. 538–539.

Tachiki, Amy. 1971. "Introduction." Pp. 1–5 in *Roots: An Asian American Reader*, edited by Amy Tachiki, Eddie Wong, and Franklin Odo. Los Angeles: UCLA Asian American Studies Center.

Tajima, Renee, and Christine Choy. 1988. *Who Killed Vincent Chin?* New York: Third World Newsreel.

Takaki, Ronald. 1983. "Who Really Killed Vincent Chin?" *Asian Week*, 29 November.

———. 1989. *Strangers from a Different Shore: A History of Asian Americans*. Boston: Little, Brown.

Tanaka, Ron. 1976. "Culture, Communication, and the Asian Movement in Perspective." *Journal of Ethnic Studies* 4 (1): 37–52.

Tanaka, Tomi. 1971. "From a Lotus Blossom Cunt." P. 109 in *Roots: An Asian American Reader*, edited by Amy Tachiki, Eddie Wong, and Franklin Odo. Los Angeles: UCLA Asian American Studies Center.

tenBroek, J., E. N. Barnhart, and F. W. Matson. 1970. *Prejudice, War, and the Constitution*. Berkeley: University of California Press.

Trottier, Richard. 1981. "Charters of Panethnic Identity: Indigenous American Indians and Immigrant Asian Americans." Pp. 271–305 in *Ethnic Change*, edited by Charles F. Keyes. Seattle: University of Washington Press.

Turner, Jonathan H., and Edna Bonacich. 1980. "Toward a Composite Theory of Middleman Minorities." *Ethnicity* 7: 144–158.

Uhlaner, Carole J., Bruce Cain, and D. Roderick Kiewiet. 1987. "Political Participation of Ethnic Minorities in the 1980s." Social Science Working Paper 647, California Institute of Technology.

Umemoto, Karen. 1989. " 'On Strike!' San Francisco State College Strike, 1968–69: The Roots of Asian American Students." *Amerasia Journal* 15 (1): 3–41.

U.S.–Asia Institute. 1980. "1980's: A Decade of Progress for Asian/Pacific Americans." Proceedings of the Asian/Pacific American National Leadership Conference, 21–22 May, Washington, D.C.

U.S. Bureau of the Census. 1943. *Sixteenth Census of the U.S., 1940*. Vol. 2: *Characteristics of the Population*. Washington, D.C.: U.S. Government Printing Office.

———. 1963. *U.S. Census of Population, 1960*. Vol. 1: *Characteristics of the Population*. Pt. 34: *New York*. Washington, D.C.: U.S. Government Printing Office.

————. 1964. *U.S. Census of Population, 1960.* Vol. 1: *Characteristics of the Population.* Pt. 1: *United States Summary.* Washington, D.C.: U.S. Government Printing Office.

————. 1973a. *U.S. Census of Population, 1970.* Vol. 1: *Characteristics of the Population.* Pt. 1: *United States Summary,* sec. 2. Washington, D.C.: U.S. Government Printing Office.

————. 1973b. *U.S. Census of Population, 1970.* Vol. 1: *Characteristics of the Population.* Pt. 34: *New York,* sec. 1. Washington, D.C.: U.S. Government Printing Office.

————. 1979. *Twenty Censuses: Population and Housing Questions, 1790–1980.* Washington, D.C.: U.S. Government Printing Office.

————. 1983a. *U.S. Census of Population, 1980.* Vol. 1: *Characteristics of the Population.* Pt. 24: *Michigan.* Washington, D.C.: U.S. Government Printing Office.

————. 1983b. *U.S. Census of Population, 1980.* Vol. 1: *Characteristics of the Population.* Pt. 1: *United States Summary.* Washington, D.C.: U.S. Government Printing Office.

————. 1983c. *Congressional District Profiles, 98th Congress.* Washington, D.C.: U.S. Government Printing Office.

————. 1983d. *U.S. Census of Population, 1980.* Vol. 1: *Characteristics of the Population.* Pt. 34: *New York,* sec. 1. Washington, D.C.: U.S. Government Printing Office.

————. 1987. "Recommendations of the Census Advisory Committee on the Asian and Pacific Islander Populations for the 1990 Census Made as a Result of the Meeting on April 23–24, 1987." Washington, D.C.: U.S. Government Printing Office.

————. 1988a. *U.S. Census of Population, 1980.* Vol. 2: *Subject Reports: Asian and Pacific Islander Population in the United States.* Washington, D.C.: U.S. Government Printing Office.

————. 1988b. *We, the Asian and Pacific Islander Americans.* Washington, D.C.: U.S. Government Printing Office.

————. 1989a. *Voting and Registration in the Election of November 1988.* Washington, D.C.: U.S. Government Printing Office.

————. 1989b. *Joint Session of the Census Advisory Committees on the 1990 Census.* Washington, D.C.: U.S. Government Printing Office.

U.S. Commission on Civil Rights. 1973. *To Know or Not to Know: Collection and Use of Racial and Ethnic Data in Federal Assistance.* Washington, D.C.: U.S. Government Printing Office.

————. 1986. *Recent Activities against Citizens and Residents of Asian Descent.* Washington, D.C.: U.S. Government Printing Office.

————. 1988. *The Economic Status of Americans of Asian Descent: An Ex-*

ploratory Investigation. Washington, D.C.: U.S. Government Printing Office.

U.S. Court of Appeals, Sixth Circuit. 1986. "United States of America, Plaintiff-Appellee, v. Ronald Ebens, Defendant-Appellant." *Federal Reporter* 800 (2): 1422–1445.

U.S. Equal Employment Opportunity Commission. 1977. "Government-Wide Standard Race/Ethnic Categories." *Federal Register* 42 (64): 17900.

———. 1979. *Job Discrimination: Laws and Rules You Should Know*. Washington, D.C.: U.S. Government Printing Office.

U.S. Immigration and Naturalization Service. 1988. *Annual Report Immigration and Naturalization Service*. Washington, D.C.: U.S. Government Printing Office.

Uyematsu, Amy. 1971. "The Emergence of Yellow Power in America." Pp. 9–13 in *Roots: An Asian American Reader*, edited by Amy Tachiki, Eddie Wong, and Franklin Odo. Los Angeles: UCLA Asian American Studies Center.

van den Berghe, Pierre L. 1981. *The Ethnic Phenomenon*. New York: Elsevier.

Vollmer, Ted. 1987. "Mas Fukai Makes It to Big Leagues." *Los Angeles Times*, 9 March.

Waldman, Tom. 1988. "The New Asians." *Golden State Report*, November, pp. 19–20.

Wang, Ling-Chi. 1989. "Report on Anti-Asian Bias in UC Admissions Process 'Seriously Flawed.'" *East/West*, 9 March.

Waters, Mary C. 1990. *Ethnic Options: Choosing Identities in America*. Berkeley: University of California Press.

Weingarten, Paul. 1983. "Deadly Encounter: Did Vincent Chin's Assailants Get Away with Murder?" *Chicago Tribune Magazine*, 13 July.

Weiss, Melford S. 1974. *Valley City: A Chinese Community in America*. Cambridge, Mass.: Schenkman.

White, Clay. 1986. "Residential Segregation among Asians in Long Beach: Japanese, Chinese, Filipino, Korean, Indian, Vietnamese, Hawaiian, Guamanian, and Samoan." *Sociology and Social Research* 70 (4): 266–267.

Wilkinson, Tracy. 1989. "FBI Joins Probe of Viet Writer's Shooting." *Los Angeles Times*, 22 August.

Wilson, William Julius. 1980. *The Declining Significance of Race*. Chicago: University of Chicago Press.

———. 1987. *The Truly Disadvantaged: The Inner City, the Underclass, and Public Policy*. Chicago: University of Chicago Press.

Woldemikael, Tekle Mariam. 1989. *Becoming Black Americans: Haitians and American Institutions in Evanston, Illinois*. New York: AMS Press.

Wone, Robert. 1990. "Low Voter Registration Retards New York Asians' Political Clout." *Asian Week*, 7 September.

Wong, Bernard. 1977. "Elites and Ethnic Boundary Maintenance: A Study of the Roles of Elites in Chinatown, New York City." *Urban Anthropology* 6 (1): 1–22.

Wong, Diane Yen-Mei. 1983*a*. "Detroit Chinese Americans Hold Demonstration for Chin." *East/West*, 11 May.

———. 1983*b*. "Relations between Vincent Chin Supporters Strained." *East/West*, 24 August.

Wong, Eddie. 1971. "Introduction." Pp. 247–250 in *Roots: An Asian American Reader*, edited by Amy Tachiki, Eddie Wong, and Franklin Odo. Los Angeles: UCLA Asian American Studies Center.

Wong, Kent. 1985. "Statement of Kent Wong, Esq., Staff Attorney, Asian Pacific American Legal Center." Pp. 172–175 in U.S. House, Committee on Post Office and Civil Service, *Demographic Impact of Immigration on the U.S. Hearings*, 99th Congress, 1st session, 19 July.

Wong, Morrison G. 1989. "A Look at Intermarriage among the Chinese in the U.S. in 1980." *Sociological Perspectives* 32 (1): 87–107.

Wong, Paul. 1972. "The Emergence of the Asian-American Movement." *Bridge* 2 (1): 33–39.

Wong, William. 1987. "Asian Americans and Political Power." *East/West*, 13 September.

———. 1988*a*. "Asian Americans Shake Off Stereotypes, Increase Clout as Political Activism Grows." *Los Angeles Times*, 23 February.

———. 1988*b*. "Riding the Census Bureau Roller Coaster." *East/West*, 24 November.

———. 1989*a*. "Bill Wong" column. *Asian Week*, 6 October.

———. 1989*b*. "Bill Wong" column. *Asian Week*, 20 October.

Woo, Elaine. 1988. "UCLA Denies Any Policy of Limiting Asian Admissions." *Los Angeles Times*, 19 November.

Woo, George. 1979. "Statement of George Woo, National President of Pacific Asian Coalition." Pp. 44–45 in U.S. House, Committee on Post Office and Civil Service, *Oversight Hearings on the 1980 Census*, pt. 3: S.F., CA, 96th Congress, 1st session, 17 April.

Woo, Michael. 1983. "America's New Wave of Anti-Asian Prejudice." *Los Angeles Herald Examiner*, 26 June.

Woon, Yuen-Fong. 1985. "Ethnic Identity and Ethnic Boundaries: The Sino-Vietnamese in Victoria, British Columbia." *Canadian Review of Sociology and Anthropology* 22: 534–558.

Wright, Theon. 1972. *The Disenchanted Isles*. New York: Dial Press.

Xenos, Peter S., Robert W. Gardner, Herbert R. Barringer, and Michael J. Levin. 1987. "Asian Americans: Growth and Change in the 1970s." Pp. 249–284 in *Pacific Bridges: The New Immigration From Asia and the Pacific Islands*. Staten Island, N.Y.: Center for Migration Studies.

Yablonka, Marc. 1989. "L.A. Lao Says Cambodians, Viets Get Most Public Funds." *Asian Week*, 15 September.

Yancey, William C., Eugene P. Ericksen, and Richard J. Juliani. 1976. "Emergent Ethnicity: A Review and Reformulation." *American Sociological Review* 41: 391–403.

Yinger, Milton. 1985. "Ethnicity." *Annual Review of Sociology* 11: 151–180.

Yoshimura, Evelyn. 1971. "G.I.'s and Asian Women." Pp. 27–29 in *Roots: An Asian American Reader*, edited by Amy Tachiki, Eddie Wong, and Franklin Odo. Los Angeles: UCLA Asian American Studies Center.

———. 1989. "How I Became an Activist and What It All Means to Me." *Amerasia Journal* 15 (1): 106–109.

Yu, Eui-Young. 1983. "Korean Communities in America: Past, Present, and Future." *Amerasia Journal* 10 (2): 23–51.

Yuan, D. Y. 1966. "Chinatown and Beyond: The Chinese Population in Metropolitan New York." *Phylon* 23 (4): 321–332.

Yung, Danny. 1977. "Prepared Statement of Danny (N.T.) Yung." Pp. 201–202 in U.S. House, Committee on Post Office and Civil Service, *1980 Census Hearing*, 95th Congress, 1st session, 9–10, 24 June.

Zane, Maitland. 1985. "Asian Leaders Accuse Demo Party of Racism." *San Francisco Chronicle*, 22 May.

Zia, Helen. 1984a. "The New Violence." *Bridge* 9 (2): 18–23.

———. 1984b. *1983 Yearbook*. Royal Oak, Mich.: American Citizens for Justice.

———. 1991. "Loo Slaying Trial Witnesses Say Piche Taunted Asians." *Asian Week*, 12 July.

Interviews

Andersen, Patrick, 5 January 1990, telephone interview.
Bagasao, Brad, 23 May 1989, Los Angeles.
Chan, Po, 2 November 1989, telephone interview.
de la Cruz, Enrique, 18 December 1989, Los Angeles.
Demonteverde, Sam, 16 August 1989, Los Angeles.
Fukai, Mas, 20 October 1989, telephone interview.
Furutani, Warren, 12 September 1989, Los Angeles.
Guerrero, Connie, 18 August 1989, Los Angeles.
Hatanaka, Herb, 18 October 1989, Los Angeles.
Hsia, Maria, 19 December 1989, Los Angeles.
Ichioka, Yuji, 2 May 1988, Los Angeles.
Jacaban, Melecio H., 23 June 1989, telephone interview.
Kokubun, Kei, 16 June 1989, Gardena, Calif.
Kwoh, Stewart, 2 June 1989, Los Angeles.
Louie, Paul, 22 July 1989, telephone interview.
Mann, Ernest, 20 June 1989, Carson, Calif.
Miyamoto, Barbara, 14 November 1989, Los Angeles.
Morales, Roy, 22 June 1989, Gardena, Calif.
Nakamura, Cayleen, 22 August 1989, Van Nuys, Calif.
Omatsu, Glenn, 30 November 1989, Los Angeles.
Ponce, Ninez, 23 May 1991, telephone interview.
Ricasa, Tony, 31 October 1989, Los Angeles.
Shimoura, Jim, 23 October 1989, telephone interview.
Strobel, Chris, 29 May 1991, telephone interview.
Watanabe, Mike, 19 July 1989, Los Angeles.
Woo, Alan, 28 May 1991, telephone interview.
Yap, Joselyn, 7 June 1989, Los Angeles.
Yip, Beverly, 19 June 1991, San Diego.
Zia, Helen, 20 October 1989, telephone interview.

Index

New York, 28, 29, 40, 84, 89, 93; in Oakland, 29; in San Francisco, 21, 45, 62, 83, 93, 183n.1; in Washington, D.C., 29

Chinese, in U.S.: acculturation of, 89; and Asian American panethnicity, 50; demographics, 26, 57, 75, 95, 105; discrimination and violence against, 21, 30–31, 36, 135, 144; dominance of, in pan-Asian organizations, 50–51, 75–80, 96–97, 98–99, 104, 108, 171; and Japanese, 20–22, 23, 27, 168; organizations formed by, 66, 77–78; political activities by, 40, 55, 60, 62, 63–64, 73, 125, 144; residential patterns of, 28, 29, 101; socioeconomic status of, 30–31, 83–84, 107; and welfare activities, 83, 88, 91, 93

Chinese American Citizens Alliance (CACA), 66, 78, 83

Chinese-American Planning Council, 93

Chinese Exclusion Act, 21, 54, 117

Chinese for Affirmative Action (CAA), 66, 126, 131

Chinese Six Companies, 89

Chinese Welfare Council, Detroit, 144, 146, 147, 160

Choices, of ethnic identity, 5–7, 15, 159, 161, 171, 174

Chu, Judy, 72–73, 182n.20

Citizenship, 22, 37, 54, 58–59, 61, 67, 125, 135

Civil rights movement, 3, 12, 25, 69

Class cleavages, among Asian Americans, 2, 11, 52, 107, 109

Class solidarity, 24–25

"Colorblind" society, 173

Cohen, Abner, 5, 8

Communist Party, 46

Comprehensive Employment and Training Act (CETA), 117

Conflicts: class-based, 2, 14, 171–172; inter-Asian, 11, 16, 18, 96, 103–109, 168–169; interethnic, 3, 137–140

Cornell, Steve, 4, 6, 7, 8, 11, 12, 14, 15, 86, 164, 165, 166

Council of Oriental Organizations (COO), 91

Cubans, in U.S., 2, 8, 124

"Cultural entrepreneurs," 52

Cultural groups: defined, 9; vs. ethnic groups, 8–9

Culture, 3, 13, 107, 165; Asian American, 9, 17, 41; creation of, 8; and ethnicity, 8–9; function of, 8, 17; and panethnicity, 9, 11–12, 13, 16–17, 164

Daniels, Roger, 20, 22, 23, 28, 29, 31, 135

Detroit, Mich.: Asian Americans in, 141, 143–144; economic conditions in, 142

Deukmejian, George, 75, 155

Din, Grant, 55, 57, 60

Dinkins, David, 68

Discrimination, 12, 69, 86, 115, 132; against Asians, 1–2, 14, 17, 28, 30–31, 36, 50, 54, 135, 174; against Latinos, 1, 174

Disfranchisement, political, 53–54

District associations, 83

"Dotbuster," 149, 188n.12

Dukakis, Michael, 62

Dutta, Manoranjan, 125

East/West, 41

East Wind, 46, 47, 183n.1

Ebens, Ronald, 141, 142, 143, 149, 188n.6

Economic competition, 137–138, 168

Economic Opportunity Act, 86

Education, 13, 35, 80, 107; discrimination, in higher, 1–2, 62, 69, 74

Electoral politics, 165; and advocacy groups, 65–69; and bloc voting, 59–61, 77; and campaign contributions, 61–65, 166; participation in, 55–59, 179n.1; and political representation, 69–75, 130, 166

Entrepreneurs, ethnic, 7, 138, 140

Ethnic bias, 97, 99

Ethnic boundaries, 9, 12, 17; construction of, 3, 9, 10; maintenance of, 2, 3; multiple, 2, 8, 10, 11, 13, 15, 36–38, 100–101, 122, 123, 131–132

Ethnic change, 2, 3, 8, 9–10, 161

Ethnic chauvinism, 80, 162; and pan-Asianism, 50, 52, 170

Ethnic "disidentification," 20–23, 134–135

Ethnic enclaves, 28, 29, 50, 162, 178n.7

Ethnic groups: defined, 9; as communities of culture, 4, 9, 52; as communi-

Piche, Robert, 157, 158, 159
Political donations. *See* Campaign contributions
Political expediency, 53, 62–63, 66, 80, 82–83, 92, 100, 101, 131, 146, 162–163, 167
Political participation and activism, Asian American, 162; against anti-Asian violence, 150–154; and Census Bureau, 123, 126, 128, 129, 133; and unity at polls, 59–61; as voters, 55–59
Political parties, 59
Political representation, Asian American, 67, 70–75, 79, 131, 167
Politics, confrontational, 17–18, 52, 53, 165
Politics of numbers, 53, 92, 103–106, 162
Portes, Alejandro, 5, 59, 134
Primordialism, 4, 9, 13, 164; critique of, 5–9
Professionalism, 11, 78, 87–91, 96–99, 106, 110, 167
Progressive Labor Party, 33, 45, 46
Puerto Ricans, in U.S., 1, 2, 13, 86, 114, 124
Purdy, Patrick, 155, 156

Race, 9, 23, 173; discrimination by, 49; importance of, 44–49, 156, 175
Racial lumping, 10, 13, 34, 122, 175; of Asian Americans, 6, 13, 16, 18, 19, 20, 21, 23, 43, 53, 73–74, 75, 83, 94, 98, 107, 122–123, 124, 130, 132, 134, 140, 159, 162, 174; of blacks, 6, 13, 174–175; of Latinos, 6, 13, 73, 124, 174; of Native Americans, 6, 13, 174; and racial violence, 7
Racial politics, 173–174
Racism, 7, 9, 12, 28, 42, 121, 137, 140, 175; and Vietnam war, 42–45
"Rainbow Coalition," 68
Raleigh, N.C., 157, 158
Reagan, Ronald, 74, 129
Red Guard (San Francisco), 45, 47, 179n.15, 183n.1
Red Power movement, 12
Redistricting, 67, 130, 132
Refugees, Southeast Asian, 96, 98, 99, 102, 105, 108, 128, 129, 150, 170; and Asian American panethnicity, 16, 184–

185n.15; public opinion toward, 137, 139; violence against, 154, 155–157
Residential segregation, 28–30, 52, 175, 178n.7
Rice, 41
Roberti, David, 108
Rock Springs (Wyo.), violence against Chinese at, 135
Roots: An Asian American Reader, 38

Sacramento, Calif., 97, 104
Samoan Service Center (Los Angeles), 90
Samoans, in U.S., 88, 90, 91, 99, 123, 184–185n.15
San Diego, 90, 91, 92
San Francisco, 1, 41, 44–45, 47, 55, 56, 62, 65, 66, 83, 84, 151, 156
San Francisco State College (now University), 34, 36, 73
Sansei, 27, 33
Seattle, Wash., 65, 71
Senate Bill 1813, Calif., 106
"Serve the People" programs, 84–85
Sexism, 12, 47–48
Shibutani, Tamotsu, 7, 9, 17
Shimoura, Jim, 144, 145–146, 148, 151, 155
Sibonga, Dolores, 65
Simon, Paul, 62
Situational ethnicity, 5, 8
Siv, Sichan, 75
Slavery, 6
Social work, professionalization of, 87–91, 96–99, 110
Socialism, 45–46
Socioeconomic status, 30–31, 83–84, 107, 184n.14
Solidarity, ethnic: multiple levels of, 161, 168–171; reactive, 134, 135
Spanish Coalition for Jobs, 1
Split labor market, 10
Southern California Justice for Vincent Chin Committee, 151
Southwest Voter Research Institute, 73
Soviet Union, 45
Stockton, Calif., 155, 156, 157
Students, 31; political activism of, 18, 20, 25, 32–40, 50; and "serve the people" programs, 84–85